FEMINISM

AND

LOVE

Tranforming
Ourselves
and
Our World

FEMINISM

AND

LOVE

Tranforming
Ourselves
and
Our World

Ruth Whitney

Cross Cultural Publications, Inc.

CrossRoads Books

Published by **CROSS CULTURAL PUBLICATIONS, INC**
CROSS ROADS BOOKS
Post Office Box 506
Notre Dame, Indiana, 46556
Phone: (800) 561-6526
            (219) 273-6526
FAX: (219) 273-5973
E-mail: Crosscult@aol.com

ISBN: 0-940121-47-6
Library of Congress Catalog Card Number: 98-71416

Acknowledgements and Loving Thanks

Heart-felt Thanks to all my family and friends

Special Help by Betsy Gannon

Edited by Diane Mason

Photograph by Davida Johns

Special Advice by Sandra Gourdine

Cover Design by Christine O'Brien and Ken Kinzel

Unique Help by Mary Kessler Lelaumier and Sue Brewer

Dedication

I thank all who loved me in their hearts,
With thanks and love from mine.
Deep thanks to all
Who paused a little near the prison wall
To hear my music in its louder parts.

Elizabeth Barrett Browning

Dedicated to taking the suffering out of life and
creating more love for all people

Contents

FOREWORD

One would hardly say that love is a radical idea. But love as synonymous with feminism? That's radical. Feminists are portrayed many ways. As activists. Warriors. Man haters. Screamers. Protestors. Not usually as lovers.

In this book, Dr. Ruth Whitney performs a marriage of the two concepts of love and feminism, proposing a model for both feminist philosophy and feminist activism that is radically new. Dr. Whitney says that "feminism is the vision and practice of love," born out of our innermost nature, which is loving. In her view, the patriarchy, and its long history of abuses against women, is the result of humankind's disconnection and separation from this innermost loving nature. In this book, she lights the way back.

My own career has taken me to both sides of the fence in the women's movement. I've been inside, as an activist, writing books for women, publishing a women's newspaper, and producing television for women. For many years, I also stood outside the movement, as a journalist for a daily newspaper. During those years, though I was friendly to feminism, I was expected to keep the appearance of professional distance. So, I've marched and I've stood on the sidelines and reported about marches. Over the past two decades, I've observed feminists struggle for power in a system that has consistently denied them power. I've also observed feminists struggle for power with each other, fighting within the ranks. This is distressing, to see women adopting the same methods that we protest against.

What happened to our vision of a new way of being with each other, finding fair ways to solve problems, changing the definition of power from "power over" to partnership? At one time, feminism's goal was to create a system where we encourage, promote, and stand up for each other, and where one person's success does not rob, but rather enhances, another's. Now, it seems that the patriarchal mindset has seeped into the movement somehow.

Historically, feminism has been a political movement. What has connected us as feminists has been shared outrage at the insults of a misogynist culture, and the desire for fairness, equality, peace, and an environment where everyone can realize her full potential, and live in health and safety with her family and children. As the underdogs, women have gone to battle to awaken society's consciousness, to right wrongs, to spotlight inconsistencies and lies, and to end cruelty. To get our message across, we've needed to take an adversarial stand, to take to the streets. We've marched, we've protested, we've challenged, and at times broken the law.

With these methods, we've won the vote, gotten our children out of sweatshops, worked to stop the violence against us on the streets and in our own homes. We've fought to end senseless killing of ourselves and animals, and to stop the pollution and destruction of our environment. We've secured better childcare, health care, and fairer wages. By a thread, we've held onto the right to have dominion over our own bodies.

In the first waves of the women's movement, our battles have been fueled by the energy of rebellion and revolt. That energy is a polarizing energy. It creates, by necessity perhaps, two warring camps. In order to be "right," someone else has to be "wrong." It's a we-versus-they mentality. Although much has been accomplished with this energy, it is an outdated model. The new model transforms polarizing energy into the energy of connection.

There are signs everywhere--in our health care, in religions and spiritual practices, even in film and literature-- that humankind may be moving toward a shift in consciousness. Scholars like Riane Eisler are writing about replacing the domination model with the partnership model. The women's movement, in it current form, may be lagging behind this planetary shift in consciousness.

We need to grow to a new level. We need to open our minds to a new way of thinking. Women have always led movements toward change. We need to lead this one, too.

Dr. Whitney's book is cutting edge, and shows us a way to transform ourselves and our world.

This book may pioneer another wave of feminism. Dr. Whitney's book suggests that in the next phase, feminism will be not just a political movement, but a spiritual one as well. Feminism will call for an expanded consciousness based on love. It will draw a wider circle. It will challenge polarizing behavior and look for ways to connect. It is a feminism that not only will work to right wrongs, but will strive to heal at the core.

Women have always been the peacemakers, the healers. We have always brought heart to the center of the action, and our protests have been against violations of our deepest, truest nature. We have always acted from a core of love. Dr. Whitney suggests a new vision of feminism that puts our love into practice, into action. She shows how our loving center is our core, how it has been violated throughout history, how we can restore it, how we can heal ourselves and the culture, and how we can create a new model for change. What Dr. Whitney is calling for has always been there. She asks us to manifest it in a new way.

This is not surrender, nor is it giving up hard-won ground. This vision does not ask us to condone the cruel and oppressive acts of the patriarchy. Our goal has always been to step outside the patriarchy and create a new way of being. In Dr. Whitney's model, we step out of the patriarchy on the wings of love.

Diane Mason
Founder and Publisher of HERS newspaper

INTRODUCTION

In spite of everything, I still believe that people are
really good at heart.
                    Anne Frank
                    Diary of Anne Frank

Love is the ultimate and the highest goal to which man
can aspire. ... The salvation of man is through love and
in love.
                    Viktor Frankl
                    Man's Search for Meaning

Feminism is ultimately the single most important
movement for planetary and social change in all
recorded history, calling for the radical transformation
of our deepest selves and the way we live our lives.

                    Char McKee
                    "Feminism: A Vision of Love"
                    The Goddess Re-awakening

Love and Feminism Are Connected

Our greatest need is to increase our love. We all want
to receive more love and to give more love to our families,
friends, co-workers, and our communities.

Our second greatest need is to decrease the negativity,
dominating behavior, and destructiveness in our lives and our
world. We have strong desires to be good and caring, but we
find ourselves being judgmental, controlling, and putting
others down. This book explains how we can learn to
become less controlling and more loving.

Feminist thinkers correctly stress the importance of
naming reality for ourselves.[1] Since my life experience

teaches me that love is our greatest need, it is essential to explain what love is. Love is our inner core. As our dynamic power and vital energy, love is our creative life force and vibrant spirit. Love is the ground of our being and the heart of our human nature. As the inner core of all life, love is the binding force that causes the ecological interdependence and unity of all people, nature, and God.

All of us are innately loving. The purpose of our lives is to become fully loving. Everything else is secondary. When we get in touch with our loving inner core, we experience a deep self-love. Then our love radiates out and we experience a heart felt communion with others and the mystical oneness of all reality. When we give love, both to ourselves and others, and are fortunate enough to receive it in return, we discover the most profound meaning of life. To love fully and freely leads to joy and happiness and even to ecstasy and bliss.

This book connects feminism and love. While it is true that feminism is a political movement to achieve equality, I believe feminists want more. Feminism works to transform our world by replacing its highest values of control and domination with feminist values.

Love is the highest value of feminism. The heart of feminism is love, including love for myself, all people, nature, and God. Contrary to the claims of its opponents and the way some people perceive it, feminism is *not* a man-hating movement. It is not a movement that only benefits women. Feminism is a movement that promotes love for all women and men.

Feminism is the vision and practice of love. Feminism is acts of love that eliminate all forms of domination; that express respect, liberty, equality, justice, and love for all women and men; and that transform our world by nurturing loving individuals and creating communities of love. Feminism is love in action.

Feminism works to heal the selfishness, prejudice, hatred, exploitation, discrimination, domination, abuse, and violence in our lives. Because it is based on our loving human nature, feminism is the most profound and most revolutionary movement in the world today.

The purpose of this book is to explain how feminism and love can help us transform ourselves and our world. Part One illuminates the power of love. Chapter One explains that all of us are innately loving. Chapter Two reveals the essence of love and the interrelationship between self-love and love for others, between solitude and intimacy. After love is described as a dialogue between giving and receiving, Chapter Three outlines eight self-help steps on how to become more loving. Because there is always more to learn, no one ever graduates from the school of learning how to love.

Part Two analyzes the love of power and the personal and social causes of human destructiveness. Chapter Four describes historically the change from an earlier, peaceful, equal, loving partnership culture to the later, warring, unequal, hierarchical, dominating patriarchal culture. The main social cause of human destructiveness is the patriarchy which is a dominating social system with the highest value of power over others. Chapter Five explains why some individuals become destructive rather than loving. After analyzing the potential for violence within all of us, it explains the individual causes of child abuse, battering, and rape.

Part Three describes the power of love versus the love of power. Chapter Six illuminates the differences between destructive and loving behavior. Chapter Seven explains over 30 ways that patriarchal, dominating leadership differs from feminist, empowering leadership. In addition, it offers several ways to deal with and change dominating leadership.

To dispute patriarchy's negative descriptions, Part Four explains feminism's true nature and the ways it creates solutions for human destructiveness. Chapter Eight describes feminism as the vision and practice of love. Through the six stages of personal empowerment and women's liberation, feminism helps both women and men become more loving and create communities of love. Chapter Nine explains why feminism is a spiritual and moral movement.

The Many Kinds of Love, Including Erotic Love

When some people hear the word love, they think only of a romantic, sexual love relationship between a woman and man, that is often called erotic love. Thus, they fail to focus on the many other types of love. I love my parents, family, friends, myself, animals, nature, work, knowledge, learning, freedom, justice, equality, beauty, truth, my home, community, country, the joy of being alive, health, life, the universe, and God. My love for all people is called universal love. Some people love their hobbies, such as sports and travel, and their possessions, such as their boats and cars, more than their spouse and children.

In this book, I hope to clarify the meaning and dynamic processes of love. This meaning applies to all the many kinds of love, not just to erotic love. Differences exist among the types of love. The depth of love varies according to the lover and the beloved. For instance, some people love their children more than anything else, while others love money more. However, the meaning and vital processes are the same for all the various expressions of love.

One important message of this book is that love is our vital energy and creative life force. As the deepest reality within us, love is present in all areas of our lives. Our friendships are our relationships made life-promoting by love. Our work is our love made visible.[2]

In our culture, the word love, its meaning, and process-es have been trivialized, distorted, misunderstood, and devalued. In addition, love's meaning has been narrowed and separated from the most crucial areas of life, except the erotic. This book attempts to correct these corruptions of love by explaining love's importance and its presence in every part of our lives.

Audre Lorde, the African American poet, writes about the erotic as "a source of power," as "what is deepest and strongest" within us. What she names the erotic, I call love. One of Lorde's important contributions is that she broadens the meaning of the erotic and reconnects it with all parts of our lives. For Lorde, the erotic is "a kernel within myself. When released from its intense and constrained pellet, it flows through and colors my life with a kind of energy that heightens and sensitizes and strengthens all my experience."[3]

As Lorde says, to survive, every oppressor must distort and corrupt the oppressed's sources of power that provide the energy needed for change. Love as our most important source of power and energy is suppressed, distorted, and relegated to the bedroom. Once feminism empowers us, we begin to demand that all areas of our lives express our love.[4]

Virginia Satir entitles her book *Peoplemaking*. This book could be called lovemaking, because the purpose of our lives is to cultivate love for ourselves and others. Unfortunately, for many people, the meaning of lovemaking is sexual intercourse and not nurturing love in all parts of our lives. Just as Lorde expands the meaning of the word erotic, I broaden the meaning of the word love to encompass every area of our lives.

Feminists Disagree about the Meaning of Love and Feminism

Feminists and anti-feminists disagree with my belief about our loving human nature. Camille Paglia criticizes feminism for being heir to Jean Jacques Rousseau's ideas about "man's innate goodness." Agreeing with Marquis de Sade, she contends "aggression comes from nature;... getting back to nature ... would give free rein to violence and lust." Paglia claims "when social controls weaken, man's innate cruelty burst forth."[5]

I vehemently disagree with Paglia. We are not innately cruel. In agreement with Rousseau, I affirm that we are essentially good, but I go beyond his ideas. In the depth of my being, I believe we are born loving. Love is our inner core and the heart of our human nature.

Feminists disagree about the nature of love. Shulamith Firestone says "love is not altruistic," but rather "love is the height of selfishness: the self attempts to enrich itself through

the absorption of another being."[6] In contrast, it is my deep
conviction that love not only answers our needs but it also
helps us nurture others and build communities of love.

Some feminists view love in our patriarchal society as
oppressive or pathological. In contrast, I assert that love is
inherently creative. As Lorde says, "the need and desire to
nurture each other is not pathological but redemptive." This
redemptive love helps us discover our power and liberate
ourselves. The patriarchy fears the transforming love that
feminism promotes.[7]

Many feminist scholars avoid the word love and write
about caring. As I explain later, caring is crucial because it is
the second step in becoming loving. We need to move
beyond caring to develop all eight steps to become fully
loving.[8]

For a variety of reasons, some feminists disagree with
my heart felt conviction that feminism is the vision and
practice of love.[9] One reason is that feminists and anti-
feminists are committed to their own diverse definitions of
feminism. Another reason is that my vision goes beyond the
standard definition of feminism as the belief and practice of
equality for women. I often wonder how any American who
agrees with the Declaration of Independence's affirmation that
"all men are created equal" can oppose feminism's struggle
for personal, political, and economic equality for women?

Transforming Ourselves and Our World

Our culture is at a turning point and faces a profound
choice. Many progressive thinkers, including feminists Marilyn
French and Riane Eisler, explain the need to change our
social system. It is crucial, I believe, that we transform not
only our culture, but also ourselves. One alteration without
the other will not provide the transformation that is necessary
to create loving individuals and new communities of love.[10]

Many women are concerned about remodeling themselves and adapting to their society. After they spend hours
in therapy and self-help programs, they do improve them-

selves. However, therapists and self-help groups often overlook the fact that our patriarchal culture is a major part of their problems. Listening to the feminist analysis of the consequences of living in our patriarchal society would help these women understand the troubles they experience.

We need to change our own highest personal value from control and domination to love for ourselves and others. Not only do we need to give our love to all family and friends, but also to our work and our community. In addition, we must transform our culture and its institutions from patriarchal, destructive behaviors to feminist, loving ways of acting.

It is important to say that there will be resistance to any strenuous effort to transform our world. The dominators will not give up their power without a struggle. A loving world will not be easy to create. There is hope because people and movements in our culture today, including feminism, have started to work. I strongly believe that they do not intend to quit until they themselves become more loving and create loving communities.

Every journey is frightening because it takes us into new territory. Every voyage runs into storms. When we begin on a new path, we never know for sure where we will end. However, uncertainty and trouble are not reasons to give up before we start, or to stop on the way. Our goal of more loving people and more communities of love is worth our efforts to overcome the doubts and difficulties. In addition, I deeply believe we have the means to reach our goal. It is not an impossible dream, because this feminist vision of loving individuals creating new communities of love is the fulfillment of our loving human nature.

Actual personal experiences are included in this book, but the names and identifying circumstances are often changed to protect individual privacy. Male pronouns traditionally refer to sexless words, like person or lover. This is a problem for the writer whose consciousness has been raised about the value of gender neutral language. Although my consciousness has been raised, the vocabulary of some writers I quote has not. Some quotations inappropriately use male pronouns to refer to neutral words like human being. When I use gender neutral words, I mean both women and men.

In the never-ending quest for the truth about human nature, love, and feminism, the insights and contributions of respected thinkers from the past cannot be ignored. Plato, Freud, and others must be listened to, even though there is no obligation to accept their ideas. It is not necessary for every generation to discover again the intellectual equivalent of fire.

Because truth is a process and not a static entity, we who search in the present need to build on the previous accumulation of knowledge. To build on the ideas of others means to reflect critically on their teachings, affirm their truthful thoughts, and perceive their errors. Then we can integrate their valuable insights with our own ideas so that together we create a fuller expression of the truth.

If we are going to create a more loving world, it all begins with you and me. It all begins when you and I develop more self-love and more love for others. This book presents my theory on how we can avoid being destructive of ourselves and others; how we can become our most loving selves; and how feminism helps create loving people and communities.

This book presents the most profound truth about life and love that I have experienced. This truth helps me survive difficult times and experience immense joy. My hope is that it will also help you get in touch with your loving inner core and become more loving.

PART ONE

THE POWER OF LOVE

CHAPTER ONE

LOVE IS OUR INNER CORE

> Love, the strongest and deepest element in all life, the harbinger of hope, of joy, of ecstasy; love, the defier of all laws, of all conventions; love, the freest, the most powerful molder of human destiny.
>
> Emma Goldman
> "Marriage and Love"

What Is Most Important to All of Us?

What really matters? What is most important? How different would your life be if you knew your own answer to these vital questions? What changes would you make in who you are and how you act? How different would your life be if you tried daily to be and to do what is supremely important to you?

To get in touch with what is deeply important to you, picture your own funeral with the flowers and soft organ music, with the faces of your family and friends. Choose four people you want to speak about you at your funeral: a family member, a friend, a work colleague, and a member of a community organization where you serve. What are the most important things that you want each of these speakers to say about you and your life? What contributions to your family, friends, work, and community do you want them to remember? What difference do you want to have made in their lives?[1]

By using our death as the criterion to examine ourselves and everything in our lives, we can get in touch with what we cherish most. Then we can make sure that whatever we do daily contributes to our deepest values rather than violates them.

What Is Most Important? My Answer Is Love.

What is profoundly important to us? We give diverse answers to this crucial question, because we have dissimilar life experiences.

My life experiences of suffering and love helped me discover my own answer to this fundamental question. In childhood, I experienced love from my parents and other relatives. I was profoundly happy when Dad read *The Wizard of Oz* as my three sisters and I snuggled close to him. Reading that book took time, but he did more. Dad read a dozen books to us. That was an extremely happy time for me. Throughout my childhood, there were many enjoyable times at home with my family and away from home with my relatives and playmates. I felt loved by my parents, relatives, and friends, and I loved them.

My childhood experiences of love led me to conclude that what is most important is to love and be loved. However, it was my experiences of suffering that solidified that conclusion. From the youngest age I can remember, the main problem in my life was Dad's drinking. Although I was too young to know the word alcoholism, I knew that Dad's drinking hurt me. I also knew his drinking hurt my mother and sisters.

Not only did I feel sad when Dad was away at some bar drinking, but I also felt unhappy when he was intoxicated at home. When he was drunk, he was unavailable to me or my sisters or my mother. Physically he was home, but psychologically he was never there for me. Dad gave me no emotional support.

At a very young age, I felt Dad was choosing the bottle over my mother, my sisters, and me. It seemed to me that the bottle was more important to him than we were. Feeling unloved, rejected, and abandoned, I was hurt, sad, and depressed.

When I was three or four years old, I devised a plan to get Dad to stop drinking. I thought a plea from one of his little girls might reach his heart. After thinking about it, I phrased my request as a question: "Dad, why do you drink?" Perhaps I sensed even at that young age that if I delivered a direct plea, he might respond negatively and critically. (Many years later, I experienced just such a hurtful, attacking response when I explicitly asked my alcoholic mother to stop drinking.)

My strategy was to ask Dad when he arrived home from work and was having his first drink, so he wouldn't be too drunk to hear. Intentionally or unintentionally, he missed my point and answered that drinking relaxed him.

Dad never talked to me about how his drinking affected me, not even years later when he joined Alcoholics Anonymous (AA) and stopped drinking. He never completed the fourth AA step of making amends toward those he hurt. Dad never helped me and my sisters deal with the effects that his drinking had on us.

My mother's response to Dad's alcoholism was, of course, more complex than I as a child could understand. Without success and without me knowing it, Mom asked the family doctor, the pastor, and others for help. All I experienced was Mom drinking with Dad.

I remember going with Mom and Dad to various bars. While they got drunk, my sisters and I played behind the bar or listened to one bartender tell stories about being a soldier during the Second World War. I'll never forget my embarrassment one night when I was standing outside a bar drinking a Coke as an elementary school classmate and his parents walked into the movies next door. Their disapproving look was just one of many humiliating experiences that my parents' alcoholism caused me.

Another of my mother's responses was to deny and hide Dad's drinking. One of Mom's main teachings was never to say anything negative. Although her message did not mention Dad's drinking, we knew what she meant. My sisters and I never talked to Mom or Dad or each other or anyone about the sad feelings our father's drinking caused us. The metaphor of the elephant in the living room applied to our house. The elephant taking up all the space in the living room was Dad's drinking. We tiptoed around it without ever acknowledging it was there, although it affected and controlled how we all lived.

Besides the explicitly stated rule, don't talk, our family implicitly taught two other rules of alcoholic families: don't feel and don't trust. Alcoholic families use these rules to keep the alcoholism a family secret.[2]

Because I obeyed these family rules, I never spoke to anyone about my father's drinking. I felt alone, because I didn't talk about what was most important to me--my unfulfilled need for love caused by his alcoholism. It was six months after Dad's death, when I was twenty-years-old, that I first told anyone. After that, I tested my friends' trustworthiness before talking about it.

Intellectually I know that there is no adequate way to compare different kinds of suffering. Yet I feel in my heart that my childhood pain was small compared with the suffering of the victims and survivors of the Holocaust, the suffering of American Indians removed from their home lands and slaughtered, the suffering endured by Africans under American slavery, the suffering of girls genitally mutilated by their elders, the suffering of children raped by their fathers, and the suffering of battered women and children.

My research into the suffering of these victims has led me to explore the questions: what is most important, who am I, who are you, why are we here, and what causes some of us to be destructive? My research confirms the answer burned deep in my heart by my own childhood experiences of love and suffering. What is most important is love. We are lovers and we are here to love. Our greatest need and the meaning of our lives are to love and be loved. We all need to give and receive love to become fully human.

In *Embraced by the Light*, Betty Eadie describes her near-death experience. She learned an important lesson after she was drawn up into a whirling black tunnel, arrived after traveling at great speed, and was embraced by the eternal light. "Love is supreme. Love must govern." Expanding on this message, she teaches "all we can do is love. ... We are to love one another. ... We are to be kind, to be tolerant, to give generous service. I know that greater joy comes through love than any other way."[3]

My life experiences of love and suffering led me to believe in the ultimate importance of love in our lives. Since love is crucial, we need to understand what love is, how we can become more loving, and why we are sometimes destructive.

The Inner Core and Basic Human Needs

Are people more like onions or peaches? This gambit raises the question: is there a common, distinguishable human nature. On one hand, if human beings are more like onions, then as layer after layer of their experiences peel off, nothing is left. There is no human nature; there are only unique individuals. On the other hand, if people are more like peaches, then they have an inner core surrounded by their unique personal qualities.[4] This inner core is their human nature that they have in common with everyone else.

To the answer the question about a common human nature, each of us must search our deepest selves. We must discover our own special uniqueness and distinguish it from that which we have in common with everyone else. One enlightening time to explore our deepest selves is the happiest moments of life when we experience joy and bliss. Another revealing time is when we face our most serious problems. Overwhelming threats, dangerous emergencies, and fatal illness expose our inner nature. When we experience physical injury, emotional trauma, social upheaval, spiritual crisis, and the loss of a loved one, we confront our innermost self.

What do I find when I delve into my own inner depths and into the depths of my family and friends? An analysis of the happiest moments and greatest suffering of myself and those closest to me leads me to the conclusion that every human being has an inner core. This inner core consists of our inborn universal human needs and our innate capacities that persist throughout our life.

One vital part of the common human nature is that people are needy. No one seriously disputes that all human beings in the various cultures around the world have needs. To survive and not to suffer and die, they must have the minimum of their needs met. To flourish, there are still other needs that must be fulfilled.

Rarely do we reach a state of complete satisfaction of all our needs, except for a short time. As one need is satisfied, still another desire pops up to take its place. Throughout our lives, we almost always want something. We are only satisfied, for a brief period, in a relative fashion, or during an ecstatic experience.

The common inner core includes the innate basic needs that every individual has, not just to survive, but to thrive and become fully human. All people have these same essential needs that do not vary with sex, race, class, or age. A poverty-stricken Chinese woman has the same basic needs as an American millionaire.

Answering the inner core's fundamental needs is the essential prerequisite for becoming self-actualized. People can be exceedingly damaged and have trouble developing if their inner core needs are not gratified. A chronic lack of satisfaction of these basic human needs produces severe problems in living, especially if the lack begins early in life. Deprivation during critical periods can cause long-lasting and even permanent injuries that make recovery extremely difficult. Studies show that babies who are not nurtured shrivel and even die. Yet even after severe deprivation, satisfying the inner core needs may cure and restore people.[5]

Safety and Growth

Two basic needs within our inner core are safety and growth.[6] These needs are matters of life or death, survival or extinction. All of us crave safety: safety produced by having enough food, clothes, and shelter; safety provided by having emotional protection and warmth; safety from fear, pain, suffering, and deprivation; safety furnished by developing the means to take care of ourselves; and safety caused by answering our inner core, physical, psychological, social, and spiritual needs.

From birth, all of us strive for growth. Unless we are stunted by debilitating experiences, we are never happy just being safe, just surviving and existing. We always want to reach out to be more, to experience more, to feel more, to do more, and to love more. Ever aspiring, we move beyond safety to growth.

The process of life is a never-ending series of choices between safety and growth.

```
safety <--------<  person  >----------> growth
safety <--------< inner core >---------> growth
```

Our inner core strives to balance our basic need for safety with our need for growth. To become our fullest selves, we need to balance our roots and our wings. Our roots provide safety and give us the courage to fly. Our yearning to fly and our attempts to use our wings are our desire to grow.[7]

The Need for Safety

To survive from conception to our deathbed, we all need to be safe physically, psychologically, socially, and spiritually. Human life is challenging and painful. We are born alone, helpless, and insecure. We die alone,[8] even when our loving family and friends are at our bedside. Totally powerless to stop death's inexorable march, we die insecure about what follows death.

Loneliness, powerlessness, and insecurity follow us throughout life from birth to death, because they are part of finite human existence. These experiences that we all encounter in different degrees result in suffering and cause us to search constantly for safety.

Loneliness Makes Us Search for Safety

My first awareness of loneliness began with my realization at an early age that Dad's drinking made him unavailable to me. I felt he could not have both his children and the bottle at the same time. These feelings caused me tremendous pain and loneliness.

Although my mother loved her four daughters and provided more than adequately for our physical needs, she never talked to any of us about any serious personal problems. With deep sadness, I recall that my mother never had enough awareness and energy to meet our emotional needs. She never helped us understand the most serious problem we all faced: our father's alcoholism.

Because of the distance the bottle created between my father and me, I felt alone. Since my mother was too busy and troubled by her own problems to be there emotionally for me, I was alone. Because my sisters and I respected Mom's rule, not to talk about Dad's drinking, I was lonely. Without anyone's help, I had to deal with my own troubles and the emotional problems that my father's alcoholism caused me. From my earliest memories, I was emotionally alone.

When I was 14, my father joined AA and stopped drinking. Since he was no longer spending so much time drinking, he had more time to be with his family. Unfortunately, he never talked about any past or present problems, so I still had to face the sadness and pain alone.

After my father's death when I was 20 years old, I met Mary who became my lifelong friend. After six months of sharing only good memories, I learned to trust her enough to reveal my deep inner feelings about Dad's drinking. I am sure Mary's ability to communicate her trustworthiness made it possible for me to share my emotional troubles for the first time. Perhaps Dad's death also freed me to talk without feeling disloyal. Since developing that beautiful friendship and many others, I have never felt as lonely as I did in my youth.

One of my favorite sayings is that, in friendship, our sadness is cut in half and our joy is doubled. Although this is an exaggeration, I believe it to be true that friends relieve our sorrow and increase our happiness. This truth does not negate the fact that in a sense I am alone in my deepest sadness and greatest joy. The death of a loved one I deal with alone. In addition, I alone experience the ecstasy in moments of great happiness: the birth of a baby, the pinnacle of achievement, and the joy of creation, whether it be a painting, a song, or a book.

Although loneliness often strikes unexpectedly during moments of profound joy or times of serious illness, it is also part of our everyday lives. Some of us even feel lonely when we are with other people. Loneliness makes us search for safety.

Powerlessness Makes Us Yearn for Safety

Powerlessness is part of human existence. We are born without any choice on our part. We die against our will. We are powerless before the forces of nature and the danger of hurricanes, tornados, and earthquakes. Facing the deadliness of cancer and heart disease, we are personally helpless.

While my mother was suffering from lung cancer, a stroke paralyzed her and destroyed her ability to speak. Then her lung cancer spread to her brain. Not only did I feel deeply sad, but I also felt helpless, like my hands were tied behind my back. Despite my urgent desire to help, I was powerless to do anything. It is impossible to imagine how helpless this previously strong and independent woman felt. She was unable to speak, to feed herself, to turn in bed, to walk, or to care for herself in any way. Powerlessness causes us to search for safety.

Feeling powerlessness is so difficult to deal with that some people who have severe experiences become power hungry. Batterers, rapists, and criminals crave power over others to overcome their helpless feelings. Adolf Hitler and Joseph Stalin are two extreme examples of men who became dictators, dominated countries, and killed millions to conquer their powerless feelings and be safe.

Insecurity Makes Us Crave Safety

Human life is fragile, finite, and limited. Our physical, psychological, social, and spiritual fragileness makes us insecure. To be human is to be finite. Being finite makes us insecure because it means we will die.[9]

Awareness of death produces anxiety and insecurity. Anxiety about death creates a healthy striving for safety and security. However, no absolute security is possible, because death always comes. Throughout life, there is certainty only about the past and the arrival of death in the future. All else about life is uncertain and insecure. Nevertheless, we strive to make ourselves as secure as possible.

When first-time parents take their newborn babies home from the hospital, they often feel both helpless and insecure. When the infants begin screaming and won't stop, parents try everything imaginable. Parents feel more power-less and insecure when nothing comforts the infants. Un-doubtedly, the infants themselves feel even more helpless and insecure than their parents, because they can't get their urgent needs met.

Two-year-old children whose feelings are hurt by their parents, no matter what the reason, feel not only hurt and alone, but also insecure. Watch them as they pull away and go off by themselves. Look into their eyes when they lay in bed unable to sleep. Insecurity is there. Insecurity is still there at age four, eight, sixteen, thirty-two, and even sixty-four, although it may lessen and express itself in different forms. Insecurity makes people look for safety.

Although insecurity is part of the human condition,

American culture exacerbates. Its patriarchal sex role socialization increases insecurity in both sexes. For many years, feminists have been writing about the damage done by this detrimental socialization process. Unfortunately, it has not changed much. It is essential that we keep analyzing its faults until we find solutions.

The patriarchal culture promotes insecurity by teaching "the two sexes are different; the two sexes are opposites; one sex is better than the other."[10] Two main sex role stereotypes are that men are aggressive, dominant, and superior, while women are submissive, subordinate, and inferior. Male dominance and female subordination are essential to the patriarchal system. Instead of teaching children to be their best self, the culture socializes them to conform to these hierarchical sex role stereotypes.

Because American culture begins teaching girls at a very young age that they are inferior, their normal, human, insecure feelings are increased. Thus, it is difficult for them to develop self-esteem and feel secure about who they are. The more that girls are socialized that they are inferior, the more insecure they feel. Most girls and women work their entire lives to overcome their feelings of inferiority and insecurity. As a result, girls and women search for safety.

Since boys are taught that they are superior, it seems logical that they would feel confident and secure about themselves. However, the paradox is that the more that boys are socialized that they are superior, the more insecure they feel. Boys unconsciously feel and often consciously know that they are not superior to girls. Consequently, their normal, human, insecure feelings are increased because they are socialized to act out a superiority they do not believe they have. Extreme insecurity causes some men to brag about their macho toughness. The insecurity underneath the fake superiority is often called the fragile male ego.

The harder some men try to prove their male supremacy, the more insecure they feel, the more they want to have power over others. Some women also try to overcome their insecure feelings by dominating others.

Some boys and men recognize that they are not superior. After affirming everyone's equality, they feel more self-confident and secure than those who believe in male supremacy. Nevertheless, both secure and insecure boys and men search for safety.

From their mothers' wombs to their deathbed, all people experience loneliness, powerlessness, and insecurity in differing degrees and in varying ways. Consequently, all individuals search constantly for safety.

The Need for Growth

Throughout our lives, we experience not only the need for safety but also the need for growth. Psychological, social, and spiritual growth are more difficult to explain than safety, because they are less concrete and discernible.

Safety helps me feel I'm OK. Growth makes it possible for me to believe that you're OK[11] and to form a relationship with you. Safety produces self-preservation, self-identity, and self-actualization. Growth promotes self-change, creativity, and connectedness with others.

When I feel safe, I can be independent. When I am growing, I can be interdependent and united with others. Safety makes it possible for me to stand alone and find inner peace, while growth gives me the strength to be creative and intimate with others. Safety is the drive for self-actualization, while growth is the drive for communion with others.

Growth is an exciting and rewarding process that fulfills yearnings and ambitions. There is always tension involved with growth because of its long-term, distant goals. When life experiences have not stunted me, growth is a continuous urge. The more I grow, the more I want to grow, so that the desire to grow is endless and can never be satisfied. The ceaseless drive for growth is a creative fire that burns in every person, a thirsting for the new and unknown.[12]

Growth is a process of risky, adventuresome undertakings. Growing involves taking chances and acting on less than certainty. The process of life always involves compromising some degree of safety. Accepting the uncertainty, fear, highs, and lows is the price we pay for a flowing and exciting life. The constructive striving to change and grow can be thwarted or warped, but it cannot be destroyed.[13]

Mutually Enhancing Balance between Safety and Growth

Safety and growth need to be in balance because they are essential to each other for full functioning. Thus, to become our fullest selves, we must balance our need for safety with our need for growth. Like a seesaw, life is a process that moves back and forth between safety and growth. Safety and growth are so connected that they cannot flourish without each other. When we feel safe, we go out from safety to grow and then return to safety again when we begin to feel insecure.

Young children clinging to their fathers' legs in a strange environment provide an illustration of the balance between safety and growth. Because their fathers' presence produces the feeling of safety, they venture out to explore the area and to discover whatever is new to them. When their fathers disappear by going into another room, the youngsters no longer feel safe. They begin to cry and search frantically for their fathers who provide their safety.

Love Is Our Inner Core and Our Most Fundamental Need

As human beings, our deepest nature is our inner core that answers our basic needs for safety and growth. What is our inner core? My life experience teaches me that love is my inner core. This is not unique to me. When I find the deepest part of myself, I have also discovered the most profound quality of human nature. Despite our characteristics, love is the heart of our human nature and our most enlivening quality. Love is our most fundamental need.

Love is the innermost core of everyone. Benjamin Spock, a pediatrician, describes the inner core of a three-month-old infant. "His core is loving and sociable."[14] As the dynamic power and vital energy that makes life possible, love is all women and men's creative life force and vibrant spirit.

What Audre Lorde names the erotic, I call love. "The erotic is a resource within each of us that lies in a deeply female and spiritual plane, firmly rooted in the power of our unexpressed or unrecognized feelings." It is "an assertion of the life force" and "creative energy empowered." With it, "we are now reclaiming in our language, our history, our dancing, our loving, our work, our lives."[15]

The American patriarchal socialization process teaches many harmful lessons that violate the inner core of love. Men, and recently women, are instructed to be dominant and competitive in the marketplace. The highest values in the business world are money, power, and success. In domestic life, women are taught to be cooperative and nurturing because they are responsible for creating a loving home.

Many people perpetuate these damaging stereotypes by stressing the socialized differences between women and men. In his recent best-selling book, John Gray incorrectly claims that *Men Are From Mars, Women Are From Venus*. Symbolized by Mars, the god of war, men value "power, competence, efficiency, and achievement." Signified by Venus, the goddess of love, women value "love, communication, beauty, and relationships."[16]

In most American homes, the highest values for both women and men are love and caring for their family and friends. However, because of their socialization, men may also value being dominant in the home as well as in the corporate world. Most people overlook the difficulties created for men when they try to act both loving and dominant. Love and domination are mutually exclusive. Acting dominant not only harms the person being dominated, but it also violates the dominator's own inner core of love.

The patriarchy rigidly divides the values of the marketplace and home, because love and caring are called feminine values. Feminine values are considered inappropriate for the rat race of the business world where masculine values reign.

Women are now active in almost all areas of the

marketplace. Nevertheless, much of the socialization process that teaches women to be wives and mothers remains the same, except there is a new female image. The super woman does it all, both at home and in the business world, and never complains. The new expectation is that women will be successful both at home and in business. The values of the marketplace and the home are still strictly separated.

The patriarchal socialization process is erroneous when it stresses dominance and competition in the business world. The separation of the values of the home and marketplace is a mistake, because the values of the home should also be the values of the corporate, financial, political, educational, medical, legal, media, and governmental world.[17]

Both women and men are innately loving. To be a father is to love. To be a mother is to love. Although many families are dysfunctional, fathers and mothers give their children love to the best of their ability and in the only way they know how.

Not only do we need to express our love to our families and friends, but we also need to give our love to our community through our work in the larger world. The patriarchy dehumanizes us by teaching us that work outside the home is only a way to make money and not a way to give our love. Work without love as its heart is unfulfilling, alienating, and even debilitating.

Since all of us are fundamentally lovers, we need a new non-patriarchal teaching that connects work with love. To work is to love. Our work is our love made visible. Our work is the gift of our love not only to our families and friends but also to the larger world.

To know an artist, study her art. Every piece of work is a self-portrait of the one who did it. We need to autograph our work with love. As an educator, I believe that to teach is to love. To teach is to help my students blossom like beautiful flowers into their fullest selves. Throughout our day, our love needs to be expressed not only to our families and friends, but also to our co-workers, customers, clients, students, and patients. Our work needs to be an expression of our deepest power, our power to love.

Three important ways to express our love are to ourselves through self-love; to our families and friends through sharing, caring, nurturing relationships; and to our acquaintances and community through our work. The more we love ourselves, the more love we have to give to our families and friends, the more love we have to contribute to the larger community and business world.

The Goal of Our Inner Core Is Love, Not Superiority or Domination

Some individuals believe that all people have the innate desire to feel superior and dominate others. Alfred Adler, a psychologist, claimed that "the psyche has as its objective the goal of superiority." At every point in life, a person is "guided and spurred on by his longing for superiority, the thought of his godlikeness, the belief in his special magical power." The origin of every bodily and mental attitude is a striving for power. Even in love, a person "desires to experience his power over his partner." Neurotics who have strong feelings of inferiority and insecurity have the goal of superiority and power over others in an exaggerated degree.[18]

It is a vitally important question whether humans have an innate inner core of love or an inborn desire to feel superior and to have power over others. The patriarchal socialization process teaches that people want to be superior and to dominate others. It claims men are superior and have the right to have power over women. Thus, the patriarchy creates a hierarchy of men over women, rich over poor, Americans over foreigners, straights over gays, and whites over people of color. Although America officially proclaims "all men are created equal," the actual message taught throughout U.S. history is that rich white powerful men are superior and have the right to dominate everyone else.

Socializing people to fit into the superior and inferior, dominant and subordinate hierarchy creates a self-defeating prophecy. Many downtrodden people internalize feelings of inferiority that they are taught. Then they feel inadequate, insecure, and even self-hating. To overcome their feelings of inferiority, some people who are treated as subordinate yearn for superiority. They want to put others down so that they can move above them on the hierarchy. When they consider someone inferior, they put them down, dominate, and abuse them to build themselves up and feel superior.

To combat their socialized feelings of inferiority, many people identify with and imitate those they consider superior. Psychiatrists William Grier and Price Cobbs say racism can result in this defense mechanism. Racism causes "the cancer of black self-depreciation and the exaltation of whites." After experiencing racists' prejudice and hostility, some African Americans internalize the whites' teaching that blacks are inferior and they feel self-hatred.[19]

According to Grier and Cobbs, some African Americans believe the only way out of racism is to imitate whites. After rejecting their own blackness, they feel superior to other blacks. African Americans who identify with whites are often rewarded by white society with status and wealth and thus believe they have chosen the right course. "They are opportunists, wretched and terrified, but going with the winner." However, reminders of their own blackness continue to produce feelings of self-hatred.[20]

The patriarchy socializes members of the dominant group to believe they are superior. Being aware that they are still somewhere down the hierarchy from the elite group at the top, they experience someone above them speaking and acting out one-upmanship. Consciously or unconsciously, they feel inferior. The existence of a hierarchy makes people, whether they are near the top or bottom, feel inferior. Hierarchies by their very nature teach people to feel inferior. Feelings of inferiority cause some people to want to feel superior and to dominate others.

We are all socialized to believe that some people are superior and others are inferior. Thus, we need to look into the depth of our heart to see if we truly believe that we are all

created equal.   Do we truly believe all women and men,
whites and people of color, gays and straights, rich and poor,
foreigners and Americans, are equal. We need to be extraor-
dinarily honest so that we can identify any cravings for
superiority and power over others when they appear.

However, I genuinely believe that our desires for
superiority and dominance are not innate.   The patriarchy
teaches us to have these desires. These internalized feelings
arise when I feel insecure or when someone causes me to
feel powerless. They develop when I feel another person is
acting in a superior, know-it-all way or when I feel someone
is trying to put me down and control me.

Despite our desire for superiority and dominance when
we feel unsafe, the depth of my being proclaims what I crave
most is not to be superior and dominate others. What I want
in my heart of hearts is to feel I am equal to others in human
dignity and human rights; to develop warm, caring relationships with others; and thus to love myself and others.   My
experiences with other people convince me that this is the
inborn nature of everyone.

Getting in Touch with Our Loving Inner Core

A question that recurs often in intellectual history is
what distinguishes human beings from their animal ancestors.
Erich Fromm, a humanistic psychoanalyst, contends that it is
not our upright posture, our tools, or our power of reflection
that distinguishes us from animals. Apes had these before
humans. Agreeing with the scientist and theologian Pierre
Teilhard de Chardin, Fromm believes what distinguishes us
from other animals is not just our knowledge and thought
because animals have the ability to think and know. What
distinguishes us is our self-awareness. We have a new and
different kind of consciousness. We know ourselves.[21]

When thinkers, like Fromm and Chardin, distinguish
between animals and humans, their thinking is often hierarchical so they imply humans are superior to animals. We need
to stop hierarchical thinking. Animals fulfill their purpose in

life by doing what comes naturally to them. Following their instincts, they live the life they were created for. Animals love, because their inner core is love. Their ability to love is more elementary or more developed, depending on how complex and conscious they are. Why do we humans insist we are superior to animals, when they accomplish their goal in life?

What is crucial is that all of us humans have a tremendous capacity to love and we are aware of it. Every one of us is essentially a lover.[22] To live is to love. To be a person is to love. To be human is to love. As our constitutive quality, love is our vital energy and the creative life force. Even though we often feel alone, we are the bearers of the most powerful love.

Our deepest, most fundamental need is to love. Disagreeing with Descartes' famous statement, "I think, therefore I am," I offer an alternative. I love, therefore I am. The more that I get in touch with my loving inner core, the more I love, the more self-actualized I am, the more I express my deepest self, the more I am in communion with others.

What is most important is to be in harmony with our loving inner core and express it as fully and freely. Some writers and therapists urge us to get in tune with our "inner child" or our "child within" or our "higher unlimited self." What they call our inner child or higher self, I call our inner core of love.[23]

Shirley MacLaine, an actor turned philosopher, says we all have a higher self that is always with us and helps us live in balance and harmony. Our higher self is our "individual soul energy" that is androgynous because it is composed of both feminine and masculine energy. "All life must work in harmony, balance, and respect for all other life." The higher self within each of us is "in touch with every other higher self. All unlimited souls resonate in harmony with each other."[24]

According to MacLaine, the higher self is the soul and the soul is "total love. ... you are each total love." MacLaine's higher self teaches that "we are all connected in love and light and purpose." To love ourselves is to love God. "The more you know your higher self, the closer you are to all other higher selves and to the Light which is the God-force."[25]

Arleen Lorrance, a philosopher, describes your Higher Self as "your own inner voice," your intuition, that monitors your body, feelings, and rational mind. "Living in the Higher Self is equivalent to living in love." To live lovingly is to keep your channels unblocked and clear, to allow your life energy to flow unsnagged and uninhibited, to "receive yourself as beautiful exactly as you are," and to "give love energy to yourself." Life in its purest form is unblocked energy. "Love is unblocked energy." Your Higher Self is "the God-self being born anew in the agony of the ecstatic life process."[26]

MacLaine and Lorrance are accurate in stressing the importance of getting in tune with our higher self. What is most important is to be in harmony with our inner core of love, which they call our higher self. Unfortunately, the phrase, the higher self, is inaccurate and even detrimental, because it indicates that we need to transcend our normal self and go beyond to something higher and better.

Our inner core of love is not a higher self, a more advanced self, or a new better self. The loving inner core is a more accurate term than the higher self because the inner core is the heart of our loving nature that is always with us. We are born in tune with our loving inner core. When we are not in accord with it, we need to get back in unity with it, and not be called to get in tune with our higher self.

It is empowering to be in harmony with our loving inner core, our dynamic power, and our vibrant spirit. Unfortunately, we can lose touch with it as a result of the patriarchal culture and our dysfunctional families. Our own destructive thoughts, feelings, and actions can disrupt the peaceful balance within ourselves, damage our caring relationships, and disturb our harmonious interconnection with nature.

Each of us has our own ways to get in harmony with our loving inner core. One way is to dialogue passionately with a close friend about what is most important to each of us. In these intimate conversations, I perceive my friend's inner beauty, goodness, spirit, and loving nature. I feel elated and fully alive.

Another way to get in tune with my loving inner core is to reflect deeply on the people in my life and how much I care about them. This helps me affirm that I am a caring person, that I am essentially a lover. Yet another way is to walk in nature and experience myself as part of the Oneness of all creation.

Spiritual reading and experiencing oneness with nature help me understand that God is Infinite Love. As Divine Love, God is within us all as our loving inner core. Thus, our loving inner core is sacred. We are all bearers of divine love. No one should mistreat or violate us, because we have the divine within us.

As lovers, we are all part of God who is Infinite Love. We are within God. God is part of all of us as our inner core of love. God is within us. God is like the ocean of love. We are all drops of love in that ocean.

When we are in tune with our loving inner core, we are in harmony with the law of life. The law of life is the law of love. The law of life, the natural law, and the divine law are all the same. All are the law of love. When we are in harmony with our loving inner core, we are aware of the underlying unity and oneness of all of life. Our cosmic consciousness perceives that love is the heart of the universe.

Our culture claims to value the individual. How has it lost sight of the sacredness of each of us as individuals? Why hasn't it understood the sacredness of our loving inner core?

What is most important is to love myself and my own goodness despite my flaws and faults. What is most important is to affirm and appreciate the loving inner core, the goodness, and the spirit of other people and nature. It is essential to feel at one with others and nature, to feel the interdependent unity of the cosmos.

To become fully functioning, we need to express our love and caring toward ourselves and others, especially those people who are part of our lives. We know what they need and we can try to support them as they work to supply what they need for themselves. It is essential that we empower others to answer their own needs by affirming their loving inner core, goodness, and spirit so that they experience their own self-love and feel loved by us. When they feel our caring because we share what we have to give, they will become empowered.

What is most important is to love ourselves and others. Thus, we take the suffering out of life, nurture loving individuals, and create communities of love.

CHAPTER TWO

THE ESSENCE OF LOVE

Love is free; it can dwell in no other atmosphere. In freedom it gives itself unreservedly, abundantly, completely. All the laws on the statutes, all the courts in the universe, cannot tear it from the soil, once love has taken root.

Emma Goldman
"Marriage and Love"

Mature love is union under the conditions of preserving one's integrity, one's individuality. Love is the active power in man; a power which breaks through the walls which separate man from his fellow man, which unites him with others; love makes him overcome the sense of isolation and separateness, yet it permits him to retain his integrity. In love the paradox occurs that two beings become one and yet remain two.

Erich Fromm
The Art of Loving

The Essence of Love

Vocalists sing about love, novelists describe it, and movies portray it. Some people chase after love, while others run away from it. Almost everyone experiences love, but no one fully comprehends it. What is this mysterious thing called love?

Nearly two thousand years ago, St. Paul wrote about love. "Love is always patient and kind; it is never jealous; love is never boastful or conceited; it is never rude or selfish; it does not take offence, and it is not resentful."[1]

In answering a class assignment that asked what is love, one student wrote a poetic description of love.

Love is believing in another
Love is deciding to stay with another
            and not being sorry
Love is being willing to take a chance
Love is wanting to grow
Love is wanting your beloved to grow
Love is trying to understand
Love is not being afraid to care
Love is enjoying each other
Love is all the smiles that you give
Love is all the tears that you cry
Love is all that you create
Love is all that you give
Love is the reason for your existence[2]

The above descriptions are beautiful and useful guides on how to become more loving, but they do not provide an adequate definition of love.

How to become more loving is an extremely important question that will be answered in the next chapter. Other questions are even more basic and therefore more important. What is love? Do I love anyone or anything in the world? Do I even love myself? These are as basic as the question, who am I, because I am what I love.

The key to answering these questions and to under-standing love is to grasp its essence. When I know the nature of love, I can answer the question: do I love anyone, even myself? Throughout history, writers of poetry and prose offer definitions of love. They range from superficial state-ments to the profound insights of Plato. Some are even incorrect, like the assertion in the novel Love Story, "love is never having to say you are sorry."

Besides the knowledge that love is our inner core, a penetrating understanding is that the essence of love is the dynamic power within us all. As our vital energy, love is our creative life force and our vibrant spirit. All kinds of love have the same essence.

Because love is our inner core, we need to love and be

loved to find out who we are. The more we express our love, the deeper the discovery of our true self and full potential. The more we love, the more we become self-actualized. When we fail to express our love, we lose part of ourselves. Consequently, we all search throughout life for love.

Because the heart of love is our creative life force, love is more than desire, although love includes desire and is sometimes triggered by it. Love is more than attraction, although love encompasses attraction and is propelled by it. Love is more than an emotion, although love causes the strongest feelings. Love is more than caring for the welfare of the beloved, although it contains caring as one of its qualities.

In his *Symposium*, Plato, speaking through Aristophanes' myth, describes what sounds like romantic love. People's intense yearning is for "meeting and melting into one another, thus becoming one instead of two." As a longing for reunion, love is "the desire and pursuit of the whole."[3]

Plato is correct that love is an intense force that moves us, but he is only partly accurate about what love drives us to pursue. Love has two drives, rather than one. The essence of love is our creative life force. The aim of love is the two drives, the drive toward communion with others and the drive toward personal development. Within its inner core, love balances these two drives. All love is the vital energy that moves us toward union with others in spirit, while each actualizes the individual self.[4]

To test whether a feeling is love is to see if it has the essence of love, a dynamic power that moves us. The way to identify whether love is a creative or damaging is to ask if it involves two drives. If love has only one drive and not two, then it will be creative, because all love is creative, but also damaging for the beloved or the lover or both. Love is damaging when it makes communion into a fusion that destroys self-actualization or when it stresses individual development and does not create relationships with others.

The reason love is the most important reality in life is because it unites the thrust toward personal development with the drive toward social connectedness. Thus, the individual and social needs are both actualized at the same time. The two basic human needs for personal safety and social growth are both fulfilled in the one act of love.

One deep sadness in my life is that for all those years my father was drinking excessively, he neglected his personal development. Because of his compulsive drinking, he lost a good deal of his ability to have deep relationships with others.

However, when Dad joined AA, he began practicing the two drives within love in creative ways. His drive for self-actualization included his stopping drinking and his efforts to change himself. One thing that makes me proud of my father and that is his greatest legacy to me is the way he expressed his drive for union with others. Dad dedicated himself to the AA work of helping other alcoholics become sober and lead positive, productive lives.

Love's Unifying and Self-actualizing Drives

Many authors neglect the self-actualizing drive and describe only the unifying drive when they define love as attachment, desire, communion, attraction, or union. Theologian Paul Tillich's definition of love stresses the unifying drive and omits the self-actualizing dynamic. "Love is the drive towards unity of the separated."[5]

When we experience any kind of creative love, we feel both the unifying dynamic and the self-actualizing drive. Love's unifying drive can be extremely powerful. In some types, such as parental love and romantic love, we must be careful that it does not overshadow love's self-actualizing drive.

The infatuation stage of romantic love demonstrates the unifying drive of love. When you and I are separated, I long to be with you again. I have trouble keeping my mind on anything but you. Daydreams about you invade my work and play. I re-create the beautiful moments we spent together in the past and I imagine the next time we will be together. Whenever appropriate and sometimes when it is not appropriate, I call you. When I cannot call, I write letters and send gifts.

When we are together, the drive for union is even stronger. If it is appropriate to our relationship, I want to wrap my arms around you in a big hug and never let go. After telling you all the beautiful things that I have been thinking and feeling about you, I want to kiss you. In sexual love, I want to touch every part of your body, while in friendship, I experience a strong desire to be in touch with your spirit.

The drive for union is unmistakable. Lovers experience this drive in their thoughts and feelings. As Viktor Frankl, who survived Nazi concentration camps, says, "love is the only way to grasp another human being in the innermost core." Love is "the experience of ultimate togetherness."[6]

In contrast, the drive for personal development that is the other drive within love is often invisible. When the drive to be with the beloved is so strong, it often overpowers the drive for self-actualization that is also part of love's nature.

The reason that I seek communion with you is not only because it is good for you but also because it is good for me. Many of us do not realize that we help each other attain a personal wholeness that is beyond our reach without our love for each other. Martin Buber, a Jewish theologian, describes love's self-actualizing drive. To become my fullest possible self, I must enter a relationship. "I become through my relation to the Thou; as I become I, I say Thou."[7] As I say Thou, I become more fully myself.

In all kinds of creative love, I want communion with you not only because you bring beauty and spirit into my life but also because loving you adds beauty and spirit to my own person. Loving you frees me to be myself. In an intimate friendship, feeling safe enough to trust and share helps me discover my deepest self. To love is not only to give for the benefit of my friend, but also to receive personal enrichment in the depth of my soul.

The power of love is the vital energy that moves the lover toward communion and self-actualization. Each kind of love varies in strength and intensity. Most people, but sadly not all, love their children more than their cars and other material possessions.

Depending on the kind, the reasons for love vary. Some causes for love are your goodness, caring, compassion, honesty, listening, understanding, trustworthiness, accepting, sharing, appreciating, courage, expressiveness, talents, looks, sense of humor, values, wisdom, spirituality, joyfulness, commitment to progressive causes, love of life, way of loving, vital life force, loving inner core, effervescent soul, or your ability to make me happy even though neither of us is fully conscious of what gives you this ability.

Your inner beauty and spirit are gifts to me that both increase my happiness and enrich my individuality. Being in touch with your spirit and beauty as well as the happiness within me that they create makes it possible for me to become aware of my own inner beauty and spirit and express them. When I am in a loving relationship, I feel myself growing happier and more peaceful.

Love Is a Dialogue

Love is a dialogue, a dynamic movement between the two drives toward personal development and union with others. When these two drives are in dialogue, they benefit each other. Love drives the individual to move out from self-actualization toward communion with others, and then back to personal development.

Just as there is no deep love without the drive for interpersonal union, so also there is no strong love without the drive for intrapersonal development. To develop fully, I must separate myself from others so that I can discover my individual integrity. However, to develop my fullest possible self, I must relate to others. When I fail to become involved with others, my separation can become alienation. If I neglect my independence, my need for interdependence can develop into dependence and clinging possessiveness. When I fail to be interdependent, my independence can grow into undependability.

Through love, I experience interdependence with loved ones, while I simultaneously grow more independent. To experience beneficial communion, I must know solitude. To be creative in my aloneness, I must know intimacy.

Pierre Teilhard de Chardin captures the all-pervasiveness of love and its essence. Love is cosmic energy, "the fundamental impulse of life." Everything is animated with the flow of love. "Love alone is capable of uniting living beings in such a way as to complete and fulfill them, for it alone takes them and joins them by what is deepest in themselves." Although love causes union, "union differentiates" because it creates personal uniqueness in the lover and the beloved. "It is through love and within love that we must look for the deepening of our deepest self, in the life-giving coming together of humankind." Love causes an exaltation that can arouse in the heart of our being all that we possess of uniqueness and creative power.[8]

The Loving Inner Core Unites Self-love and   Love for Others

Self-love is love's first drive toward self-preservation and self-realization. Love's second drive toward communion with others can be called love for others. These two drives are united within the inner core of love.

self-actualization <-----< love >-----> communion with others
        self-love <-----< love >-----> love for others

Thus, the inner core of love consists of the two active drives toward self-love and toward love for others.

The fundamental quality necessary to be fully functioning is love, including the dialogue between its two drives, love for self and love for others. If many other characteristics are present, but love is absent, people will never reach their full potential. Fully functioning people not only express and practice love for themselves but also love for others.

Self-love and love for others answer our needs for

safety and growth. Our most important safety need is our need to be loved. Our need to be loved includes the simple need to be recognized by acquaintances and the intense need to be loved by our family, friends, and romantic partners. Our contact with acquaintances and our intimate communion with friends provide different degrees of sharing and caring that answer our need to be loved.

Most of us search throughout our lives for people to love us, and fortunately many of us are successful. Some of us, however, feel unhappy because we are not loved in the way we want. A crucial challenge of life is to realize that the best way to feel safe is to love ourselves.[9] It is wonderful if others love us, but the surest means to feel safe is to love ourselves. Self-love provides safety when we feel rejected, abandoned, betrayed, ostracized, deserted, or simply left alone by others.

Self-love is the drive toward self-preservation and self-actualization. It unites my separated parts into a unique personal wholeness. Many easily spot their faults, but fail to see their own goodness. Self-love accepts all my parts, including my strengths and weaknesses. It accepts me even when I feel unacceptable. Self-love affirms my life, my goodness, and my love.

My most important relationship is my relationship with myself. How I view myself is more significant than how others view me. My character is what I am. It is the outward manifestation of my loving inner core. My reputation is what other people say that I am.

Although it is important to listen and even be influenced by what others say about me, it is more important to be influenced by what I say about myself. Of all the people in the world, I know myself better than anyone else. If I look hard enough into myself, I will see my own good qualities, and even more crucial, my own loving inner core. When I believe that I am good and loving, I can accept my faults and mistakes. When I believe in myself, no one can take that belief away from me.

It is rewarding to find someone I like, but it is essential

to like myself. Although it may be thrilling to realize someone else is good and decent, it is indispensable to view myself that way. It is a delight to find people who are worthy of respect and love, but it is vital to believe that I deserve these things. I cannot find myself in anyone else. Of all the people I will know in my lifetime, I am the only one that I will never leave and never lose. To the question of my life, I am the indispensable answer. To the problems in my life, I am the most crucial solution.

Just as the best answer to the most important safety need is self-love, so also the preeminent answer to the most vital growth need is loving others. Love for others drives toward communion and promotes growth.[10]

Fully functioning individuals are capable of extremely close personal relationships. As Maslow says, self-actualizing people are "capable of more fusion, greater love, more perfect identification, more obliteration of the ego boundaries than other people would consider possible."[11]

After fully functioning people extend their love beyond themselves to their family, friends, and neighbors, they expand their love to humanity, to all people everywhere. Because they believe all people are members of one human family, they have compassion and love for humankind. Self-actualizing individuals want to help solve the problems facing the whole human race.[12]

Self-actualizing people give respect to all people just because they are human. They feel kinship with all people, because they are part of the human family. Because of their love for all people, they are realistic and disapprove of others' harmful activities. Criticizing wrong doings but not the actor, they speak harshly about dishonest, prejudiced, power-hungry, and violent acts.[13]

Gandhi loved both the oppressed and the oppressors. He helped free India from British colonial power by preaching *ahimsa*, which means nonviolence. "In its positive form, ahimsa means the largest love, greatest charity. If I am a follower of ahimsa, I must love my enemy." Loving those who hate us is the "grand law of love." Although it is the most difficult thing to do, Gandhi urges people to do it. "It is not nonviolence if we merely love those that love us. It is nonviolence only when we love those that hate us." For Gandhi, this law of love is a universal principle governing all people. When love is accepted as the law of life, "it must pervade the whole being and not be applied to isolated acts."[14]

Gandhi's activities were motivated by universal love. "My life is one indivisible whole, and all my activities ... have their rise in my insatiable love of mankind." Gandhi strongly affirms the importance of love when he says "it is love that sustains the earth. There only is life where there is love. Life without love is death. ...we can conquer the whole world by truth and love."[15]

Many people, both the unknown and the famous, preach and practice lifelong dedication to love others. Elizabeth Cady Stanton and Susan B. Anthony worked for over 50 years of their lives for women, as they struggled for women's right to vote, both nationally and internationally.

Love Balances Self-love and Love for Others

Love is a mutually enhancing balance between self-love and love for others. Before loving others, fully functioning people need the safety provided by loving themselves. When they feel safe, they have the strength to express their love for others. After their love for others promotes their own growth, they need to create new feelings of safety through self-love, before going out to love others again. Thus, love balances self-love and love for others.

We can only love others as much as we love ourselves. Self-love and love for others are inseparably connected rather than mutually exclusive. Respect and love for our own self cannot be severed from respect and love for another.[16] The deeper our love for ourselves, the more we are able to love others. The greater our love for others, the stronger our self-love.

Jesus' second great commandment, "love your neighbor as yourself,"[17] stresses both self-love and love for others.

The message of this commandment is that self-love and love for others are equally important. You are not to love yourself more than your neighbor. You are not to love your neighbor more than yourself, but as yourself.

According to Alcoholics Anonymous (A.A.), the underlying problem for alcoholics is both their inability to form constructive relationships and their lack of self-love. A.A. believes that many alcoholics suffer the most from their twisted relationships. Failing to recognize their "total inability to form a true partnership with another human being," alcoholics sometimes manipulate and dominate other people. Other times they lean on others far too much,[18] because they want to be taken care of as though they were children.

To assist alcoholics with their low self-esteem and inadequate connections with others, A.A. works to help them develop genuine self-love and creative relationships. "Courtesy, kindness, justice, and love are the keynotes by which we may come into harmony with practically anybody." A.A. also helps alcoholics "see truth, justice, and love as the real and eternal things in life."[19]

In A.A., it is not enough to see the importance of justice, truth, and love. The twelfth A.A. step teaches members to take action by carrying the A.A. message to other alcoholics to help them become sober and develop the joy of living. Helping others solve their personal problems is a profound act of loving others. It is also a way for A.A. members to practice self-love and stay sober, because they see alcoholism as it really is in the lives of the drinkers they are helping.

Psychiatrist M. Scott Peck explains the need for both independence and communion by comparing pure communism and pure capitalism. The philosophy of pure communism claims that "the purpose and function of the individual is to serve the relationship, the group, the collective, the society." The destiny of the individual is of little or no concern.[20]

In contrast, pure capitalism stresses "the destiny of the individual even when it is at the expense of the relationship, the group, the collective, the society." The fact that poor women and children may go hungry does not prevent individual entrepreneurs from taking enormous profits. Peck contends that neither pure capitalism nor pure communism provides an adequate solution for the need for both independence and relationship. "The individual's health depends upon the health of the society; the health of a society depends upon the health of its individuals."[21]

Love, Self-love and Love for Others
are like Tao, Yang and Yin

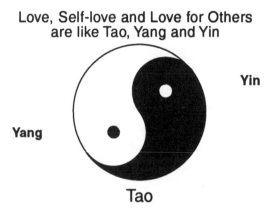

Yin

Yang

Tao

Thousands of years ago, Chinese philosophy said there is an ultimate reality, called the *Tao*, that underlies and unifies all things. Tao is the undefinable reality that is difficult to translate and even more difficult to explain. Perhaps the best English translation is "the Way." Lao Tzu, the legendary founder of Taoism, began his classic *Tao Te Ching* with the assertion, "the Tao, the Way, that can be trodden is not the enduring and unchanging Tao. The name that can be named is not the enduring and unchanging Tao."[22]

The Tao is the cosmic way, the "transcendent origin and guiding force of the universe."[23] As the fundamental law of life, the Tao is the primal energy that unifies all life processes and governs everything. The Tao is the dynamic interplay of two modes of energy, the yin and yang, that make up everything in existence.

According to Chinese philosophy, everything has within it the yin and yang life principles. In some things, yang dominates, while in others yin prevails. Fire and heaven are more yang, while water and earth are more yin. For the Chinese, yang is masculine, while yin is feminine. Yang is active, warm, dry, light, high, strong, spiritual, and positive. Yin is passive, cold, dark, weak, material, and negative.

Ancient Chinese philosophy is accurate when it declares that the Tao is the ultimate reality of the universe. In my philosophy, love as the cosmic energy within all life is like the Tao, the governing principle of existence. For the Chinese, the essential element of life is the Tao that is composed of the duality of yin and yang. In my philosophy, the fundamental element of human nature is love that balances the drive toward communion and the drive toward personal development. As the dynamic power of life, love unites the two drives, the yang, the drive toward self-love, with the yin, the drive toward love for others.

Chinese philosophy is accurate that Tao has two drives, the yin and yang. It is inaccurate in describing these two drives as masculine and feminine or as positive and negative. The two drives are sexless. In addition, they are both positive because both are necessary to reach full humanness.

Fully functioning women and men are lovers who balance self-love and love for others, safety and growth, the drive for personal development and the drive for communion. Love harmonizes these drives.

Person = Lover =
Our Inner Core of Love =
self-love <------< love >-----> love for others
self-actualization <------< love >------> communion with others
safety <------< love >-----> growth

Lao Tzu teaches the importance of both self-love and love for others when he creates the ideal of the sage. Sages both perfect themselves and benefit others. "The sage does not hoard: the more one does on behalf of others, the more one has for oneself; the more one gives to others, the more one is enriched."[24]

Providing meaningful ideas on how to reach peace and happiness, Taoism teaches non-interfering and letting be. Barry Steven's title, *Don't Push the River*, captures non-interfering. Lao Tzu's words describe letting be. "The sanest man ... takes everything that happens as it comes."[25]

The underlying assumption of Taoism is that there is an interdependent unity of life. All of life is innately good and naturally harmonious. If people accept themselves and life, they will experience the peace and happiness that are an inherent part of life. When they resist the flow of life and try to impose their own way, they lose the harmony.

To be happy, we must accept our place within the interdependent unity of life and harmonize with it. We must accept ourselves as we are. One thing that we must accept about ourselves is that we have two driving forces within us that must be actualized. One thrust is to accept life as it is and flow with it. This force is our self-love, our drive for personal development that provides safety and creates a creative self-identity. The other drive is to exert effort, to go beyond ourselves to love and unite with others. This causes us to grow and change.

To be happy, we need to actualize both drives: the acceptance of life and the urge to exert effort. We need not only to feel safe and peaceful but also to strive and grow. Passiveness leads to peace and harmony, while activeness produces accomplishment and achievement. All of us need both to attain harmony and happiness.

The Progression of Love

Love progresses from self-realization to intimacy. First, I move toward my own self-actualization. As a child and adult, it is natural for me to meet my own needs and develop myself. After I take care of myself and feel safe, I relate to the beloved. Many of us then move back toward our own improvement again.

After uniting with our loved ones, some of us progress toward a second type of self-realization, the personal development of our loved ones. We want our loved ones to fulfill their potential. We have as much commitment to their self-realization as we do to our own. After we cultivate our beloved's actualization, we again work to improve ourselves.

The progression of love starts with the drive for my self-actualization and then moves toward intimacy with the beloved. Sometimes this leads to the drive for the beloved's self-realization. Then I again work to develop myself, and the progression continues.

The Progression of Love =
drive for my own self-actualization --->
drive for communion with the beloved --->
drive for the beloved's self-realization --->
drive for my own personal development --->
drive for intimacy with the beloved --->
and so on

All the parts of love are difficult to do. Because living in a patriarchal culture damages us, our love is fragile and needs to be nurtured and treated with care. Love can be snuffed out anywhere along the progression of love by harsh words or actions. It is challenging to be loving toward ourselves, especially if we were raised in dysfunctional families where we were put down and abused. It is hard to love ourselves when our culture teaches us that we are inferior and other people are above us on society's hierarchy. It is exhausting to feel self-love when are dominated by others in most areas of our lives.

When we grow up feeling put down and inferior, it is difficult to feel safe enough to be intimate with others. Conversely, it is hard to develop equal, mutual relationships when we are taught in childhood that we are superior and supposed to dominate others.

However, one extremely difficult part of love is helping the beloved become self-actualized. It is challenging to assist the self-actualization of our friends when we do not live with them every day. Even more effort is required when we daily share our lives with the beloved. Most mothers and fathers want the best for their children but are drained by their constant, ever-present needs. Extreme care is necessary to support and help our loved ones without doing for them what they can do for themselves.

The most challenging problem in love is to balance our own needs with the needs of our beloved and thus produce mutuality and intimacy. When we are in a loving relationship, our needs will always clash. Our needs even collide when we suppress our own needs so that we are not aware of them. In this case, the clash is covert rather than overt. Negotiations are necessary to meet both our individual needs. When negotiations are not successful, creative healing of wounded feelings is required.

When we feel that our needs are balanced in a way that is good for both of us, our independence and intimacy grow. Each of us becomes more self-reliant, as our closeness matures. The more we take care of our self-actualization; the more we can unite with the beloved. The more we care about our loved one's self-realization; the more independent both of us become; the more interdependent we are; the more our mutual partnership grows; the more intimate we become.

In love, the dynamic striving for communion involves giving. The quest for our personal development involves receiving.

Love Is a Dialogue between Giving and Receiving

Just as love is a dialogue between self-love and love for others, so also love is a dialogue between giving and receiving. Giving is sharing and communicating rather than sacrificing. What do givers share? What is most important is not that they give material things, but that they share their inner selves. It is only when they share themselves that they truly give. If they withhold their love and giving, they will never become fully alive.[26]

Lovers give all that they have to give. They give their

time, understanding, pain, feelings, thoughts, happiness, sadness, goodness, empathy, laughter, vulnerabilities, values, their most profound concerns, and most important, their deepest selves. Even when they choose to give material goods, these often symbolize the gift of themselves.

Just as there is no love without giving, so also there is no love without receiving. It seems to me that Fromm's view becomes unbalanced when he says that "love is primarily giving, not receiving,"[27] because love's giving and receiving are always in dialogue. When I love you, I not only share with you, but I also grow in my own sense of aliveness. Through acts of love, I experience my own power, strength, and vitality. This creates joy within me. This is the minimum that I receive from loving; sometimes I receive much more.

Giving is an obvious part of love. Receiving is not only less obvious; it is sometimes a hidden and unrecognized part of love. It is well known that teachers give knowledge to their students. It is unknown to many, including many teachers, that teachers learn from their students. Actors not only give their performance to the audience, but they also receive stimulation from it. Clergy perform acts of kindness for individuals in their congregations and grow psychologically, socially, and spiritually from interaction with them. Love is the ultimate two-way relationship.

Parents give to their children, and they also receive from them. Christine Gudorf, a feminist theologian, and her husband adopted two physically disabled and developmentally backward children, ages two and five. After spending most of their lives in institutions, the children were severely deprived. The younger child had never formed any relationships and totally refused any after adoption. He could not walk or talk, refused all food, and he did not respond to speech. After the parents shared a great deal, these needy children gave their parents "love, trust, a new view of people in general, and hope that the world can be made significantly better."[28]

Because their eldest son was a refugee, Gudorf and her husband became involved in the needs of refugees. Seeing the world in radically different terms, they chose sides because they realized that in the face of injustice, there is "no neutral attitude." These new communities, causes, perceptions, and loyalties led to new identities. "The children gave us not only themselves, but ourselves, and in more than one way." Helping the children learn to participate in society gratified the parents' own self-interest. "Every achievement of the child is both a source of pride and a freeing of the parent from responsibility for the child."[29]

Many people claim that we should love and never request anything in return. While it is true that love does not ask for anything in return, we nevertheless receive many joys in return. We receive the joy of giving, the joy of the presence of our loved one, the joy of knowing the beloved, the joy of loving and sometimes being loved in return. As Buber teaches, the I-Thou relation is mutual. "My Thou affects me, as I affect it."[30] Both the lover and the beloved are receivers. In fact, we are all receivers.

When lovers give to their loved one, something new is born from which they each benefit. When people are successful in loving, they transform the beloved into a lover. Powerful lovers can create love in other people. Lovers help others become givers. They promote love by expressing it. Just as violence begets more violence, so also love creates more love. Genuine love transforms both the lover and the beloved into more loving people. Both are surprised and blessed by the joy of giving and receiving.

Those who want only to give and never to receive block the development of love. Feeling insecure, they do not want to be in debt to anyone, because they want to be ahead of others in giving. For example, picking up the tab helps overcome some of their feelings of unworthiness and makes them feel that they have a right to be with others. This need to be constantly giving and never receiving may cause their own ability to give to dry up, because a lifetime of hidden resentment has built up.

Those who receive and seldom give are selfish people. Trying to build up their poor self-image, they take everything for themselves and give nothing in return. Their taking is insatiable because what they are receiving is often superficial things and what they need to receive is love. They are attempting without success to cure the symptoms rather than the cause of the problem. Because they do not love themselves enough, they are unable to love others.

Although changes are slowly occurring, women are socialized that their main purpose is to give everything to their husband and children, no matter what the cost to themselves. This selfless giving can be destructive, if it is not balanced with self-love.

In many ways, the patriarchy teaches women to give and men to receive. It socializes women to take care of men's physical needs for food, clean clothes, and an attractive home; their social needs for companions and entertainment; and their emotional needs for support and love. Men are taught to expect that their physical, social, and emotional needs will be met by women.

Another way that the patriarchy socializes women to give and men to receive is during sexual intercourse. In earlier times, women were taught to give men sexual pleasure, even if it was painful for them. This has changed, but some states still have marital exemption laws that say husbands cannot be prosecuted for raping their wives. A man's home is his castle and his wife is expected to be sexually available to him whenever he wants. When women's groups have tried to abolish these laws, there is resistance. Sadly, the practice of spouse abusers wanting sex and even raping their wives after beating them has not stopped.

Some people still defend men's right to have sex with women whenever they want. The Republican candidate for Governor of Texas during the 1992 campaign said something similar to the old sexist maxim, "if rape is inevitable, relax and enjoy it." Although his statement may have contributed to his loss in the Governor's race, his way of thinking is far from dead.

The patriarchy socializes men to believe that their main purpose in life is to provide for their family's financial needs. The most important sign of being a good breadwinner is to feed, clothe, and shelter their wives and children adequately, if not luxuriously. If necessary, men are expected to work at jobs they hate. Thus, men's main responsibility, like women's, is to give, no matter what the cost to themselves.

Both Christianity and American culture teach it is more blessed to give than to receive. Both stress giving and rarely teach anything about the importance of receiving. Neither speaks about the importance of balancing giving and receiving.

When people are taught their purpose is to give to others and not to receive, they feel guilty when they spend time, money, and energy on themselves. Women seem to experience this debilitating guilt more than men.

When men provide adequately for their families through their work, they feel they have accomplished their main purpose in life. In addition, success in their work gives them an additional sense of self-satisfaction and achievement. Once they have provided for their families' needs, men feel their time, money, and energy are their own to use as they please. In contrast, women's work of taking care of their husbands, children, and homes is never ending and never done. Thus, when women work outside the home or do things for themselves, they often feel guilty in ways that men do not.

Our culture flaunts romantic love before the public as the be-all and end-all of life, in novels, movies, television, and advertisements. As a result, many people who are not in erotic relationships experience themselves as unhappy failures. Instead of valuing their many other ways of loving, they feel unhappy because they fail to conform to the romantic standards of the patriarchal culture.

Unhappy individuals who feel unable to love sometimes ask in moments of despair: Do I love anyone? Do I even love myself? Not seeing themselves clearly, depressed people question their own ability to love.

More helpful ways to ask the questions are: Do I want to be with anyone? Do I want a relationship? Do I wish for personal improvement? If the answer to any of these questions is yes, then we are beginning to love. How loving we can be depends on how capable we are of giving and receiving.

Giving and receiving are part of the essence of love and the expression of love. The essence of love is the dynamic power that drives us toward both giving and receiving, that moves us toward both personal development and communion with others. Giving creates intimacy with others, while receiving produces individual self-actualization. To overcome the feeling that we are not loving, we need to experience and respond to these two drives. Then we are learning how to become more loving. Then we are on the road to love.

CHAPTER THREE

LOVE AS DIALOGUE

Love is within us. It cannot be destroyed, but can only be hidden.

Marianne Williamson
A Return to Love

Man is nothing else but what he makes of himself.... Man is at the start a plan which is aware of itself, rather than a patch of moss, a piece of garbage, or a cauliflower; nothing exists prior to this plan; there is nothing in heaven; man will be what he will have planned to be.... Man is responsible for what he is.

Jean Paul Sartre

Introduction

After knowing each other for years, John and Rose developed a romantic love relationship. One day in a dimly lit restaurant, they were talking about their struggles to make a contribution at work. Suddenly, John said that he was worried that he hurt her by complaining about her asking about his feelings. Rose responded that several months ago she would have been deeply wounded, but now she had a new understanding.

Rose realized that his complaints were just another example of his game playing. His criticisms were attempts to control her and push her away. Previously she tried to get him to stop trying to dominate her, but she had given up because attempting to break through his armor just bruised her. Now she decided to accept the fact that their relationship would probably stall at this level because of his fear of intimacy. Instead of trying to change him, she decided to change herself in ways that were growth-producing and accept him as he was.

John's face tightened for an instant, then began to soften and give way to the tears and the deep emotions he was trying so hard to conceal. Months before when Rose had attempted to break through his shell, she had gotten nowhere. Unexpectedly, when she was not trying to change him, his strong feelings made him stop playing games.

As John sat in silence with a pained look, his resistance against telling her what he was feeling was as strong as ever. Waiting patiently, Rose asked him with loving eyes and a soft caressing voice what he was feeling. Deathly afraid of self-revelation, he said "let's leave." Fearing that this would allow him time to suppress his emotions, Rose stayed where she was and gripped his hand tightly. Slowly he said with genuine feeling, "there is reality behind my game playing, I truly love you." In this experience of honest sharing, John and Rose lived out the eight steps of becoming more loving.

Discussing the weather, without being able to do anything about it, is often to kill time. Discussing love, without suggesting that we can do something about it, is often to kill hope. There is hope. We are all essentially lovers. The eight steps to become more loving are not beyond any of us.[1] These steps that help us fulfill our loving potential may also be viewed as the eight qualities of the loving person. We are familiar with them and already possess some, if not all, of them.

After reiterating the socialized differences that women value love and relationships, while men value power and achievement, John Gray claims that women and men's primary love needs are different. Women need "caring, understanding, respect, devotion, validation, and reassurance," while men need "trust, acceptance, appreciation, admiration, approval, and encouragement."[2] Although Gray accurately describes some qualities of love, he is also inaccurate. The primary love needs are the same for both women and men. Both need to give and receive the same eight qualities of love.

Love is a dialogue between giving and receiving. Accepting, understanding, appreciating, and forgiving are the receiving qualities of love. Responding, sharing, apologizing, and trusting are the giving elements. Since receiving comes before giving, the eight steps on the path to becoming more loving are:

accepting
    that leads to responding
        which produces understanding
            that grows into sharing
                which breeds appreciating
                    that leads to apologizing
                        which brings about forgiving
                            that culminates in trusting.

Accepting Is the First Step in Becoming More Loving

The beginning of love is accepting myself and others. The easiest step in being loving is accepting the beautiful parts of myself and others. Love sees myself and others as magnificent and splendid, as unique in all the world. Love also accepts my own and others' flaws. We are all finite and therefore imperfect. Love accepts our faults and imperfections.

Accepting myself is the first step toward loving myself and the necessary requirement for loving other people. To love myself and be happy, I need to affirm my deepest self. I need to believe that I am a good person, just as I am, just by being myself, without doing anything to prove myself. The best way to accept myself as I am is to get in touch with my loving inner core. Then I can be genuine and not wear masks, honest and not phony. If I act on the expectations of others instead of my own inner messages, I will not only be false to myself, but I will also lose my self-acceptance.

To accept myself does not mean that I must like everything and never want to change anything about myself. Self-acceptance is the affirmation of my inner goodness in spite of my faults. Accepting myself means that I admit my shortcomings and talents, anger and friendliness, my sorrows and joys. Once I accept myself as I am, I can accept others as they are.

Another way of describing this first step is respect, which Fromm calls one of the four basic elements of love.[3] Respect is the ability to see people as they are with all their strengths and weaknesses, their unique individuality and flaws. Respect is being open to others as they are, not as I want them to be.

Accepting is listening love. Our first task as lovers is to listen to who we are and who other people are. No intimate relationship is possible without mutual listening. We all ask others to listen to us both verbally and non-verbally. We want others to understand who we are.

Concentrated, uncritical, and perceptive listening is hard work. Listening shows that we take people seriously and want them to reveal their true selves. Listening love tries to know others without arguing with them, judging them, criticizing them, or changing the subject. Making us fully alive in the present, listening becomes the only thing that matters.

As a powerful and influential technique in human interaction, listening is a creative force that not only derives from affection but also expresses affection. I am attracted to those who listen to me. When others listen, it makes me unfold and expand; it creates happiness and freedom within me. Listening allows the creative fountain within me to spring forth.

Daniel Maguire, a moral theologian, says "respect is always the first breath of love. ... Respect is the opposite of insult." The absence of respect is unbearable. Sexism, "the belief that women are inferior," lacks respect and maims love. Acting superior or inferior is only compatible with being dominant or subordinate and not with mutuality and love. Sexist hierarchies in relationships are devastating to love. "The fact that when some women become feminist, their marriages fail, does not indict the woman seeking mutuality, but the man denying it." For there to be love and mutuality, respect is essential.[4]

Some couples suffer from extreme togetherness.

Because they believe that unity is a sign of a healthy relation-ship, they speak for each other, defend each other, and present a united front.   When these couples are open to change, they learn to accept each other's separateness and individuality. They see respect as the only foundation upon which real love can grow and a mutual partnership can be based.[5]

All individuals have the right to demand a minimum of acceptance. They have the right to be respected as human beings who possess human dignity and human rights.   To show respect for humanness, the least that people can do is to see others as they are and to listen to what they have to say.

Acceptance, respect, listening, and affirmation are necessary for love to begin and to grow, because they provide safety. This minimum of acceptance and respect can develop into the maximum kind of love, if both parties are open to giving and receiving.

Responding Is the Second Step in Becoming More Loving

When we truly listen to ourselves and other people, we hear our own and their needs. Responding to those needs is the second step on love's path.

Responsibility, which Fromm calls a basic element of love, does not denote duty or something imposed upon us from outside.[6] Coming from our inner core of love, it means to respond to our own and other people's needs, whether they are expressed or unexpressed.   Some shout about their needs, while others whisper. Still others complain about their less important needs to hide their more crucial needs.   No one's needs remain completely unexpressed, since total silence is itself a cry for help.

Some of us experience physical or psychological problems, others have social, economic, political, or spiritual troubles. We all need other people in some way, because we are all interdependent. As the novelist Fyodor Dostoevsky says, "each of us is responsible for everything to everyone else." When the French philosopher Jean Paul Sartre says "a man is responsible for himself," he does "not only mean that he is responsible for his own individuality, but that he is responsible for all men."[7]

In the Bible, Cain asks "am I my brother's keeper?" Am I my sister's keeper? Loving people answer yes. Each of us is responsible for all of us. The poet John Donne expresses this beautifully. "No man is an island entire of himself. Every man is a piece of the continent."

Responsible individuals recognize their interdependence and act to help others whenever possible. From taking the time to check in their pockets to see if they have change for a dollar to spending time with a grieving friend, loving individuals respond to those in need.

Before we can be responsive to others, we must first experience and respond to our own feelings, thoughts, and needs. Once we get in touch with our own needs, we are better able to recognize the needs of others. After we take care of ourselves, we are more sensitive to others.

Audre Lorde claims when we are in touch with our own life force and the power of love, we begin to be responsible to ourselves. "When we begin to live from within outward, in touch with the power of the erotic within ourselves, and allowing that power to inform and illuminate our actions upon the world around us, then we begin to be responsible to ourselves in the deepest sense." When we are in touch with our loving inner core and respond to ourselves, we stop being satisfied with self-denial, powerlessness, depression, and suffering.[8]

Although Fromm distinguishes between responsibility and care, two of his four basic elements of love, care is part of responsibility. Care is active concern for the life and growth of others.[9] Where concern is missing, my love is diminished. To care for others is to be devoted to them and to work for their self-actualization. If I love others, I care for them. If I care for them, I love them. I want them to experience fulfillment and the best things that life has to offer.

Genuine concern always involves helping loved ones.

Love lives and grows through laboring for the beloved. Love always produces action. Sometimes that action is only to be present and listen. This is often the action required by the mourner. The alleviation of need is an important part of caring for the beloved. Where there is no help, there is no caring love. An African proverb refers to this aspect of love when it declares "he may say that he loves you. Wait and see what he does for you."

All help springs from love and creates greater love between the giver and the receiver. It is important to help people do things they cannot do for themselves. To do for others what they can do for themselves sometimes causes more harm than good. As the slogan says, it is better to teach people to fish than to give them fish to eat. Thoughtfulness is crucial in effective helping.

To be caring is to affirm the others' inner goodness, support their work, and encourage them to be their fullest possible selves. Besides helping others grow in ways they themselves envision, caring people help develop the potential that they may not even perceive. Loving eyes see what others are blind to. Caring individuals may spot hidden talents covered by years of neglect and help to resurrect them.

Caring involves giving happiness as well as help. A psychologist brings out this point about caring when she says love is "that condition in which the happiness of another person is essential to your own."[10] Moving beyond responding to needs, caring people work for the beloved's happiness.

When I say that I care for you, it means that I respond to your needs and help you. I want you to be happy. I have good feelings for you. I am emotionally involved with you. You have a place not only in my thoughts but also in my heart. When I perceive your beauty and spirit, I am delighted, I am excited, I am ecstatic. Joy flows through me. I soar.

According to a recent poll, 99 percent of American women affirm caring is a positive trait that applies to them. 78 percent describe themselves as self-sacrificing.[11]

When women express their feelings, they often get in

touch with their own needs and then they are better able to recognize and respond to others' genuine needs. However, some women do not get in touch with their own needs and consequently they have trouble being aware of other people's true needs. Sometimes they even unconsciously disguise their own needs and claim they belong to those they want to help. By responding to their own distortion of others' needs, they risk damaging the individuals they intend to help.

The patriarchy teaches men to provide financially for their family. Many men make being a breadwinner their top priority and responding to others' needs a lower priority. Men are taught to suppress their feelings because being emotional is unmanly. When they suppress their feelings, they do not get in touch with their own needs and thus are less able to recognize or respond to others' needs.

In his sermon on the mount, Jesus preached about the plank and the splinter. "Why do you observe the splinter in your brother's eye and never notice the plank in your own?" How can you take the splinter out of your brother's eye, when you haven't removed the plank from your own? "Hypocrite! Take the plank out of your own eye first, and then you will see clearly enough to take the splinter out of your brother's eye."[12] There is tremendous truth here. Christian clergy sometimes forget this truth when they lead you to believe you should suppress your own needs and care exclusively for others.

However, it must be admitted that I am not able to take the plank completely out of my own eye because I never reach perfection. Can I heal others when I am still sick? Can I liberate others when I still need to free myself? I emphatically answer yes. If I do not know what sickness is, how can I understand another person's yearning to be well? If I do not comprehend what it is to be in bondage, how can I empathize with everyone's righteous passion to be free? None of us is totally liberated. Everyone is both free and unfree. We must give others what we have already found and be willing to receive what they have that we lack.

When people are loving, their responses are caring

rather than critical. A supportive response says "you're OK." A critical response conveys "you're not OK."[13] The American socialization process stresses critical responses more often than supportive ones. In the home, mothers and fathers often put their children down with criticism and seldom builds them up with praise and encouragement.

Schools put students down by making 100%--perfection--the standard. Few students are ever able to reach this goal. Teachers and parents often speak critically about youngsters' behavior and infrequently show their appreciation and approval. Their response is usually "you did that wrong"; it is rarely "good work." To express love is to give supportive, empowering responses.

To be supportive does not mean that individuals must squelch their critical faculties. Constructive criticism is a caring, helpful response. If people are doing something harmful to themselves or others, loyal friends will tell them and even try to stop them. Some people think of loyalty as going along with their friends. My friend, right or wrong. My country, right or wrong. That is being a "yes" person, and not being loyal. Genuine loyalty is being honest and offering constructive criticism when my friend is wrong.

When President Richard Nixon engaged in illegal Watergate activities, his White House workers were "yes" men who went along instead being genuinely loyal by offering constructive criticism. In contrast, when Secretary of State George Shultz thought President Ronald Reagan's trading arms for hostages was unwise, wrong, and possibly illegal, he voiced his criticisms to Reagan in private and in meetings with Reagan and his top advisors.[14] His honesty was constructive criticism and an act of loyalty.

To allow others to engage in destructive behavior is to neglect their need for help. No one's first choice is to be destructive. When people are negative and hurting themselves or others, they would prefer doing more growth-producing deeds, but they do not have the strength. When responsible persons see the problem, they offer constructive criticism and concrete help on how to begin to behave more lovingly.

Destructive criticism puts down both the actors and their acts. In contrast, constructive criticism begins with some honest appreciation and approval of our good acts and then offers suggestions about how to alter specific harmful behavior. When we are constructive, we criticize the wrongdoing, but help the doer improve. Constructive criticism is an invitation to grow and change. Supportive responses promote love, while critical responses damage love.

Daniel Maguire claims justice is "the first response to the value of persons."[15] The minimum we need to do to honor people's value and worth is to answer their human needs and treat them with respect, liberty, equality, and justice. The maximum is love.

When we deny people what they need to be fully human, we proclaim we are worth more than they are.[16] Love is harmed when we show disrespect by treating others in unfair, unequal, unjust, dominating, abusive, and violent ways. When one person is considered superior and dominant and the other is treated as inferior and submissive, love is severely perverted. Disrespect, sexism, racism, classism, and violence deny people's value and damage love.

As Maguire says, "in friendship and in love we respond lavishly."[17] Answering human needs, respecting people's worth, and providing liberty, equality, and justice are the beginning steps on the way to the fullness of love.

Understanding Is the Third Step in Becoming More Loving

After describing knowledge as a basic element of love, Fromm asserts that it is not possible to respect people without first knowing them.[18] In contrast, I believe that it is not possible to know them without first respecting them. I must accept them as they are before I can know them. Listening and responding lead to knowing. This knowing is the third step on the road to the fullness of love.

Before I can know others, I must know myself. The

further I dig into the depths of my soul, the more I find to explore. I both know myself and simultaneously I do not know myself. Just as I shall never have complete knowledge of myself, so also I shall never have complete knowledge of others, even my most dearly beloved. I both know others and simultaneously I do not know them.

Through knowing others, I learn more about myself. In penetrating to the heart of others, I not only learn about them, but I also learn about myself. This is particularly true in intimate discussions and personal quarrels. In both cases, as my loved ones lay bare their souls and values, I begin to expose my own loving inner core and priorities. In knowing myself and my beloved, I learn about that which is deepest in us both and thus I learn about all people.

The only way to know other people fully is through the act of love that does not stay at the periphery but goes to their innermost core. The deeper the love, the fuller the knowledge. Knowing love actively penetrates the beloved so that the desire to know is satisfied by the exquisite experience of communion.

The similarities between love and knowledge are that both unite the separated and both overcome the gap between the subject and object. However, the difference between them is that knowledge is part of the mind, while love is the dynamic power of the entire being. Love is the whole being's movement toward unity, while knowledge is the mind's effort to unite the knower and unknown. Thus, knowing is part of love.[19]

Two ways of knowing people are analysis and synthesis. Coming from the Greek word meaning to break up, analysis separates the whole into its component parts. It can identify, name, examine, classify, compare, evaluate, and understand the relationships between the constituent parts and the entire reality.

Coming from the Greek word meaning to put together, synthesis combines the parts into a whole, so that the entire reality can be understood. Synthesis involves making connections between things that seem separate and unconnected in order to form a more holistic view. The human being is seen as a unity, and not merely as distinct qualities. The person is perceived as more than the sum of the parts, just as the melody is more than the sum of its notes.

Surface and deep knowing describe two kinds of knowledge. In surface knowing, people are what they appear to be. Surface knowing learns the external facts about people, such as their physical appearance, hometown, occupation, and personal characteristics. In deep knowing, we go below the surface to learn who people really are. Deep knowing participates in the other's inner self as far as one human being can penetrate another. Maslow calls this deep way of knowing a peak experience.[20]

Surface knowing is a safe, non-threatening way, while deep knowing is a risky, growth-producing way. As a peak experience that transcends the parts and perceives people as unique, complex, whole, and ineffable, deep knowing sees below the surface into their loving inner core. This requires the gift of self-revelation that comes in love. Only in this way can they be fully known.

The best way to know other people is to be in communion with them through love. I know others because I love them. Love sees them face-to-face and knows the center of their being. Enduring love is not a blind love, but a seeing love that looks beneath the surface appearance to the person's depths. As Tillich says, "there is no strangeness to love; love knows; it is the only power of complete and lasting knowledge."[21]

In the I-Thou relation, the other person becomes present not merely in my feelings, but in the depth of my spirit. I experience the mystery of the other's being in the mystery of my own. I speak to the Thou with my whole being. I know the whole person. I behold the Thou as splendid and radiant.[22]

Although knowing is an appropriate word for the third step in becoming more loving, understanding is a more accurate description. Before understanding is truly possible, a degree of personal safety is necessary. The more secure we feel; the less we allow our personal fears, prejudices, or defensive feelings to color our vision; the more we see people as they are; the more we can truly understand them.

More than intellectual knowing, understanding involves both the head and the heart, knowing and feeling, reason and affection. Understanding blends rational insight with intuitive, sensitive, valuing affection. It includes both intellectual thought and affectionate feeling. Since emotion is central to the experience, understanding creates excitement.[23]

The patriarchy teaches women to be emotional and men rational. When this socialization is successful, men are more likely to know with their heads and not understand with their hearts. Women are more likely to understand with both their feelings and thoughts, their hearts and their heads.

For Lorde, the statement that this feels right to me is "the first and most powerful guiding light toward any understanding." Understanding is the handmaiden of "that knowledge deeply born" and "the erotic is the nurturer or nursemaid of all our deepest knowledge." A grave responsibility exists within us not to settle for the expected, the convenient, or the safe. "Our erotic knowledge empowers us, becomes a lens through which we scrutinize all aspects of our existence."[24]

The best way to avoid false perception is to move beyond objectivity to empathy, the deepest kind of understanding. Empathy is the process of putting myself in other people's moccasins, walking with them, and seeing the world from their point of view. To empathize is to be totally with others, to sense their feelings, and to perceive their inner world of meaning and chaos as if it were my own. Empathy is non-judgmental understanding from the inside rather than judgmental knowing from the outside. When individuals have serious problems, the best way to be loving is to empathize. When people find themselves accurately and warmly understood, they find solutions to their problems and grow.[25]

The desire to be understood by others is one of our most important needs. Those who understand us perceive our inner beauty, spirit, and goodness. To those who

understand, we are never ugly.   When they observe our
faults, they know from our personal history why we have
these flaws. Witnessing our mistakes, they comprehend why
we made them. In contrast, we may appear ugly to individuals who notice our shortcomings but do not understand them
or us. Those who understand know our character. Those
who do not understand see only the masks that we present
to the world.

Sharing Is the Fourth Step in Becoming More Loving

Through accepting, responding, and understanding, we
incorporate others' inner beauty, spirit, and goodness into
ourselves. Then we long to give ourselves to them because
they are such a magnificent addition to our lives. To share is
to give our deepest self to others so that we enhance their
happiness. Sharing is the heart of the loving process. Where
there is no sharing, there is no love. Where there is sharing,
there is love.

What do we share? We share all that we have to give.
We share our feelings, time, humor, laughter, strengths,
weaknesses, fears, pains, faith, doubts, sorrows, joys, hopes,
values, spirit, love of life, and our deepest selves.

By putting us down, our patriarchal society damages
our self-esteem and makes us question what we have to give.
The most important thing we have to give is our loving inner
core. This is a magnificent gift, because our loving inner core
is our spirit that is part of the Divine Spirit and Infinite Love.[26]

Lorde says "the need for sharing deep feelings is a
human need." Love provides the power to share deeply with
another person.   "The sharing of joy, whether physical,
emotional, psychic, or intellectual, forms a bridge between the
sharers which can be the basis for understanding much of
what is not shared between them, and lessens the threat of
their difference."[27]

When we are with our beloved in times of happiness,
we share our feelings of delight. We simply bubble over with
joy. We talk because we feel. We talk to our loved ones

because we want them to know how we feel. Once we start talking, we are like volcanos erupting because we just go on and on. We want to tell them everything about ourselves. The only thing that holds us back is that we want to hear what our loved ones have to say. Their response is important to us, but once they answer, it is like they pulled the trigger because we are off and running again.

Our loved ones' presence makes us want to talk. Because we feel their acceptance, responsiveness, and understanding, we feel safe enough to express our inner self that we normally hide from the world because self-exposure makes us vulnerable. Talking to the beloved, we not only feel safe but we also feel ourselves growing as we share our innermost spirit. As the beloved learns about us, we also deepen our knowledge of ourselves. We only become fully conscious of what we express to someone else.[28] Our understanding of our own character remains a vague intuition until we communicate with the beloved.

In times of sorrow, we need to tell the beloved why we are so sad. Those of us with good self-images can survive without discussing our troubles with anyone, but strong people know that sharing their difficulties with trustworthy listeners is a sign of strength rather than weakness. When talking about our problems will lessen the burden more quickly, hiding these difficulties is detrimental, not wise.

Talking about our troubles has many helpful consequences. Airing sorrows lessens them because conversing about problems puts them in proper perspective so that they no longer seem like such unbearable burdens. Digging into our troubles brings alternative solutions to mind. Sharing our difficulty means that we no longer carry it alone. At a minimum, our loved ones respect the way we are dealing with the problem. At a maximum, they share part of our load.

Most of us realize that we need to share our joys and sorrows with the beloved, but we fail to understand that we must also share our constructive criticisms. When constructive criticism is expressed in a spirit of love and in an atmosphere of support, it can be helpful and growth-producing rather than damaging and harmful. On the other hand, if criticism is suppressed, it will eventually come out in a distorted and sometimes unrecognizable form that will be destructive. Supportive feedback is always helpful. Negative criticism, even though it may be painful, is better than no feedback at all. Nothing is learned from no response, while something can be gained from either caring or critical responses.

When our feelings are hurt, we often become critical. Launching a verbal attack is a defense mechanism to hide hurt feelings with a show of strength. Criticism that echoes our own self-condemnation is extremely painful.[29] Care must be taken before such criticism is expressed or excessive pain will result.

Deep communication is not talking at you; it is not talking about someone or something. Talking at or talking about are conversations, not communication. Deep communication is talking with you. Authentic communication is a dialogue between two people who are willing to reveal themselves and change.

As Hugh Prather says, "if I truly communicate, I see in you a life that is not me and I partake of it. And you see and partake of me. In a small way we then grow out of our old selves and become something new." To have this kind of sharing, I must enter the conversation with openness rather than closedness. I must uncover myself and discover you, while you uncover yourself and discover me. We must both be willing to change and reveal our changes to each other. "I must give myself to the relationship and be willing to be whatever grows out of it."[30]

Two levels in any conversation are the verbal and the emotional. Words spring from thoughts and feelings. When you want to share, you will inform me with your words as accurately as possible what you are feeling and thinking. However, there is always more emotional content than can be expressed in words. "If I ignore the emotional plea and respond only to the words, I will not be communicating with you, there will not be a flow of understanding between us, I will not be feeling you."[31]

A good sign that I am not receiving your feelings is that either you or I feel frustrated, because we are not understanding one another. Then we need to stop and ask "what are you really trying to say?"

An essential ingredient in sharing is honesty.[32] In a love relationship, I expect both of us to speak honestly about everything. Self-deception and lying are the antithesis of love. The more honest we are with ourselves and others, the more loving we are. The more dishonest we are with ourselves and others, the more we damage love.

Reliability is another element in sharing. Reliability means you can count on me to be present and share myself in whatever way is appropriate in times of joy and sorrow. Sharing with its components of honesty and reliability helps build trust.

C.S. Lewis calls sharing Gift-love. Gift-love longs to give the beloved protection and happiness. In contrast, his Need-love describes the feeling that I cannot live without my loved one, while his Appreciative love rejoices at the wonder of the beloved. An example of Gift-love is the love that a woman and man have for their family that makes them plan, work, and save to provide for their needs. Gift-love is boundless giving; it is God-like. Gift-love wants to actualize whatever is best for the beloved.[33]

The patriarchy socializes women to give themselves limitlessly to their husbands and children, while men are taught to share financially. Because men are socialized not to be emotional, women often do the emotional work for the men and create the emotional environment of the home. In trying to live up to the image of the strong, silent type, many men keep their feelings and problems to themselves. Most women share their deepest feelings and thoughts, joys and sorrows, with their closest family and friends.

While Fromm describes respect, responsibility, care, and knowledge as the four basic elements that are common to all forms of love, he also says "love is primarily giving."[34] As giving love, sharing is essential to love's development, because it leads to mutuality and communion.

Appreciating Is the Fifth Step in Becoming More Loving

What Lewis calls Appreciative love is the fifth step on the journey toward becoming more loving. Appreciative love admires your uniqueness and marvels at your splendor. I delight in your presence and I offer thanks. This thanksgiving is gratitude for the gift of your inner beauty and spirit. My appreciation makes me see your goodness and spirit as outstanding. I feel privileged to know you.

One of my students defines love as "digging the differences."[35] One meaning of digging the differences is appreciating the beloved's uniqueness. I love you because you are different from me or the same as me or in spite of our similarities and differences. It also means I love you because you are you, and you are worthy of love. Digging the differences points to love's two drives, communion and self-actualization. To appreciate is to unite with you in spirit. To accept the differences between you and me is to rejoice in our personal uniqueness.

The experiences of accepting, responding, understanding, and sharing prepare the way for appreciating love. Antoine de Saint-Exupery's Little Prince moves through the initial steps of love by accepting the rose as she is, responding to her needs, knowing her beauty, and sharing with her by listening, watering, sheltering, and touching her. In addition, he forgives her pretending, boasting, and grumbling.

Because the Little Prince went through these steps, he came to appreciate her in a new way. When his rose is in his life, it is as if the sun is shining only on him. Her voice is music; her movements are a dance. His rose is not a common rose, like a hundred thousand roses. The Little Prince's rose is "unique in all the world."[36] To love appreciatively is to experience and revel in the beloved's uniqueness.

My initial reaction in appreciating your inner beauty. goodness, and spirit is to stand in awe. The ultimate response is to celebrate. An important sign of appreciation is celebration. To celebrate is to express outwardly the pleasure and excitement that I feel deep within myself. By celebrating, I spontaneously affirm life and its goodness. Celebration allows the tremendous appreciation bottled up inside to explode into the joyous activities of singing, dancing, shouting, hugging, laughing, kissing, drinking, and breaking bread.

Apologizing Is the Sixth Step in Becoming More Loving

As the sixth step in becoming more loving, apologizing comes after making a mistake or after quarreling. When there is conflict in a relationship, the cause is often two-sided. Both parties have something to apologize for and something to forgive. One essential element in an apology is to acknowledge when our mistakes hurt someone.

The human tendency is to repress past mistakes because remembering them is too painful. We repress what we cannot stand to face. However, repressed memories influence the unconscious and sometimes covertly express themselves in feelings and actions, often in distorted and harmful ways. The best method to liberate ourselves from past mistakes and the suffering they caused is to apologize for them and not repress them. To apologize is to feel sorry about our mistake, to acknowledge it to others, to try to correct the harm done, to attempt not to repeat it, and to leave it behind by doing good deeds.

Sometimes we say that we are sorry and mean it, but unless we correct our mistake, our apology is incomplete. Apologizing is admitting genuine sorrow by actions as well as words. In a genuine apology, we not only try to heal the injury but we also work not to repeat the same harmful acts again. To be sorry is to renew ourselves internally and to change ourselves externally.

Some of us torture ourselves about our faults and withhold our best energy from the work of changing ourselves for the better. We add self-indulgence to our other faults. Instead of continually worrying about past mistakes, we should apologize and move on to new creative activities. By constantly thinking about past deeds, we fail to cast our mistakes out of ourselves. Once we truly apologize, we can move on.

Love's course is never smooth. Human interactions inevitably provoke mistakes, conflict, hurt, anger, and resentment. Love can only endure if the lovers freely express, discuss, and deal with any difficulties. Talking together fosters love. However, the airing of troubles must not include accusations, blaming, temper tantrums, or arguments which play the same old record repeatedly.

After complaints have been expressed, forgiving and apologizing set the stage for a constructive discussion of the problems. Only if I understand what caused the trouble can I work to avoid repeating it. To deny you the opportunity to talk with me about the difficulty is to be unfair to you and to put a new and additional conflict in our relationship. To impose silence when communication is called for is to fail in one necessary requirement for being a loving person.

An apology is obviously necessary when I intentionally or unintentionally injure you. But it is also important on other occasions. My feelings toward you are always ambivalent. I love you and yet I have negative reactions to some of your thoughts and deeds. When I recognize your weaknesses, I try to accept them. Because I am not perfect, I condemn and reject some of your faults. Despite my love for you, my acceptance has a limit. These ambivalent feelings of both love and disapproval are not something to hide and be ashamed of because all lovers experience them. If I am loving, I acknowledge my ambivalent feelings, apologize for the inadequacies of my love, and work to improve.

Forgiving Is the Seventh Step in Becoming More Loving

We always hurt each other because we cannot give and receive perfectly and because living in a patriarchal culture damages us. Sometimes you act in ways that cause me to suffer, while other times I myself bring about the pain. I cannot fully comprehend your feelings toward me because

I am not you and your way of loving is unique to you and different from mine. On the occasions when I misunderstand the special gift of yourself to me, I feel wounded.

Although we are all good and loving, we are also, because of our imperfections, capable of behaving in very harmful ways toward others, even toward those we love. As the seventh quality of love, forgiving is accepting your faults as well as your strengths. Forgiving is a later step because I must know your goodness before I can forgive you and because in the initial steps of love I concentrate mainly on your virtues. Forgiving love makes it possible for me to accept not only your unique gifts but also your ugly behavior. To forgive is to affirm you and your worth in spite of the fact that I have witnessed and suffered from your faults.

Forgiving is not loving the unlovable, but concentrating on the good in every person, while accepting the unacceptable. To forgive is to love the sinner, while hating the sin. In forgiving, I love you even though you were disrespectful and abusive to me. Revenge is alien to love. Once I forgive you, I try to trust you again even though you were untrustworthy before. Forgiving is always proof of the strength of love because it fulfills one of the two drives within love, it unites the separated.

To grow, I must take risks. To love is always to risk. When I love, my heart will be touched, very likely it will be bruised, and possibly it will be broken. There is only one way to insure that my heart remains intact and that is not to give it away. "To love at all is to be vulnerable."[37] The more I love, the more vulnerable I become.

Those whom I love passionately can hurt me most deeply. When I am indifferent to you, I am not vulnerable to you. Any wound means I care for you enough to be vulnerable. This is why the injury itself is a sign of the past love, while forgiveness is a sign of the new love that is created after the hurt and because of the hurt.

Forgiving re-establishes my relationship with you even though you injured me. It does not forget the damage because a wound may never be completely forgotten. Every psychological hurt leaves a scar that may later be torn open. To forgive is to accept you in spite of damage you did to me.

Many of us do not love others enough to forgive them and their faults. To be unable to forgive means we are unable to affirm their goodness and unable to accept their mistakes. If we are unable to forgive, our love for others and ourselves is stunted. "Forgiving others is the only way to forgive ourselves." Running away from others' faults is a way of running away from our own. Failing to see that our judgment of others is an extension of our judgment of ourselves denies healing to both of us. Only when we show each other the worst side of our natures are we ready for the forgiveness that leads to trust and the fullness of love.[38]

When love exists, there is a lifelong bond created that may change forms as well as increase and decrease in intensity, but it never ceases to exist. In Tillich's words, "love lasts; love alone endures, and nothing else besides love, nothing independent of love."[39] Not to forgive is not to affirm and honor the love bond which is permanent. Not to forgive is not to accept the hurting which is transitory. Not to forgive is not to allow the power of love to work within ourselves to heal and overcome the difficulty. Not to forgive is to refuse to love.

Trusting Is the Eighth Step in Becoming More Loving

The most difficult quality to practice in becoming more loving is trust. Erik Erikson, a psychoanalyst, correctly asserts that trust is the first stage of psychological growth and therefore the prerequisite for all the other stages.[40] Nevertheless, deep trust is the last quality to develop in becoming more loving. The trust that infants develop toward their parents slowly grows into the trust that loving people have for their friends and lovers.

Before I can trust others, I must trust myself by affirming my essential goodness in spite of my flaws. To trust others is to believe in their basic goodness in spite of their faults. When I trust others, I believe that they will be supportive, honest, understanding, caring, and not intentionally harm me. To trust is to count on people to be there for me. The highest degree of trust is to expect others to deal with my feelings, words, thoughts, values, and inner self with the same degree of seriousness and sacredness that I do myself.

The deepest trust occurs only after a conflict is overcome through forgiveness and apology. The newly solved problems expose the strength of ourselves and our relationship. After passing through an ordeal, trust grows firmer. Once we conquer the difficulties, my belief in your goodness is more secure because it has been tested and proven true in terrible circumstances. The future never again holds such heavy fears because when dangers occurred, we both found the fortitude to meet them. My renewed trust in you is well-informed and robust. My love is stronger.

After stressing the importance of balancing intimacy and solitude, Stephanie Dowrick explains the connections between trusting and feeling alive. "Trusting ourselves, we feel alive; feeling alive, we can reach out and trust others. Trusting others, we can cherish what they have to give. Taking what they have to give, we feel more alive."[41]

According to Leo Buscaglia, "love is trusting, accepting and believing, without guarantee." Loving people speak in supportive rather than negative language and stop using labels, like dago and communist, that create distance and even hatred between various groups. Saying Yes produces a growth in love. "A lover says 'Yes' to life, 'Yes' to joy, 'Yes' to knowledge, 'Yes' to people, 'Yes' to differences." Love creates joyous expression.[42]

Perfect love is an impossibility. Our capacity for loving is limited even when we try to love with our whole heart, mind, body, and soul. We never possess total love because it is infinite and beyond our finite grasp. Moreover, love is always incomplete because it is not a state but rather a process. As lovers, we constantly ask others for more of themselves. Love is only true to itself if it requests more of us and our loved ones. Love is only genuine to the extent that it is willing to become more tomorrow than it is today.

Trust helps us attempt the impossible, but deeply desired, task of giving ourselves totally. Trust strives for the ideal of complete honesty and participation in the beloved's life. When we are trusting, we hold nothing back. After we have practiced the other seven qualities on the road to love, we are ready to reveal ourselves entirely. Of course, none of us totally knows ourselves so we can only give what we consciously know. Thus, no matter how hard we try, our gift is always incomplete.

In the final step, lovers do not want to keep any secrets from their loved ones, even when sharing causes pain. The goal is total psychological nakedness. Genuine trust means there is completely open and honest communication and participation in each other's lives. As the African proverb says, "let your love be like the misty rain, coming softly but flooding the river."

One thing that is shared in love is our commitment to the beloved. Commitment encompasses all eight qualities of love. To be committed is to accept our loved ones as they are, to respond to their needs, to understand their goodness and weakness, and to share ourselves as fully as possible. Appreciation often comes spontaneously, but if it doesn't, committed lovers work to develop it. Apologizing, forgiving, and trusting take strength and character that lovers never know they have until circumstances and commitment demand them. To be committed is to be accepting, responding, understanding, sharing, appreciating, apologizing, forgiving, and trusting.

The dialogue between the giving and receiving qualities forms the spiral of love. The steps of the spiral of love are first receiving and then giving.

The Spiral of Love

**Receiving
Qualities of Love**

**Giving
Qualities of Love**

Trusting enough to give myself
completely and totally

Forgiving your mistakes

Apologizing for my mistakes

Appreciating your goodness

Sharing my deepest self

Understanding your inner self

Responding to your needs

Accepting you as you are

Love is the complex reality that includes all these steps, although some phases are more intense than others, depending on the kind of love. The quality of our love can be measured by discovering how many of the eight steps on the spiral of love we have practiced in a particular relationship. To become more loving, we must master each step because the more difficult ones depend upon and require the less difficult ones before they can be fulfilled. To stop along the road is to stunt love.

Certain people, while living intensely the first five steps, never progress beyond appreciating to the apologizing, forgiving, and trusting stages so their love remains unfulfilled. Others live every step less intensely, but because they climb all the way to the top of the spiral, their love has the potential to deepen to the fullest possible love.

PART TWO

THE LOVE OF POWER:
CAUSES OF
HUMAN DESTRUCTIVENESS

CHAPTER FOUR

THE SOCIAL CAUSES OF HUMAN DESTRUCTIVENESS

Patriarchy began and spread as a war against women.

Marilyn French
War against Women

The war is men against women; the country is the United States. Here, a woman is beaten every eighteen seconds: by her husband or the man she lives with, not by a psychotic stranger in an alley. ... Woman-beating, the intimate kind, is the most commonly committed violent crime.... A woman is raped every three minutes, nearly half the rapes committed by someone the woman knows.

Andrea Dworkin
Letters from a War Zone

Introduction

Three deer hunters were in the woods looking at pornographic magazines, when they saw a thirteen-year-old blond child. After catching the girl, they gang-raped her. Later, the girl testified that while calling her names, "two men held their guns at my head and the first man hit my breast with his rifle and they continued to laugh." After the first man raped her, they made jokes about her virginity.[1]

After the second man raped her, "the third man forced his penis into my mouth and told me to do it and I didn't know how to do it." After one man pulled the trigger on his gun, she tried harder. When the third man had an erection, he raped her. Continuing to make jokes, they kicked her and told her if she wanted more, she could come back the next day. This young girl didn't tell anyone about her gang rape until she was 20 years old.[2]

Why did these men gang rape this young girl? Why do American men rape an estimated one million women every year? Why are more than three million children abused? Why do an estimated two million American men batter the women they claim to love? Why have over a hundred million young girls around the globe been genitally mutilated? Why did the Nazis slaughter six million Jews and make war on the rest of Europe? Why do humans savagely abuse and kill each other and damage the ecosystem?

If humans are good and loving, why isn't the contemporary culture peaceful and loving instead of dominating and violent? Why are there so many dysfunctional families? Why are so many people unhappy and destructive of themselves and others? Are humans by nature dominating, destructive killers? Was human culture always as violent as it is now? Why is there so much prejudice, domination, and violence in contemporary and past cultures around the world?

Are the rapes, murders, and wars proof that people are inherently dominating and destructive, and not good and loving? Are individuals formed by nature or nurture? Does the environment change humans from being loving to being destructive and thus create a violent culture?

In 1969, American scientists solved the mind-boggling problems that made it possible for our astronauts to travel 238,000 miles to the moon, walk around, and then return safely to earth. 238,000 miles away! Incredible! Why can we solve the problems of science so that we can walk on the moon, but we cannot solve the serious social problems that plague us as individuals and as a human community?

Politicians and professionals talk about the severe problems here on earth, while the difficulties increase in seriousness. At home and abroad, prejudice, domination, and violence result in people hurting each other. Innocent children, women, and men are injured and murdered everywhere. On the international scene, wars and the threat of war are grave, relentless tragedies. The possibility of nuclear war and its ultimate result, the total annihilation of the human race, hangs over our heads like a dark, ever-present cloud.

An important step in solving our personal and social difficulties is to become aware of the problems and discover their root causes. Once we have found the core of our troubles, we can begin to create solutions. Unless our answers address the root causes, we will only be dealing with the symptoms, not the problems. Just as using morphine to kill the pain doesn't cure the disease.

The root cause of our personal problems is that we do not live in accord with our loving inner core that is our innate human nature. When our inner core of love is damaged by our dysfunctional families and patriarchal culture, it is difficult to love ourselves and others.

The root cause of our social problems is that our institutions and cultures promote the patriarchy's highest value of having power over others. These institutions do not respect, support, and nurture our loving human nature.

How can we live in harmony with who we are as lovers when our culture is pushing us in another direction? Sometimes we can, because our loving inner core is the strongest power within us, but it is extremely difficult because we are definitely influenced by our culture.

We Are Born into a Community and the Interdependent Web of Life

Although it is debatable, I strongly believe that we are all born loving, even Adolf Hitler. Our love drives us to actualize ourselves and unite with others. As products of an evolutionary process that is millions of years old, we are born into the interdependent web of life. We are interconnected with fish, reptiles, mammals, and other humans because we all developed through evolution.[3]

We are not self-made people. Our mother and father provide our biological heritage. Belonging to a family, we are born into ongoing relationships, whether caring or rejecting. Our cultural heritage is a community of people who have a language, traditions, values, and a power structure. Our culture's language and values form our way of thinking, acting, speaking, and viewing the world. Our culture and its institutions affect who we are.[4]

Matricentric Animal Culture

It is my belief that the values of the earliest human cultures grew out of people's loving inner core. Thus, thousands of years ago, these earliest cultures were nurturing, sharing, cooperative, and loving, because the earliest people were innately loving.

In documenting these life-promoting cultures, Marilyn French analyzes animal behavior and its relationship to human patterns. The center of the social group for mammals is the mother and children. Primates' social organization is matrifocal and matricentric, which means their society focuses and centers on the mother and children.[5]

Although not all adult mammals have a complete society, the universal nuclear unit is the mother and children. Among larger animals, matrifocal society is essential because the young are born helpless. Youngsters would die without their mothers to care for, feed, and teach them about the environment. Among elephants, the mothers, aunts, and sisters remain together throughout life in cooperation and harmony.[6]

Chimpanzees, bonobos, and gorillas are among the closest animals to humans both structurally and genetically. As French says, they are "gentle and sociable; they live in large social communities and know each other well." Although the mother is the primary caretaker and teacher of baby chimps, other females play with, hold, and give affection to the young and thus "all female primates learn to mother." Chimps are sociable, cooperative. and affectionate. Although conflict exists among chimps, it is not frequent and not lethal.[7]

Some scientists claim bonobos, who share more than 98 percent of their DNA with humans, are the closest primate in the animal kingdom to humans, "the missing link." Female bonobos strongly bond with one another, spend their time in the company of other females, and control the resources of their group. Throughout their lives, most male bonobos stay close to their mother and their status depends largely on their mother's. Bonobos use sexual expression to ease tension, keep their society together, negotiate favors, and make friends. Sharing their food, they are social, gentle, playful, empathic, and peaceful.[8]

Since humans evolved from primates, all the traits that are used to distinguish animals from human beings need to be questioned. Both animals and humans use tools. For example, termites, ants, beavers, and chimps use tools. Humans and animals both communicate. Birds sing and animals vocalize. It is possible that dolphins and whales have a kind of language. French contends "the only absolute difference between humans and animals may well be simply male-dominant, coercive hierarchical organization of the human type."[9]

Matricentric Human Culture

Evidence exists that hominids, an early form of humans, lived in Africa about three and half million years ago. Between one and two million years ago, hominids were gathering, hunting, and inventing containers, tools, and fire. The image often perpetuated of these early human ancestors is extremely brutal, male dominant cavemen hitting each other over the head with clubs and dragging women around by the hair. As French says, most probably this is a false image; it is likely that the early humans were gentle, peaceful, and playful.[10]

Evolving from their primate ancestors, the earliest humans centered and focused their societies on mothers and children. Thus, their cultures were matricentric and matrifocal, but not matriarchal, which means a social group ruled by the mother. As French says, "there is no evidence that a matriarchy ever existed on earth," either an animal or human matriarchy. Societies with powerful rulers are unnatural and artificial.[11]

Matricentric societies were natural. Since human infants were born totally helpless and dependent, mothers fed, cared for, and educated their children until they could take care of themselves. The strong bond between mother and children taught young females and males how to share. Mothers had positions of leadership because of their skills and knowledge. The purpose of the mothers' leadership was to make their children independent[12] and interdependent.

The wider circle of the community beyond the center of the mother and children was her sisters, other mothers, and their children. Since early humans' did not know that sexual intercourse caused pregnancies, the males' role in procreation was unknown and fathers were not recognized. The mother's brothers, partners, and other adult males were all part of the matricentric community if they were cooperative, shared their food, and helped protect the group. French contends that "group life centered in child care and sharing.... Intense aggressiveness would have destroyed the species."[13]

Hominids were sociable and friendly. Relationships between the sexes and among members of the same sex were harmonious and egalitarian. The period from two million years ago until 10,000 years ago was peaceful. There are no signs of weapons being used against humans and no remains of humans being slaughtered. As French says, "early humans probably lived in close, affectionate groups, with a strong bond between mother and children, affection among young-sters playing together, and friendship among all members."[14]

The gatherer and hunter groups that continue to exist today have customs that vary from extreme male domination to equal societies. As French says, "one factor is universal: all live by sharing." Some self-protective aggressiveness is necessary for survival, but extreme "aggressiveness is culturally induced: where it is not valued, it is not strong." In early human cultures, social skills were developed that stressed cooperation, sharing, and seeing the self as part of the larger group. When conflicts and aggression occurred, the antagonists were encouraged to depart and join another group.[15]

It is important to recognize the existence of the early matricentric societies because this means there is an alternative to the dominator social system. Learning about early egalitarian cultures challenges the inaccurate teaching that male dominance is universal.[16] It also helps us envision and believe in the possibility of changing our patriarchal culture into communities of love.

Hominids evolved into our own species, homo sapiens, somewhere between 200,000 and 30,000 years ago. Early human communities still did not know that men played a role in procreation so they were not only matricentric, but also matrilocal with the husband living with his wife's family. They were also matrilineal, that is, the inheritance of any possessions was passed down from the mother to her daughters.[17]

These small matricentric cultures survived because their values of fertility, nurturing, caring, cooperating, and sharing preserved and enhanced life. These cultures were egalitarian and peaceful, because they were based on a life-promoting partnership between all people.

Throughout recorded history, longevity rose. Estimates say that life expectancy was about 20 years in ancient Greece, 33 years during English Middle Ages, about 35 years in the Massachusetts Bay Colony, about 41 years during British nineteenth century, and 47 years in 1900 in the United States.[18] Because people died at a very young age in early prehistoric cultures, women were highly honored and valued. By giving birth, women kept the tribe alive and thus prevented its extinction.

These early matricentric cultures had high esteem and

respect for women and their reproductive powers, because these cultures did not know men's part in procreation and because only women could produce the children the group needed to survive. Women shared in the group's decision making. According to French, people ruled themselves without need of chiefs, leaders, or rulers.[19]

Women's work was as highly valued as men's work, because women's function of raising the children ensured the survival of the tribe. Despite the fact that people owned their own containers and tools, there was communal possession of land and animals rather than private property.[20]

For small groups of early humans trying to survive, the greatest mystery was the miracle of creation. Who was the creator of the universe? Who was the source and sustainer of all living things? Since it was thought that women alone produced babies, it is not surprising that females were connected to the miracle of creation, including divine creation.

Around the world, archaeological evidence, including customs, myths, and artifacts, especially statues of Goddesses, indicates that the earliest known religion was the worship of the Great Mother Goddess as the creator of life. Possibly as early as 25,000 B.C.E., the Great Mother Goddess was the principal divine being.[21]

Scholars have documented that the religion of the Great Mother Goddess encircled the globe. Around the world, the Goddess was worshiped under many different names, including Isis, Astarte, Ishtar, Oshun, Kali, Venus, and Gaia. For thousands of years all over the world, the Goddess was supreme, male dominance was not the norm, and there were no signs of war.[22]

Archaeologists have documented matricentric, egalitarian, peaceful, Goddess worshiping partnership cultures in Catal Huyuk in Turkey from 9,000 to 6,000 B.C.E., southeastern Europe from about 7,000 to 3,500 B.C.E., and India from 4,000 to 2,000 B.C.E. A Goddess worshiping partnership culture that existed in Minoan Crete from 3,000 to 1500 B.C.E. was matrifocal, equal, and peaceful. As an urban society with cities numbering as many as a hundred thousand inhabitants, Minoan culture had a centralized government, a flourishing art, joyful play, equitable sharing of wealth, matrilineal inheritance, and egalitarian relationships between the sexes. The women, queens, and priestesses had high status.[23]

Which came first, Goddess worship or the partnership culture or the high status of women? The answer to this question remains buried in prehistory. Nevertheless, there is an interrelationship between these factors. The evidence shows that during the thousands of years when Goddess veneration remained dominant throughout the world, women were active and admired participants in the partnership society and often enjoyed an independent social and economic position.[24]

The Change from the Matricentric Partnership Culture to Patriarchy

The change from the matricentric, egalitarian, cooperative, peaceful, Goddess worshiping partnership cultures of the early humans to the dominating, hierarchical, competitive, aggressive, warlike, male God worshiping patriarchal cultures happened over thousands of years in different places around the globe. How did these life-affirming partnership cultures change into our current violent, patriarchal cultures? No one knows for sure, because the changes happened before recorded history.

Some feminists contend that sexual inequality as it is practiced today was probably unknown in prehistory. Patriarchal power relationships of dominance over others did not exist then. In these early societies, men treated women as equals because they admired their procreative power. However, with admiration came the fear of women. Women had the power to give birth. Men lacked that power. Powerlessness created fear. Women's life-creating power caused both admiration and problems.[25]

Women's mysterious loss of blood every month did not harm them. In contrast, when male hunters lost blood fighting animals. they were weakened and sometimes died. Again women appeared to have strength that men lacked. Men respected and feared women and their strange powers.

One important change probably led to the establishment of the current dominating social system. Men's attitudes, values, and behavior changed from respect, equality, and sharing with women and nature to superiority, control, and power over them. A major factor that probably caused this change was a new awareness that men played a part in procreation.

By watching the planting of seeds and reproducing of animals, men eventually figured out that they impregnated women. The infants were the men's children as well as the women's. Although men claimed they still honored motherhood, some now wanted to control women's procreative power. This was seen as the most important power that humans possess. With the beginning of men's domination of women and their reproductive powers, the change from partnership to patriarchal society was underway.

The discovery that males played a part in procreation led to the change from egalitarian relationships between men and women to males dominating females, because men wanted to possess and control their wives and children. Men also began to believe they could transcend death by passing on the male line through their children. This produced the change from matrilineal to patrilineal descent and inheritance. In addition, matrilocal marriage changed to patrilocal.[26]

There is no definite information about women's earliest responses to male domination. Some myths suggest a power struggle between women and men. Somewhere lost in prehistory or even erased from history are women's struggles against and then their acquiescence to male dominance and superiority. Men need to take responsibility for exerting male power over women and changing the culture from peaceful and egalitarian to warlike and male dominating. Women need to question why they allowed the change to occur and why they complied.

Also important was the change in humans' attitudes

and behavior toward nature. Early people had a close relationship with nature. Living within nature, they participated in it and believed themselves to be part of nature and connected with natural processes. As gatherers, humans shared the same food, water holes, and natural environment with animals.

The invention of tools, containers, weapons, fire, cooking, cave dwelling, clothing, painting, and rituals separated humans from nature. The development of hunting altered humans' relationship with animals and began their control over the natural world. Starting about 10,000 B.C.E., the development of horticulture and then agriculture and the domestication of animals furthered their control over nature.[27]

Frederick Engels contends that the transition from matrilineal to patrilineal descent led to the first oppression, men's domination of women. "The overthrow of the mothers' rights was the world historic defeat of the female sex. ...the woman was degraded, enthralled, the slave of the man's lust, a mere instrument for breeding children." Economics also caused the change from partnership to male dominating culture. With population increases and the development of agriculture and animal breeding, the economic system changed. The plow and herds of animals created the need for labor and the coercion of animals, slaves, and women to do the work. Agriculture and animal herds produced surpluses, profits, and wealth.[28]

This new wealth led not only to the transition from matrilineal to patrilineal inheritance. It also caused the shift from communal property to private property and from egalitarian relationships to the formation of classes, the rich owners and the poor workers. Greed propelled the desire for even more wealth and this led to wars to gain land, workers, and other possessions.[29]

Population increases expanded villages into cities and created new political systems. Kinship groups, customs, and peace were replaced by laws, states, armies, wars, conquest, empires, and the stratification of people into rulers, owners, workers, and slaves. In the newly created hierarchy, the powerful elite viewed themselves as superior and dominated the inferior masses. Men had power over women, the rich over the poor, masters over slaves, the rulers and military over the people.

According to Engels, the state was created to protect the interests of the wealthy owners when the exploited workers struggled against them. French claims that although the law can be concerned with human rights, "it is concerned above all with property. ... Lawyers have been serving the interests of the wealthy from their first emergence." The legal system is mainly devoted to power as the highest value and to stratification, dominance, and control over low-status groups.[30]

Another important change was the religious change from the worship of the female Goddess to the male God. First, the Great Mother Goddess was supreme. When the male role in procreation was discovered, belief systems that described the creation of the universe by the Goddess alone began to include a male God as secondary to the Goddess and then as an equal. Mother Earth and the Sky God gave birth through sexual union. Then in some religions, the Goddess was eliminated altogether and the male God became the creator.[31]

Which came first: religious changes leading to social and political changes or societies changing first and religions following? Did the Goddess' loss of status lead to women's devaluation or did males' growing power over females lead to the Goddess' loss of existence?[32]

By either invasion or slow alteration, the egalitarian, peaceful, Goddess worshiping partnership cultures were changed into dominating, warlike, male God worshiping, patriarchal cultures. Before 4,500 B.C.E., southeastern Europe was a matrifocal, Goddess worshiping partnership culture that was an unstratified, equal society with no classes of rulers and laborers. Starting about 4500 B.C.E., Kurgan invaders from the East brought in a socially stratified, patriarchal society with an ideology that glorified the warrior. Their principal Gods, such as the sky and sun Gods, carried weapons. The earlier culture was matricentric, settled, and peaceful, while the later one was patriarchal, mobile, and warlike.[33]

Excavations have revealed the urban Harappan culture existed in India from 4,000 to 2,000 B.C.E. The discovery of many figurines indicate the religion of the Great Mother Goddess. What is particularly interesting about India is that the Harappan worship of the Goddess was not destroyed by the invasion of a warlike people. The patriarchal Hindu religion with its male Gods absorbed the early Goddesses so that today this religion includes the worship of many Gods as well as Goddesses, like Kali and Aditi, the boundless Mother of All.[34]

If all the early human cultures were peaceful and treated women as valuable and equal, how did the invading patriarchal groups develop? One totally speculative theory is that the peaceful cultures banished troublemakers rather than imprisoning or killing them. Banding together, the exiled troublemakers multiplied over time. Being angry and dominating, they conquered and imposed their patriarchal ways on the peaceful cultures.[35]

In some cultures, the change from a partnership to a patriarchal society was gradual. Shifting the highest value to domination was probably the most influential factor. Once men knew their part in procreation, they wanted to control women and their reproductive powers. After developing hierarchical systems of control with unequal status and power, they forced people to submit to the new power structures. As French says, "the fundamental nature of patriarchy is located in stratification, institutionalization, and coercion."[36]

Partnership Versus Patriarchy

In her book, *The Chalice and the Blade*, Riane Eisler calls matricentric cultures the partnership model. Symbolized by the chalice as the source of life, the partnership's highest values are "the generative, nurturing, and creative powers of nature--not the power to destroy." Patriarchy is the dominator model. Symbolized by the blade, the dominator model's core value is "the power that takes, rather than gives, life." The norms for this system are "male dominance, male violence, and a generally hierarchic and authoritarian social structure."[37]

In her anthropological study of 156 worldwide cultures spanning 3,000 years from 1750 B.C.E. to 1960 C.E., Peggy Sanday theorizes about why societies with female power changed into male dominant cultures. One factor that led to the evolution of male dominance was the culture's response to stress. When resources diminish, cultures develop male dominance because they believe that group survival depends on male aggression. "Men almost always respond to stress with aggression" and preserve their threatened identity by competition and force, while women respond in a conciliatory way.[38]

In defining the differences between the two kinds of cultures, Sanday says in female power societies, women have domestic and economic control, political participation in public decision making, and female solidarity. In male dominant cultures, women lack power; men are aggressive and macho; the sexes are separated; and the incidence of male violence and rape is moderate to high.[39]

Why is it important to discuss the causes of patriarchy? For those who want to create a culture where all people are treated with respect and equality, some causes, like those discussed next, point to possible solutions.

A new definition of manhood was essential to the development of the patriarchy. Although there is no evidence what the definition was in prehistoric cultures, in patriarchy to be a man meant to dominate women, children, and other men, especially minority men. This new definition of men as dominators was "the foundation stone and the *raison d' etre* for patriarchy."[40]

With the new definition of manhood, relationships between men became competitions for power. However, male solidarity was based on their superiority and domination over women.[41] Listen to the contempt for women that male locker room talk often expresses. Watch some men close ranks to support a man who is definitely guilty of sexual harassment.

French believes the patriarchy had to take away women's power in three ways to establish male dominance. First, it broke the bond of mutual affection and love between women and men and substituted male power over females. The relationship between the sexes was the domination of superior men over inferior women rather than equality and love.[42]

Second, to cause women to focus their energy and attention on men, the patriarchy broke the bond of unity among women. Patriarchal institutions socialized women to see themselves as inferior and thus to have contempt for women. Because women were taught to believe men were superior, they turned to men for leadership and protection. In addition, women's solidarity was damaged by the change to patrilineal and patrilocal families.[43]

Third, the patriarchy broke the bond of love between women and children and stressed parents having power over children. The emphasis in child-rearing was changed from nurturance and love to obedience and control.[44]

While some feminists call American culture patriarchy, Anne Schaef names it "the White Male System." Like pollution, it is everywhere; we all live in it. We are all trained in its educational, economic, political, legal, and religious institutions. Although many think our survival depends on our supporting this system, Schaef concludes that the White Male System is destructive, addictive, and death-oriented. She says the Emerging Female System is a Living Process System that is "life-supporting and life-producing."[45]

Patriarchy Causes Human Destructiveness

Patriarchy is the dominating social system that uses socialization, education, language, media, business, medicine, law, government, religion, and violence to have power over women and dictate what part they play in society. Even when women act as equal providers in the family, they very early

deliver their children over to the patriarchal system of socialization, education, and religion.

The dominator system excludes women from decision
making in almost all areas of life except the home. It controls
women and the things women produce, including children. In
the hierarchies it always creates, the vast majority of men,
especially men of color, are not near the top of the pyramid,
even though they are above women.

Once patriarchy consolidates its power, it develops an
ideology to justify male dominance. It teaches men are
superior and dominant, while women are inferior and submissive. It also claims men are to be productive, while women's
place is in the home. Preaching the same ideology, patriarchal religions teach that these definitions of women and men
are unchangeable because they are God's will. When both
women and men internalize these distorted external definitions of themselves, they are damaged.[46]

According to feminist Marilyn Frye, a crucial part of
male supremacy is "man-loving" which means that all people
reserve exclusively for males "respect, admiration, recognition,
honor, reverence and love." What men want from women is
"devotion, service and sex." Frye claims "woman-hating is an
obvious corollary of man-loving."[47]

Maguire asks if the word hatred is too strong and
answers that hatred is "the perfect word for the macho
attitude toward women." Hatred is "sustained anger and
disdain" that is marked by degradation and aversion. Exclu-
sion is one mark of hatred. For more than 200 years, the
United States has excluded women by maintaining a 90
percent monopoly for white males in decision making in
almost all the centers of power.[48]

Although it is often unrecognized, contempt for women
is a common thing in American culture. This contempt is
expressed in the fashion and advertising industries, in popular
entertainment, such as stalking and rape in movies and
television, in pornography, and in actual women battering and
rape. Frye says, "woman-hating is a major part of what
supports male-supremacy." The functions of woman-hating

are multiple, including supporting male solidarity and superiority by putting women both below men and apart from men.
Woman-hating helps maintain a definite boundary between
the male ingroup and the female outgroup.[49]

The strongest evidence of women hating is the murder
of women that Diana Russell and Jill Radford name femicide,
the misogynist killing of females by males. Femicide comes
in many different forms: marital femicide when husbands kill
their wives, racist femicide when white men kill black women,
homophobic femicide when heterosexual men kill lesbians,
femicide by rapists who kill their victims or give them AIDS,
serial femicide, and mass femicide.[50]

The first domination was males subjugating females so
that women were responsible for the tedious domestic work
and men were free to enjoy, create, and control the political,
economic, and religious world. The ideology of patriarchal
elitism in which men were considered superior created a
hierarchy of dominance of men over women.

Having learned how to maintain control over women,
the patriarchal elite began dominating other groups. Once the
hierarchy of dominance of men over women was established
and legitimated, it was transferable to rich over poor, masters
over servants, and whites over people of color. Sexism,
racism, and class dominance are interconnected in the
overarching system of white, ruling class, male domination.

Like many feminists, Rosemary Ruether identifies
sexism as "the first and basic model" for the subjugation.
Sexism is "the expression of a primal psychology of domination and repression." Patriarchy is, according to Adrienne
Rich, "the relationship at the core of all power relationships,
a tangle of lust, violence, possession, fear, conscious longing,
unconscious hostility, sentiment, rationalization."[51]

During the transition from the partnership to the
patriarchal society, the normal process of the young child
learning to distinguish between the self and the other was
used by the elite to create hierarchies of men over women,
the ingroup over outgroup, and humans over nature. The
patriarchy defined the self as the male who was superior,

competent, and good, while the other was females, other tribes, and nature who were inferior, less capable, less than human, and sometimes evil. The elite's positive perception of itself was reinforced when it gained power and reduced the others to servile status.[52]

The patriarchal ideology that justifies the subjugation of women is the model for dominating and making inferior the other oppressed groups. Subjugated people are described with similar stereotypes, not because they are alike, but because the same dominant group does the defining. Thus, the stereotype for dominated groups is similar to the stereotype for femininity. Subordinated people are described as lazy, emotional, dependent, submissive, inferior, and overly sexual. In contrast, the dominant group is the model of true humanity because its members are hard working, rational, independent, powerful, and superior.

Patriarchy criticizes and rejects the egalitarian way of relating as unrealistic and unworkable, while advocating domination and subordination. Patriarchy produces cultures, including our own, in which dominating is the main way of relating not only for individuals but also in the institutions of the family, school, business, law, medicine, government, politics, the military, and religion. Husbands have power over their wives, parents over children, men over women, rich over poor, teachers over students, lawyers over clients, doctors over nurses and patients, whites over people of color, government officials over citizens, and clergy over laity.

Methods Used by the Patriarchy To Dominate and Control

How does an elite group of rich white men control the masses of women, poor men, and people of color? The main method used by the patriarchy is mind control. When people internalize the patriarchy's values, there is no need for harsher methods of social control. Mind control is more effective, more efficient, and less costly than other forms of domination, including verbal abuse, discrimination, and physical violence.

For the patriarchal system to maintain itself, children must be trained to play their proper sex roles and to believe these roles are natural. Over thousands of years, women have been socialized that men are superior and that women's role is to raise children and take care of men's personal and emotional needs.

According to Jessie Bernard, the division of women and men into two groups is more important than the content of the differences assigned to them. The division into two groups is primary. The assigned differences are secondary. It makes no difference whether boys are rational and girls emotional or the other way around. What is crucial is that a difference is made. The division by sex is the fundamental fact.[53]

The patriarchy's division of women and men accomplishes several purposes. First, it makes it possible for the patriarchy to teach that males are superior to females. As Pogrebin says, the patriarchy teaches "boys are better. Girls are meant to be mothers." Male supremacy and compulsory motherhood are "the raw essentials of a patriarchal system."[54]

The second purpose is to divide and conquer. When the patriarchy divides men from women, it socializes both to believe that males are superior and females are inferior and therefore men have a right to dominate women. When women and men internalize these beliefs, they accept male domination of females. This belief in the superior elite's right to dominate creates the ideology of domination which socializes people to believe that a small group of elite rich white men who consider themselves superior has the right to control the masses of women, poor men, and people of color.

While the division into two groups is important, the assigned differences also have a major impact. In 1902, Carrie Chapman Catt, a leader of the women's suffrage movement, said "this world taught woman nothing skillful and then said her work was valueless. ... It forbade her to speak in public, and said the sex had no orators. It denied her the schools, and said the sex had no genius. ... It taught her that every pleasure must come as a favor from men, and when to

88

gain it, she decked herself in paint and fine feathers, as she had been taught to do, it called her vain."[55] Both women and men internalize the devaluation of women.

The patriarchal socialization process spends billions to teach the differences between women and men. Movies, magazines, television, music, and pornography create a standard of feminine beauty and masculine power. The advertisement industry is an over $100 billion business that advocates a feminine standard of beauty. Women spend billions to conform to the patriarchal standard of beauty that results in a $33 billion-a-year diet industry, a $20 billion cosmetic industry, and a $300 million cosmetic surgery industry.[56]

Some male psychologists perpetuate the patriarchal stereotypes that control women and men's minds. Maslow sustains the stereotypes when he sees the woman as able to be motherly and holy and "to strike awe into the heart of the man." Females are given the nearly impossible tasks of simultaneously "nursing, feeding, giving birth, taking care of children, cleaning the baby, being beautiful, being sexually exciting."[57]

Many women internalize the patriarchal teaching of male superiority and female inferiority. As Kay Hagen says, they believe the false messages that women are sex objects whose goal is to please men, average women's bodies are not beautiful enough, women are unable to take care of themselves without a man, and females need male approval in order to feel like real women. Women accept these patriarchal messages rather than listen to their own inner voice.[58]

According to Hagen, females internalize and echo "the woman-hating at the core of society." It is "not just men hating women, but women hating women and me hating myself." Male domination depends on "our unconscious, automatic self-hatred for its stability." Patriarchy teaches women to hate themselves, since "self-hatred insures both our collusion with the system of dominance and its continued success."[59]

When mind control is working properly, women acquiesce in their own subordination. For example, some women believe the patriarchal myth that women are raped because they asked for it by wearing provocative clothes or being in the wrong place at the wrong time. Because they believe patriarchal teachings are the truth, they are not consciously aware of choosing them.

Mind control insures women's unquestioning obedience to patriarchal values, so that they grieve when they fail to conform. Women's collusion with the patriarchy is complete, when they are asked whether they are dominated and they answer no. As Hagen says, "women may be the only oppressed group in the world who, by and large, have difficulty recognizing our own oppression."[60]

Usually women blame themselves for their own problems and deny any connection between these troubles and the patriarchal system. The patriarchy encourages both women and men to blame women for their difficulties and also for the problems of their children. Women blaming has become an art form in the patriarchy. Why does the patriarchy blame women? If women believe that they are to blame for everything that goes wrong, they are going to stay until they fix it.[61]

Besides mind control, the patriarchal elite uses harsher methods. These other methods of patriarchal control form a continuum from least harsh to most harsh. The continuum ranges from mind control to verbal abuse, discrimination, violence, and finally to the most severe type, murder.

Verbal abuse and emotional abuse control women in harsher ways than mind control. Still more severe types of domination are the restrictions on women's reproductive freedom, the separation of the private world of love from the public world, all forms of prejudice and hatred, and all ways of viewing women as only breeders or sex objects.

All kinds of discrimination, exploitation, and sexual harassment are other harmful ways to dominate. Prostitution which allows men to buy women's bodies for temporary use for whatever they want is another serious kind of domination.

More violent types of domination from the ancient times until today include Chinese foot binding, women battering, rape, child sexual abuse, genital mutilation, Indian suttee, and witch torture and burning. Female infanticide and murder are the most extreme forms of domination.

Mind control is used throughout the continuum. From the least harsh to the most harsh methods of domination, mind control is central so that those who are dominated blame themselves for the troubles that the patriarchy causes.

CONTINUUM OF PATRIARCHAL METHODS TO CONTROL AND DOMINATE WOMEN

Least Harsh Methods
    mind control
        socialization process produces a standard of feminine beauty and masculine power
        advertisement industry
        Harlequin romance novels
        diet industry, cosmetic industry
        cosmetic surgery
        movies, television, music, and pornography
    verbal abuse and emotional abuse
    restricting reproductive freedom, birth control, abortion
    viewing women only as breeders or sex objects
    all forms of prejudice, hatred, and discrimination
    segregation such as purdah
    work place discrimination and sexual harassment
    prostitution
    Chinese foot binding
    women battering
    rape and child sexual abuse
    genital mutilation
    Indian suttee
    witch burning
    female infanticide
    murder
Most Harsh Methods

Patriarchal institutions do not stop but rather encourage and support violence against women, including battering and rape. When the masculine mystique, that teaches males are superior and dominant, is carried to its logical conclusion, it leads men to violently impose their physical and sexual dominance on women. Before men rape and batter, they often verbally abuse and discriminate against women.

The media treats stalking, beating, raping, and murdering women as entertainment. This encourages the trivialization of these crimes. Many newspapers sensationalize these crimes to sell papers. Robin Morgan claims pornography as sexist propaganda is the theory, while rape is the practice. Many officials in the criminal justice system do not take rape and battering seriously. Few rapists and batterers are arrested, prosecuted, convicted, sent to prison, or rehabilitated.[62]

Dominance and subordination are the foundational values at the heart of the patriarchy. As long as these values remain intact, there will be no end to sexism, racism, classism, environmental destruction, militarism, war, and the increasing violence, destructiveness, and murders.

The patriarchy with its dominating hierarchy of superior over inferior damages people's inner core of love. The more their loving inner core is injured; the less self-love they have. The greater their feelings of insecurity and powerlessness, the more they want to dominate others or submit to the powerful to overcome their insecure and helpless feelings; the greater their destructiveness toward themselves and others.

To stop human destructiveness, its social causes must be abolished. The patriarchal model of dominance and subordination must change to the loving partnership model that promotes self-love and love for others as the most important values and actions.

CHAPTER FIVE

THE POTENTIAL FOR VIOLENCE WITHIN US

Normal men have killed perhaps 100,000,000 of their fellow normal men in the last ... years.... It is quite certain that unless we can regulate our behavior much more satisfactorily than at present, then we are going to exterminate ourselves.

R.D. Laing
Politics of Experience

Even as we are loved and cared for in families, we are simultaneously taught that this love is not as important as having power to dominate others. Power struggles, coercive authoritarian rule, and brutal assertion of domination shape family life.

Bell Hooks
Feminist Theory

I don't think we are going to understand violence in American society until we understand violence in the family.... The home is where violence primarily occurs.

Murray Straus

Introduction

Charles Manson gathered a group of followers he called his Family. In 1969, he ordered his Family to murder all the people at Sharon Tate's home on one night and at the La Bianca house on the next evening. In two nights, they murdered seven people and one unborn child.

Susan Atkins, age 21, a Manson Family member, described the murder of the pregnant Sharon Tate. "It felt so good the first time I stabbed her." When Sharon screamed, "it did something to me, sent a rush through me, and I stabbed her again." Susan said "I just kept stabbing her until she stopped screaming." Killing is "like a sexual release.... Especially when you see the blood spurting out. ... More you do it, the better you like it."[1]

Susan claimed she looked straight at Sharon and said "I don't care if you're going to have a baby. ... You're going to die, and I don't feel anything about it." After the murders, Susan said "I felt so elated, tired, but at peace with myself. I knew this was just the beginning of helter skelter. Now the world would listen."[2]

What caused Charles Manson, Susan Atkins, and other Family members to become mass murderers? If all human beings are essentially lovers, what causes them to become destructive of themselves and others?

Three Kinds of Aggression

The patriarchy is the main social cause of human destructiveness. It teaches people the highest value is domination and creates hierarchies in which elite individuals have power over the masses. Through its dominating hierarchies, the patriarchy encourages and activates the human potential for destructiveness.

Erich Fromm describes two kinds of aggression: defensive benign aggression and destructive malignant aggression.[3] He does not recognize a very significant third type, self-assertive aggression. Self-assertive aggression is people's drive to express themselves and participate actively in the world. Assertive individuals work to actualize their talents and accomplish their goals with perseverance, no matter what the obstacles.

Self-assertive aggression is part of the growth drive within the inner core of love, while defensive aggression is part of the safety drive. Defensive aggression responds to any threat to vital interests.[4] It removes the danger by talking, negotiating, fleeing, assuming a protective posture, or by attacking if nothing else works.

Defensive aggression is innate in both animals and humans. Animals react when danger threatens their vital interests, such as their life, food, territory, freedom, and children. Humans' range of vital interests is wider than animals'. Not only do humans defend their life, food, home, freedom, and family, but also their possessions, country, and sacred values. Thus, the reasons for defensive aggression are greater among humans than animals.[5]

Defensive aggression is the innate drive for self-preservation, safety, and self-love. Its purpose is not a lust for destruction, but the preservation of life, the survival of the individual and the species. Once the threat passes, the aggression ceases because it is life-serving, and not self-gratifying.

Self-assertive and defensive aggression account for most aggressive actions. However, destructive malignant aggression seems more pervasive because it captures more headlines and does more damage. Attention focuses on acts of savagery that horrify most people, but titillate some. A few disturbed people try to imitate these hideous atrocities to gain attention and fame.

Malignant aggression is dominance, cruelty, destructiveness, and killing. As Fromm says, destructive aggression is characteristic only of human beings and "virtually absent in most animals." Humans differ from animals because they are the only primates that torture and kill members of their own species without any reason and feel satisfaction in doing so.[6] Malignant aggression is harmful not only to the people who are attacked but also to the attackers because it violates their loving human nature.

Malignant aggression is not inborn. There is no innate human destructiveness. As Fromm says, "destructiveness and cruelty are not instinctual drives."[7] As a distorted form of the drive for safety and self-preservation, destructive aggression is defensive aggression carried to a perverted, warped extreme. Although it is a human possibility, it is an unnatural malformation of the natural safety drive.

The Human Potential for Destructiveness

Basic insecurity is normal, because we are all born helpless and need the protection of others to survive. When our dysfunctional family or patriarchal culture deprive us of safety, our basic insecurity becomes exaggerated and grows into a constant feeling of helplessness, powerlessness, and hopelessness in a dangerous world.

Excessive insecurity and helplessness cause fear. Like pain, fear is an uncomfortable feeling. People will do almost anything to get rid of it.[8] Fear creates the urge to fight or flight. Many flee literally by leaving the situation or figuratively through alcohol, drugs, or other self-destructive practices.

The most helpful and creative method of dealing with fear is to face it directly and try to solve it. Other constructive, but less direct and less helpful ways are work and play, socializing and solitude. A nihilistic, malevolent way of getting rid of fear is to become destructive. When people get out of the passive state of fear and begin to attack, the painful nature of fright disappears for a time. Becoming the attacker makes insecure, fearful individuals feel less like powerless victims.

One married couple's experience illustrates how excessive feelings of insecurity and powerlessness led to destructive behavior. Barb was upset because she was having trouble with her mother and difficulties at work. When her husband Jim came home, she told him about her problems. After she stopped crying, she went to bed. When Jim came into the bedroom, she held out her arms to embrace him. Climbing on top of her, he began punching her face and body. Because his body held her down, her only defense was to put her arms in front of her face. After pinning her arms above her head, he continued beating her.

Later Jim said the reason he battered Barb, whom he claimed to love, was he felt powerless to help her. Feeling fearful and helpless made him want power so he attacked her. His explanation may not be trustworthy because his motives may be unconscious and he may be lying to himself

and others. When people with a damaged inner core feel
they cannot reach people in any other way, they lash out
verbally or physically.

We have to believe in ourselves to affect others. We
have to be able to influence others to believe in ourselves.
When we do not believe in ourselves, we feel insecure and
powerless. Many of us with damaged inner cores think of
ourselves as helpless so we try to control others in order to
feel powerful. Some even use domination and violence to
overcome the fear caused by feeling powerless. In contrast,
those of us with healthy inner cores recognize others without
belittling ourselves and assert ourselves without putting others
down.

The purpose of defensive aggression is self-defense.
Its goal is to stop any danger that threatens. Defensive
aggression ceases when the threat has passed.

The purpose of malignant aggression is also self-
defense against a threat. Both its aim and the threat are
more complex than they are in defensive aggression. The
obvious threat is in the present, but the hidden threat is
always in the past. The previous damage to the loving inner
core is a constant threat to the well-being of injured people.
The threats caused by the earlier wounds to the loving inner
core may be unconscious, but they have powerful effects on
people's behavior. The more damaged the loving inner core,
the more distorted the aggression.

Unprovoked cruelty and killing of people whom murderers do not even know are not the result of innate human
destructiveness. As distorted methods of trying to stop their
own pain, they are a way of getting revenge for the damage
that was done to them in the past. The greater the damage
done to them earlier, the more brutal will be the expressions
of their retaliation now.

At birth, infants are complex and fragile. They are
extremely sensitive and easily injured. Children's innate inner
core of love is damaged when they are abused physically,
verbally, emotionally, or sexually. When they are mistreated,
their suffering can be severe and excruciating because they

experience not only physical pain, but also psychological anguish, social problems, and spiritual distress.

Infants will die without proper physical care. Lack of adequate love damages their loving inner core. Scarcity of love is painful and harmful. The less love, the more pain children experience. Too much agony from heartache mutilates their loving nature so that they become sad, angry, negative, hostile, hateful, destructive, and even violent.

Severe injury to the loving inner core can result from parental maltreatment. Sometimes parents scapegoat their children and project their own self-hatred onto them. Even if parents do not blame their children for their own failings, their destructiveness not only inflicts pain but also hurts the children's self-identity and loving inner core.

When children are mistreated by their parents, they suffer harm and sometimes assume that they deserve this poor treatment because they are bad. Children who do not receive enough parental love assume that they are the cause of this lack of love and they develop a negative self-identity. As M. Scott Peck says, "raised without love, children come to believe themselves unlovable."[9] Perhaps children cannot perceive their parents as unloving because they need to see them as providers of safety. Thus, youngsters believe that the unlovableness resides within themselves.

As Maslow says, "no deprivation is more to be feared than being deprived of self-esteem and security."[10] No psychological suffering is more severe than that caused by feeling absolutely worthless and unlovable. The loving inner core is injured and may be permanently wounded when safety, self-identity, and self-love are damaged.

Many youngsters receive some love, but not enough to foster their safety and growth. Being given some love helps them express part of their loving nature and to protect themselves against attack by using defensive aggression. However, others are starved of love throughout childhood and this distorts their natural drive for self-preservation into malignant aggression.

Destructive and violent urges may begin to reveal

themselves in childhood or they may remain dormant until they become adults and have the freedom to express these dangerous impulses. Some provocation unconnected to the real causes of the belligerency often triggers these destructive inclinations.

It is important to acknowledge that some people who experience a lack of love and tremendous pain in childhood become destructive, while others do not. Why only some and not the others? It does not matter how many similarities there are in two individuals' backgrounds. No two people ever experience life in the same way, so they do not receive the same amount of love or suffer the same degree of pain.

In addition, people have different tolerance for pain. Possible ways to assess whether individuals will become loving or destructive are to study their threshold for pain as well as the amount and quality of the love they receive. Whether people become loving or destructive depends on whether they receive enough love and whether they receive more pain than they can handle at a given time. Only one person can say for sure what is enough love and what is too much pain, and that is the individual who experiences it. However, people may not be able to predict accurately their own need for love, tolerance for pain, or breaking point until after the fact.

It is crucially important to say that parents are not the sole cause of whether their children become destructive or loving. Although parental harm to children's loving inner core aggravates their potential for destructiveness, the patriarchy damages parents before they become adults. Besides having their loving nature damaged when they were children, parents learn from the patriarchy to have power over others. The patriarchy and its dominating institutions, such as the family, school, medicine, and businesses, are the main cause of human destructiveness and they negatively affect all children and adults.

The Causes of Child Abuse

Love begets love. When children receive love, they become loving adults. In addition, violence breeds violence. When children are treated violently, they are more likely to become violent adults. Most child abusers were abused as children. Most women batterers either witnessed their mothers being beaten or were abused themselves as children. Most rapists were sexually traumatized, abused, or raped as youngsters. Most child molesters were sexually victimized when they were young. This is the generational cycle of violence.

In 1962, C. Henry Kempe, a pediatrician, described the serious problem of children being battered. More recent studies also show that "child abuse causes immediate and often permanent physical and emotional trauma." Besides the physical wounds, battered children are at greater risk of poor self-image, depression, poor peer relationships, apathy, learning disabilities, deviant acts, and aggressive behaviors.[11]

Vincent Fontana, a pediatrician, says the forms of child abuse may vary, but the abusive family environment is usually characterized as "unnatural, uncomfortable, unstable, unwarm, unprotective, unnourishing, unloving, and hostile to the development of a whole human being." Fontana is sure that in a study of the childhoods of murderous criminals, an abusive family environment would be found.[12]

The similarities between the qualities of abused children and abusive parents show that, unless abused children receive help so that they can overcome their problems, they may become abusive parents. Both the children and parents think of themselves as worthless and unlovable. Feeling fearful and angry, sometimes under a quiet manner, they are unable to revise their poor self-image.[13]

Being unable to trust anyone, abused children and abusive parents are lonely and have trouble making friends. At the slightest sign of disappointment, they relapse into distrust and discard their relationships. Although they want to be nurtured, they quickly find fault with others. Although they need help, they find it difficult to ask for it. Unless the cycle of child abuse is broken, the distorted relationship between the parents and children that deprives the young-sters of consistent love and nurturing will continue in the next generation.[14]

The Causes of Women Battering

Just as abused children are more likely to become abusive parents, so also children who either witnessed their mothers being beaten or were abused themselves are more likely to become spouse batterers. Erin Pizzey, who estab-lished the first battered women's shelter in the world, says men who batter their wives are children who were abused and not helped. The life histories of batterers show that they were either beaten as children or watched their mothers being assaulted so that the violence goes from generation to generation. Maria Roy's study of 150 battered women shows that over 80% of the abusive husbands came from homes where they either witnessed violence or were abused them-selves as children.[15]

Women battering and child abuse are interconnected. When husbands violently attack their wives, the children suffer also, either emotionally or physically or both. In Roy's study, 100% of the battered women said they believed their children were negatively affected when their mothers were beaten. About 45% of the batterings were accompanied by physical assaults by the father on at least one child in the home.[16]

In addition, battered women in their desperation may strike out at their children. They may scapegoat their chil-dren, as they feel that they have been scapegoated by their violent husbands. In one survey, 37% of the abused wives admitted taking their frustrations out on their children.[17]

Children who witness their fathers assault their mothers suffer emotional trauma. They feel shocked and scared because the safety that their homes previously provided is either threatened or gone. Not knowing what to do to stop the violence, they feel helpless. Male children who observe their fathers physically attack their mothers are more likely as adults to be violent with their spouses than those who never saw their parents fight.[18]

Murray Straus, Richard Gelles, and Suzanne Steinmetz interviewed a national sample. The 2,143 families with 960 men and 1,183 women had 1,146 children at home between the ages of three and seventeen. The results show that growing up in a violent home is predictive of future spouse and child abuse.[19]

Those whose parents did not hit their children and did not hit each other are more likely to be nonviolent. Those whose parents battered each other and hit their children are the "most violent people." When children who experienced the "double dose of violence" become adults, the chances of their becoming violent spouses or parents are greatest of all. About 25% of the males who grew up in the most violent households use some physical force on their spouses in one year. Over 25% use enough violence to risk seriously injuring their children. Each generation learns to be violent by participating in a violent family.[20]

The Causes of Child Sexual Abuse and Rape

The evidence also shows that most men who become rapists and child molesters were sexually victimized as children. After working with over 500 sex offenders for more than a decade, Nicholas Groth stresses that rape serves multiple psychological aims. Although rape appears to be a sexual act, it serves primarily nonsexual needs. Rape is an expression of anger and power, more than sexuality.[21]

Groth says during their formative years, 80% of sexual offenders, both rapists and child molesters, remember experiencing sexual trauma. He defines sexual trauma as any sexual activity witnessed or endured that was emotionally disturbing and upsetting. Those who were sexually victimized may try to combat their feelings of helplessness by identifying with the sexual abusers. By becoming powerful aggressors, they attempt to overcome feeling like defenseless victims.

Thus, sexual offenders' crimes may be in part a repetition of the sexual abuse they were subjected to as children. This acting out is a maladaptive effort to work through early unresolved sexual traumas.[22]

In one study, Groth compared the experiences of sexual offenders to other criminals and to college males. He discovered that while 80% of sex offenders were sexually abused as children, only 9% of college males and 28% of other criminals had this experience.[23]

Groth contends that many factors cause people to become rapists and child sexual molesters. Nevertheless, he cites the background of physical abuse, neglect, and their own sexual victimization as children as important causes. Sexual offenders' early experiences of sexual abuse shape their adult behavior.[24]

The evidence is overwhelming that there is a generational cycle of violence. Children who grew up experiencing or witnessing violence are more likely to become violent adults. Nevertheless, the whole burden of violence cannot be placed on childhood victimization. According to Murray Straus, some adults, whose fathers did not abuse them or their mothers, become violent even though their rates of violence are "a fraction of the rates for those who came from violent homes." There are other causes of violence, besides the generational cycle of violence. "The family may be the main training ground for violence, but in a violent society like ours, this role is shared with others."[25]

Besides childhood victimization, some other causes of destructiveness and violence are patriarchal power, sexism, racism, classism, elitism, prejudice, discrimination, poverty, hunger, crime, drug abuse, and alcoholism. Still other causes are the promotion of the masculine mystique, hierarchies of superior over inferior, violence used in movies and television as entertainment, the cultural acceptance and encouragement of all kinds of violence, including military violence.

The Root Cause of Human Destructiveness and Violence

The root cause of human destructiveness and violence is the patriarchy's teaching that the highest values are domination and power over others. The belief in the right to dominate others leads to the formation of various hierarchies of superior over inferior, men over women, rich over poor, and whites over people of color. To preserve themselves, these dominating hierarchies use prejudice, lies, verbal abuse, manipulation, discrimination, dehumanization, hostility, and violence.

When the 1993 U.S. Congress discussed ways to stop crime and violence, they wrote bills that increased the numbers of police officers, the length of prison sentences, and the waiting period for handgun purchases. Newspaper articles claimed hundreds of billions of federal and state dollars were needed to solve the problems of crime and violence. U.S. Senator Joseph Biden said "no one wants to be honest with the public about the cost of fixing the system."

The real cost to fix the system is not in dollars. Although there will be financial costs that the taxpayers must pay, the most significant costs are the psychological and social changes. All people in positions of power in patriarchal institutions, including the Congress, must give up their belief in their own superiority and right to dominate others.

Leaders with wealth, status, and power in patriarchal institutions are greater road blocks to the changes that are necessary to stop destructiveness and violence than the public who must pay the financial costs through their tax dollars. In fact, the public would be more willing to pay if they could believe that the system was serving all the people and not just benefiting the powerful.

The Potential for Violence within Us

While we criticize the brutal acts of others, we find it hard to admit that the potential for destructive actions is also within us. We are all potential dominators, abusers, and even killers. Our controllingness and destructiveness begin when we are socialized to believe that the highest value is domination and when we are mistreated as children. As adults, we act out the control and abuse we experienced.

Although it is true that we are all potential killers, we are not tempted to murder others, unless someone tries to destroy us. Killing does not come naturally to us. We only raise our hands to strike others after we ourselves have been struck. However, we all experience the destructiveness of the patriarchal culture as children so that we all have been figuratively struck. Thus, the potential to strike back, even if it is not at the same person who struck us, is there waiting for some provocation.

The only way to free ourselves from destructive urges is to recognize when we are feeling them, acknowledge them, and choose not to follow them. Through self-love, we begin to accept the disowned, destructive parts of ourselves and deal with them.

Men are socialized and rewarded for being dominant and aggressive. They are punished and called names, such as wimp and sissy, for exhibiting the opposite traits. Men are encouraged to turn their anger into aggression. If other methods fail, men are taught to solve their problems through physical violence. From childhood on, attacking physically is considered an acceptable way for men to deal with insults and threats to their power.

In contrast, the patriarchy not only praises women for being gentle and submissive, but it also calls them unfeminine for being aggressive. Women are taught that hitting other adults is masculine behavior and thus an unwomanly, unacceptable way for them to solve problems. Because anger is considered unfeminine, they are encouraged to turn their anger inward, where it becomes depression. Because they don't express their anger, they are more likely to be selfless, dependent, possessive, and passive-aggressive.

Both females and males are innately aggressive. Both are born with self-assertive and defensive aggression, but not with malignant aggression which is only a potential. Thus, destructiveness and violence are not innate, but both women and men have the potential to become killers.

Margaret Mitscherlich, a German psychoanalyst, claims that it is unrealistic to hold up an image of a nonaggressive, peaceable woman and an aggressive, warring man. Both sexes from birth onward are aggressive. Both females and males need their aggressiveness to become self-actualized. As a fundamental part of the human nature, aggression has a survival value. Socialization explains the differences in the ways females and males express their aggression.[26]

Mistakenly, Mitscherlich lays the sole responsibility for stopping violence on women. She says, if men are unwilling to give up their power, it is up to women to dismantle male domination and female submission.[27] Instead, I believe both women and men have a responsibility to stop the malignant aggression that perpetuates destructiveness.

The patriarchy claims women provoke men's violent actions. It teaches people to blame women for rape because they asked for it by the clothes they were wearing or by being at the wrong place at the wrong time. Both females and males are socialized to believe that men are provoked into brutally battering women because of nagging or poorly cooked food. Male violence is considered acceptable and masculine, while females shoulder the blame. Women blaming is as old as the patriarchy. Both males and females need to stop the violence and the women blaming.

Societal and Parental Abuses Cause Destructiveness

The damage done to Manson from his earliest years by both his parents and society caused him to become belligerent. His father refused to marry his 16-year-old mother or claim his son. When Manson was five, his mother went to the state prison for several years for robbing a service station. When she was paroled, she reclaimed her eight-year-old son from a very strict aunt who believed that all pleasures were sinful.

After Manson lived with his heavy drinking, promiscuous mother for several years, she attempted to put him into a foster home.   When none was available, the court sent twelve-year-old Manson to a caretaking school for boys. After ten months, he ran away and returned to his mother.

When his mother did not want him, Manson ran away and began robbing.   Police caught him and sent him to various correctional institutions.   He ran away more than eighteen times. By age 32, Manson had spent over 17 years in correctional institutions.   His history of violence included armed robbery starting at age 13, homosexual rape at age 17, wife beating at age 20, car theft, forgery, and pimping. When he was outside prison, he never held a job or went without law-breaking activities for more than a short time.

When Manson was to be released from prison the last time, he begged the prison authorities to let him remain in prison.   Telling them that prison had become his home, he said he did not think he could adjust to the outside world. The prison authorities denied his request. Two years after he was released from prison, his Family killed Sharon Tate and six other people. The causes of Manson's destructiveness, both toward himself and others, are evident in his history.

It is easier to say that Manson is innately mentally ill or destructive or evil than to face the real causes. To call him mentally ill is to make him seem different from ourselves. It makes us believe that we could never do what he did.   To describe Manson as evil is to mystify him so that he is separated from us. It is almost as if we are saying that Satan made him do it.   To say that his innate destructiveness produced his actions is to detract attention from the real causes.

Manson is not innately mentally ill, destructive, or evil. Nevertheless, he is extremely violent. The violence within him frightens us because it makes us aware of our own potential for murder. One method we use to escape from our own destructiveness is to explain violence away as though there is nothing we can do about it. When we say that other people are pathological or evil, we turn them into things that are different from us. We blame their illness or evilness for their bizarre behavior and remove the causes of their actions from the social situation in which we become who we are.

The society that was supposed to provide Manson with a nurturing environment maimed him and thus produced his violence. His mutilation was started by the patriarchy's damage to his parents who then passed it onto him. His 16-year-old mother had too many problems of her own to give her son the love he needed. His father failed to love him and outwardly rejected him. His relatives may have tried, but the wounds inflicted by the patriarchy and his parents were too severe.

When Manson's mother no longer wanted the 12-year-old boy, she turned him over to the institutions built by society to care for children whose parents are having trouble. Those institutions continued the wreckage begun by his family and the patriarchy. The psychologists missed their opportunities. Other officials contributed to his ruination. Society's institutions utterly failed him. The most important cause of Manson's destructiveness and violence is the lack of love in his life.

It is easier to say that there is something wrong with Manson than to admit that our institutions marred his humanity and thus produced a killer and a trainer of other killers. We do not want to admit that the institutions we support are more harmful and damaging than helpful and corrective.

We prefer to avoid criticizing our social structures by blaming the individual. We do not admit that our institutions are not serving us well. Thus, we refuse to make the needed changes. The fact that we must confront is that our social structures breed destructive people.

Although individuals sometimes damage themselves, most often the cause of the damage to human beings is outside themselves. Lack of love damages the inner core of self-love and love for others. This lack of love comes in many forms: child abuse, incest, neglect, poverty, maleducation, mistreatment, authoritarianism, discrimination, injustice, inequality, exploitation, alcoholism, drug abuse, women battering, sexual abuse, and abandonment.

Radical changes in the social and political structures are needed to create the conditions that will make love the supreme goal of society. As Fromm says, "genuine freedom and independence and the end of all forces of exploitative control are the conditions for mobilizing the love of life, which is the only force that can defeat the love for the dead."[28]

The ancient Greek Aeschylus said "our purpose must be to tame the savageness of man and make gentle the life of the world." The suggestion that Kate Millett offers for taming human savageness is change. But change is not enough. "If we are to succeed, if change is to come, there must be mercy. There must finally be love."[29]

The criterion to judge social institutions is: do they serve human life? Do they promote respect, liberty, equality, and justice? Do they encourage self-love and love for others? Any structure that damages human life and love needs to be changed.

Self-actualized people are aware of the insensitivity and cruelty within the familial, social, educational, political, economic, legal, governmental, military, and religious institutions and attempt to change them whenever possible. They are also aware of their own potential for destructiveness. There is nothing they can do to stop this potential from existing. However, they can choose to express love and curb any violent tendencies.

The damage to the inner core of love that causes brutality is reversible under the right circumstances. People whose inner joy has been deadened can learn to experience it again so that they feel good and happy instead of worthless and miserable. People who feel unloveable can develop self-love so that they can love others.

Twenty-five years after they took part in the murders, two of Manson's female followers admitted their profound remorse and their immeasurable everyday sorrow. While still in prison, their desire to make amends for their actions caused them to work to make positive contributions. In contrast, Manson still claims he was not responsible for the murders, even though both women now call him a liar and contend he gave the orders.[30]

Love is the best cure for any damage to the inner core. As Maslow says, "for a child who hasn't been loved enough, obviously the treatment of first choice is to love him to death." Maslow suspects that love works nine out of ten times.[31] Because the most important cause of human destructiveness is the lack of love, to stop violence both individuals and societal institutions need to become more loving.

PART THREE

THE POWER OF LOVE VERSUS
THE LOVE OF POWER

CHAPTER SIX

LOVING VERSUS DESTRUCTIVE BEHAVIOR

> Interviewing 200 working prostitutes in San Francisco, Mimi Silbert and Ayala M. Pines discovered astonishing patterns. ... Of the 200 women, 193 had been raped as adults and 178 had been sexually assaulted as children. That is 371 cases of sexual assault on a population of 200 women.
>
> Andrea Dworkin
> *Letters from a War Zone*

Introduction

Mary's father was a corporate executive and a lay minister in Nebraska. Behind closed doors, he was also an alcoholic and a child molester. When Mary finally spoke about it, she says "my incest story begins before pre-school and ends many years later." Besides her father, her uncle and a minister sexually abused her. "My father forced me to perform sexual acts with men at a stag party when I was a teenager." Three times between ages nine and sixteen, he forced her to be a pornography model. Today Mary calls herself "an incest survivor, ex-pornography model, ex-prosti-tute," and a feminist fighting to stop violence against women.[1]
What caused a father, an uncle, and a minister to molest Mary? How could men at a stag party force sexual acts on the daughter of a man they knew? How did Mary

survive these multiple sexual abuses and fight to protect other
women? If all people are born loving, what causes some
individuals to become destructive and others loving?

Loving Versus Destructive Behavior

Since love is the essence of human nature, love is the
single best criterion for judging behavior. The best way to
distinguish between fully functioning and destructive behavior
is to find out how well people express love for themselves and
others. As Virginia Satir says, love is "the highest form of
expressing my humanness."[2] To be self-actualized is to love
fully and freely. In contrast, destructive behavior is any action
that is anti-love or anti-life.

Sigmund Freud said the criterion for mental health is
"*leben, lieben, arbeiten*," which means "to live, to love, to
work." Ashley Montagu's criterion is similar, "to love, to work,
and to serve." People's need for love is as compelling as
their need for food. "Without love there can be no healthy
social behavior, cooperation, or security." After defining love
as relating to others, Montagu says "every neurosis has at its
core the failure of healthy involvement, of relatedness to
others." Putting it another way, "men who do not love one
another are sick."[3]

All people are loving. However, because some have
been mistreated by their caretakers, life circumstances, and
the patriarchy, they are afraid to make themselves vulnerable
by expressing their love. When their love does come out,
defense mechanisms conceal its identity and distort its form.
Sometimes the damage that the individuals have suffered
causes them to express themselves in destructive behavior
rather than in loving acts.

Besides giving love to themselves and others, individuals also need to be loved in order to be fully functioning. Self-
actualized individuals are in touch with their loving inner core,
gratify their basic needs, fulfill their creative talents, solve their
own problems, express their unique selves, and give love to
themselves and others. Unfortunately, many people are not

fully functioning. The continuum that ranges from fully loving to totally destructive behavior indicates how fully functioning individuals are. At one end of the continuum are fully loving actions, while at the other extreme are the totally destructive acts, such as rapes and murders.

Between the continuum's two extremes are the actions of people with problems. Such problems include disliking themselves, rejecting intimacy, having weak inner signals, not knowing what they want, neglecting their own needs, failing to grow, experiencing excessive grief over a lost love, losing hope, submitting to others, and dominating others in order to feel superior.

Fully loving behavior is acting in a deeply loving way toward the self, all people, and nature. Destructive behavior is loving in a deformed way or not loving at all. Full functioning behavior balances self-love with love for others. When this balance is disrupted, the centered self is damaged and destructive behavior follows. When self-love is not balanced with love for others, it becomes selfishness. When love for others is not connected to self-love, it leads to selflessness. Both imbalances result in destructive behavior.

Too much concern for safety wrecks possibilities for growth. Too much activity and change can lead to chaos. Excessive concern for either safety or growth destroys personal wholeness. Fear makes people cling exorbitantly to safety. After excessive concern for safety stunts their development, they become apathetic, alienated robots who go through the motions of life without really living.

One example of clutching safety too tightly is the adult man who clings to his mother's apron strings so that he never creates a life of his own. Another example is a woman who lives vicariously through her husband and children because she is afraid to use her own talents. Yet another example is the intimidated employee who quakes every time the boss speaks.

If people fail to respond to their self-creative drive to go out from their safe haven into the social world, then alienation results. Alienation is extreme separation from other people.

In becoming alienated, they become society-less. Alienation is a cancerous self-preservation that corners them in dark loneliness and violates their innate drive for communion with others. Alienation causes them to lose their self-identity, emotional ties, and finally their orientation to reality.

Excessive concern for safety leads to self-destruction that comes either slowly or quickly. In its extreme form, it comes quickly by suicide. However, there are ways to kill ourselves even though we are still alive. Becoming apathetic, we totally withdraw from reality and do absolutely nothing. We talk to no one and have only our own mind for company. Slower, less severe forms of self-destruction are mental problems, alcoholism, drug addiction, criminality, and other kinds of anti-social behavior.

Too much activity and change is another type of destructive behavior. Constantly rushing from one activity to another damages our wholeness and self-identity. Growth not balanced with safety causes us to lose our centered self. When change runs wild, we become formless dynamos running around with no place to go and no purpose in going.

In large cities, people are bombarded by constant stimulation when they walk the streets and turn on the radio and television. Alvin Toffler calls "future shock" a physical and psychological disease of too much change too fast. Confronted continually with a deluge of innovations, people do not have time to assimilate them and are stretched beyond their limits.[4]

Examples of too much change and activity are executives who work such long hours that they have no time for their families or friends. Constantly running from one social event to the next, wealthy socialites never stop to look into themselves to understand their real needs. Because poor women workers are exploited, they slave long hours in dehumanizing factories and then spend the rest of their waking hours caring for their husbands and children.

To be fully functioning, solitude and communion must be kept in balance. When solitude becomes extreme, it develops into isolation. When union with others becomes fusion, it leads to a loss of self. Severe aloneness produces detachment from others. An overabundance of attachment to others results in possessive love.

The following chart shows how loving behavior balances self-love with love for others and how imbalance leads to destructive behavior.

Loving versus Destructive Behavior

Destructive Behavior	Person = Lover = Inner Core of Love = Loving Behavior		Destructive Behavior
selfishness	self-love	love for others	selflessness
excessive concern for safety	safety	growth	too much activity and change
egoism	self-actualization	communion	possessiveness
self-indulgence	self-identity	self-change	self-loss
undependable	independent	interdependent	dependent
rugged individualism	self-preservation	self-change	shatteredness
dominator	self-interest	altruism	dominated
malignant, destructive aggression	defensive, benign aggression	self-assertive aggression	no self-assertion

Excessive concern for self-preservation overflows into rugged individualism. Exorbitant independence expands into undependability, while the superabundance of interdependence produces dependence. Too much need for control and concern for self-interest makes people into dominators. However, there can be no dominators without submitters. Individuals who are too concerned with pleasing others will allow themselves to be dominated rather than offend others.

Because the patriarchy socializes men to be independent and not interdependent, they need to be careful not to become selfish and undependable. Because women are taught to take care of the needs of others and not their own, they need to guard against becoming selfless and dependent.

Thomas Harris correctly teaches that the only way for people to have a sense of well-being is to act out the I'm OK and You're OK life position.[5] When love balances self-love with love for others, it balances the belief that I'm OK with You're OK. Destructive behavior results from actions that express either You're not OK or I'm not OK or both. Patriarchy socializes both women and men to believe that men are OK and women are not OK. This socialization is destructive and untrue, because both women and men are OK. Both women and men need to believe I'm OK and You're OK, even when their behavior is flawed.

The I Win/You Win mentality is an interdependent way of relating where we both win and where the results are mutually beneficial for both you and me. The I Win position is an independent frame of mind where I am only concerned about my own aims.[6] The I Win mentality creates safety, while the I Win/You Win interaction produces growth.

When the I Win mentality is not balanced with the I Win/You Win way of thinking, it becomes the I Win/You Lose interaction. This is a competitive, dominating frame of mind where I want to get my way no matter what the cost. I use power over others and any means necessary to reach my goal, even unethical methods.[7]

One problem with the I Win/You Lose way of thinking is that most of life involves cooperative, interdependent interaction rather than competition. The I Win/You Lose mentality makes cooperation difficult.[8] Both people are often harmed when the loser becomes angry and tries to get even with the winner.

When the I Win/You Win mentality is not balanced by the I Win way of thinking, the I Lose/You Win interaction results. When I do not preserve my independence and become selfless, I let you have your way. Because I am intimidated by your ego strength, I am afraid to express my feelings. In order to be accepted, I do anything to please you.[9]

One problem with the I Lose/You Win mentality is that you may treat me as a doormat to be walked on. Although I may suppress my feelings of anger and resentment, these unexpressed feelings never die. Instead they are buried alive and come forth later in ugly ways. The I Lose/You Win way often ends up as the I Lose/You Lose interaction where both of us are losers because we do not have a mutually beneficial relationship.[10]

The patriarchy socializes men to use the I Win/You Lose interaction. Since birth, most of us have been taught by our family, peer group, and schools that the I Win/You Lose mentality is the best way of thinking. Despite this, women are expected to practice the I Lose/You Win way.[11]

The Continuum from Fully Loving
to Totally Destructive Behavior

A continuum ranges from fully loving behavior at one extreme to totally destructive behavior at the other. Love is on one end, while hatred, domination, and violence are on the other end. Between these two extremes are different degrees of destructive behavior.

When self-love maintains a balance with love for others, people act in loving ways. Individuals act in destructive ways when the balance is disrupted. Then their actions fit somewhere down the continuum toward destructive behavior.

Fully loving behavior is rare. In a patriarchal culture, love is often flawed. Loving people, such as Gandhi and Eleanor Roosevelt, worked throughout their lives to improve themselves and to serve others. Yet they often fell short because no one is perfect. However, most of their actions deserve to be placed near the fully loving end of the continuum because they expressed love for themselves and others. Most people try to improve themselves and help others, but often their actions fall somewhere between the two extremes.

Hitler epitomized totally destructive behavior. In the twelve-year reign of the Third Reich, he ordered his followers to overrun countries, slaughter millions of innocent people, and rule the survivors by means of terror. Finally, as his empire collapsed around him, he ordered the devastation of Germany, and he killed himself and his wife. The behavior of mass murderers and sadistic rapists comes close to being totally destructive because they often think of suicide, before or after they torture and kill their victims.

Destructive behavior is acting against love and life. In its most extreme form, destructive behavior is violence against the self and others. Psychiatrist R.D. Laing claims love and violence are opposites. It is more accurate to say love and violence are at the opposite ends of the continuum between fully loving and destructive behavior. Laing correctly says "love lets others be, but with affection and concern. Violence attempts to constrain the other's freedom, to force him to act in the way we desire, but with ultimate lack of concern, with indifference to the other's own experience or destiny."[12]

Carl Rogers formulated a continuum of personality change with seven stages. Whether there are three stages or 50, Rogers stresses there are the two extremes and some intermediate points. People's behavior clusters in a narrow range. It is unlikely that individuals would be at one end of the continuum in one area of their lives, while being at the other extreme in another part. At one end, people's functioning is rigid and impersonal. Since they are out of touch with what is going on within themselves, they do not own their feelings and are not able to relate to others. Either they see themselves as having no problems or they blame others for their problems.[13]

In contrast, people at the other end of the continuum are in touch with their loving inner core and use it to guide their behavior. Not only are they responsive to events outside themselves, but also to the ever changing experiences within themselves. After owning their feelings, they express them when appropriate. Their way of thinking is flexible so that fresh meanings are drawn from new experiences. They relate well to others and recognize their responsibility for many of their own problems.[14]

Once people move away from rigid, destructive behavior at one end of the continuum toward loving acts, they do not want to go back to being rigid and destructive again. Instead they want to progress,[15] even though they make many mistakes and have multiple setbacks.

Susan B. Anthony and Martin Luther King's loving behavior can be placed near the continuum's fully loving extreme. Moving further down the continuum are actions that expose varying degrees of minor problems. Examples are a self-conscious man who cannot gather the courage to call a friend for a date and a student who cannot settle down to study and fritters away her time watching television. Other examples are a woman who constantly complains of fatigue and headaches for which no cause can be found and a successful businessman who cannot relax on his vacations and keeps calling the office.

Moving even further down the continuum away from fully loving behavior toward destructive behavior, the signs of difficulties become more obvious. The commonplace troubles shift to more severe problems. Examples are a quiet choir boy who steals cars and a young woman who belittles her friends so persistently that they ultimately are alienated from her. Other examples are a shy man who exposes himself in the library and a woman who is unable to sleep because of her fear that someone will sneak into her home and murder her family. Still another example is an alcoholic father who spends all his time and money in the bar and neglects his wife and children.

Markedly severe problems are so destructive of the self and others that they are evident to all who encounter them. One examples is a isolate who seems perennially unhappy, speaks of weird experiences, and shouts at persons unseen by others. Other examples are a mother who sexually abuses her own child and a man who brutally beats his wife and children. Still more examples are a woman who attempts suicide because she is rejected by her lover and the robber who shoots an unarmed shopkeeper. A final example is a rapist who has no remorse after he brutalizes and murders an eighty-year-old woman.

The Continuum from Game-Playing to Game-Free Living

We find ourselves in many types of relationships. Some are based on equality, such as two friends. Our patriarchal culture turns many other relationships into hierarchies. These patriarchal hierarchies include husbands over wives, parents over children, teachers over students, doctors over patients, bosses over workers, and whites over people of color. Violent hierarchies include batterers over battered, rapists over raped, and murderers over murdered.

Except for violent relationships that are by nature dominating, these relationships can be acted out in one of two ways, either game-playing or game-free. Normally two equals relate in a game-free way. Relationships between parents and children or teachers and pupils, that are often viewed as unequal, can also be game-free. Unfortunately, controlling people can distort any relationship into a game.

Another way of describing the continuum from loving to destructive behavior is the continuum from game-free living to game-playing. People's behavior can be placed on the continuum from fully loving to totally destructive by finding out the extent and seriousness of their game-playing. The more fully loving their behavior, the less they play games. The more destructive their behavior, the more they play games, the more serious are the games they play, the more control they exert over others.

The extent of game-playing varies from playing games all the time in all relationships to playing them occasionally or not at all. The seriousness of the games ranges from harmless amusements to the deadly serious games of manipulation, exploitation, domination, torture, battering, rape, murder, and war.

Game-playing is a form of destructive behavior and it always involves dishonesty. Playing games is a way of relating in which we attempt to hide from, manipulate, and control others. People who play games do not treat others as equals. Instead they dominate and put others down so that they feel superior and those they control feel inferior. As a defense mechanism, game-playing prevents a genuine exchange of feelings, thoughts, values, and actions and thus avoids intimacy.

As a way of expressing love, game-free living means that two people relate to each other honestly and respectfully. Neither tries to control or put the other down. Relationships where one person is trying to help the other are game-free when they are both understanding, accepting, sincere, forthright, trustworthy, considerate, and caring. Neither lies. Neither takes a dominant or submissive role. Neither tries to manipulate, exploit, or abuse the other.

In game-free living, two people interact honestly and respectfully to accomplish a mutually agreed upon purpose. For example, Rose asks Sarah for reassurance. After Sarah gives the requested reassurance, Rose thanks Sarah. However, this simple transaction can be turned into a game.

Every game involves a dishonest switch in roles. This gives the person who switches the roles control over the other and a payoff that is unexpected by the other who is therefore conned. The reason the game is played is to gain control over the other and to receive the hidden benefit of the payoff.[16]

Using the same example, Rose asks Sarah for reassurance and Sarah gives it. Then Sarah turns Rose's request for reassurance against her by criticizing her. For instance,

Sarah ridicules Rose for being too needy. Sarah switches her role from being the helper who gives reassurance to the controlling persecutor who knows it all. The dishonesty is that Sarah is on the surface helping Rose, while in reality she is putting Rose down. Sarah switches Rose's role from being a needy person to a victim of Sarah's persecution. The hidden payoff to Sarah is just that; it is hidden. It depends on Sarah's particular psychological needs. In this case, it could be her need to build herself up by putting others down.

When two people play everyday games, three roles are often used: victim, rescuer, and persecutor. Each person takes one of these roles and then continually switches to another. They trade places indefinitely because they are playing the no-win game of trying to control each other.

Some couples use these three roles in their daily interactions. When a husband comes home late for dinner, his wife takes the victim role by complaining that the dinner is spoiled, while he takes the rescuer role and tries to comfort her. Then she switches to the persecutor role and harangues him for always being late and not caring about anyone but himself. Taking the victim role, he says that he was busy supporting the family. Playing the rescuer, she tries to reassure him. Next he switches to the persecutor role and complains about her nagging. This game is an endless cycle of accusing, comforting, blaming, placating, and criticizing.

In everyday games, individuals are autonomous, but they try to control aspects of others' lives. Some people who relate in dominating ways call themselves friends. However, they do not have a friendship, because having power over the other is the antithesis of love and friendship.

Sometimes when people play games, they do it consciously and intentionally. Other times the people who initiate the games are not aware of their own game-playing. Sometimes the games are harmless, but other times they are serious games with deadly consequences.

One common game is dishonestly switching a non-controlling role to a controlling one. This kind of action is devious because it is cloaked under a role that is not supposed to be controlling. Some game-playing ministers outwardly care about their parishioners and try to help them grow spiritually, while inwardly and unconsciously they attempt to control them and thus stunt their growth.

Playing a role is not by its nature playing a game. Playing a role is performing certain functions with the aim of achieving a specific goal. Sadly, a role can be turned into a game if individuals try to control other people, to force them into an inferior position, or to put them down. Being a teacher is a role that involves teaching and learning with particular students. When teachers try to dominate their students, they turn their role into a game.

Regrettably, even love is turned into a game when it becomes possessive, jealous, obsessive, manipulative, exploitative, or controlling. Love that becomes damaging is always a game, because love by its very nature is creative and to turn it into something injurious is to switch its role dishonestly and thus to play a game.

Robin Norwood identifies "loving too much" as being addicted to relationships. Loving obsessively is a more accurate phrase than "loving too much." Women love obsessively when they constantly look for someone to love them and when they care for partners who are unloving and afraid of intimacy. They also love obsessively when they stay in relationships in spite of the ever-present pain caused by their partners' put-downs, dishonesty, manipulation, domination, womanizing, alcoholism, drug abuse, battering, and sexual abuse.[17]

Often a woman who loves obsessively suffered from a lack of love in her childhood because of the dysfunction in her family. Because her pain was too great in childhood, she denies her feelings and tries to control her environment. First she obsessively tries to find a man to love her. Then she attempts to control him by taking care of all his needs. Sometimes she tries to rescue and change an uncaring, unavailable, unloving man, even a man who abuses drugs and batters her.

Most often these women do not realize that they are

controlling others through their obsessive love. Because they fear the pain that would result from dealing with their feelings, they deny their feelings of insecurity and unlovableness that are the underlying reasons for their controlling behavior. Since they deny their own feelings, they are not able to be truly honest about who they are and what they need, even with those they claim to love.   Loving obsessively is a dishonest, controlling game.

Over-protective fathers and mothers claim to love their children and do, but in a harmful way. Their possessive love smothers their children's individuality and does not allow them to have a life of their own. Clinging mothers and fathers purport to be acting for their children's own good when they are actually attempting to control them.

Some parents who love their children dearly cannot understand why their children develop behavioral problems. These parents do not recognize the fact that they put their children down with negative humor, sarcastic remarks, and a constant barrage of belittling statements. Because children's fragile identities are still developing, parents' negative statements can do serious, long-term damage to children's inner core of love. To help children develop good self-images instead of negative ones, parents need to stop this unconscious game of putting their children down.

The patriarchy socializes both men and women to play games. Men are taught to be masculine and to act dominant and aggressive. Even though being dominant and aggressive does not feel natural, they are expected to act that way. Women are socialized to be feminine and to act submissive and passive. Even women who want to be assertive and active are expected to act subordinate and docile.

Since mutuality and partnership are essential to game-free living, being either dominant or submissive is playing a game. Both women and men engage in overt and covert forms of game-playing, such as manipulating, lying, and dominating.

The partial control in everyday games is more devious but less lethal than the game of oppression. Coming in many forms, oppression varies in how severely it damages its victims. Pimps and johns oppress prostitutes. Hitler oppressed the Jews. In most forms of oppression, the subordinates know who their dominators are and the extent of their control. However, some wives do not recognize when they are controlled by their husbands.

The foremost cause of this game is the oppressors who impose their power on unwilling victims. However, if the oppressed remain victims instead of resisting, they collaborate in the oppressors' power game.

Once a game is started either by other people or by ourselves, the first step in stopping it is to recognize it as a dishonest, controlling game. Next we need to confront the game-players about their devious, dominating behavior. The third step is to refuse to play. We must refuse to be either manipulated or manipulators, dominated or dominators. As President Abraham Lincoln said, "as I would not be a slave, so also I would not be a master."

Even when someone else chooses to play games, we can refuse to play and choose game-free living. When other people have the physical, psychological, economic, political, or military power over us, we can still choose to live game-free, although it is difficult.

When teachers act controlling, students have several choices. Some students submit to the teachers' domination. Other students work behind the teachers' backs to manipulate them. Still others attempt to live game-free by trying to express their talents despite the teachers' dominating actions. To stop the game-playing, the teachers and students must not control each other, must not take the superior or inferior stance, and must not put others down or allow themselves to be put down.

When game-playing employers act controlling and treat their workers as inferiors, their employees have several choices. Some obey their bosses and exert power over those below them. Others have the integrity to refuse to play the bosses' game and courageously attempt to live game-free. Workers who live game-free do all their work to the best of their ability, but refuse to participate in anything that is unfair, discriminatory, or unethical. Even in the most difficult circumstances, people can say no to oppression and live with integrity.

Although people are born both interdependent and independent, they often give up some of their autonomy and adapt to parental programming. This includes learning to play their parents' games and following the life script written for them. To define their own identity, people must learn to reject their parents' games, while affirming their game-free living. Then they become autonomous individuals who take responsibility for their own lives and cease being controlled by others.

What is necessary to achieve creative game-free living instead of just surviving by destructive game-playing? Game-free living is being honest and expressing love for the self and others. Thus, it involves all the qualities of being loving, including accepting, responding, understanding, sharing, appreciating, apologizing, forgiving, and trusting. Acting true to their loving inner core, people who live game-free reject parental and patriarchal prohibitions. Because they shun artificiality and falseness, they live simply and act spontaneously.

People with good self-identities want game-free living. The better their self-image, the less they want to play games. Because they feel secure and not defensive, they accept themselves and others as they are and refuse to play games, even when others try to force games upon them. Not allowing themselves to be put in either a superior or inferior position, they refuse either to dominate others or submit to others.

Self-actualizing people believe that love is the best guide for their actions and that the ends do not justify the means. Game-playing as a means to even good ends is dishonest and therefore unacceptable. Since they distinguish between people and their actions, they condemn game-playing, while they continue to respect those who play games.

People play games to overcome their insecure,

powerless feelings. The deeper their helpless feelings, the less their self-love, the less their love for others, the more they play games, the less they are able to live game-free. Because they do not feel safe, they are not able to accept themselves or others. Their defensiveness, false fronts, and masks are supposed to protect them from others. Their lies and game-playing are used to control others so that they can hide their insecurities.

However, people who play games know, either consciously or unconsciously, that their power over others is tenuous because it is based on dishonesty. Thus, their insecurities are exacerbated because they live in fear that people will become aware of their duplicity and expose them for what they really are. Fear of discovery leads to even more game-playing.

People whose loving inner core is damaged can love in only a limited or distorted way. The more damaged their inner core of love, the more deformed their way of loving themselves and others, the more they play games. To overcome their feelings of unlovableness, they try to control others. When they have power over others, they feel no one can hurt them. Since their control over others is not total, they sometimes become frightened and strike out at others, because their inner fearfulness threatens to overwhelm them.

The choice between game-playing and game-free living is difficult and ever-present because so many people attempt to force us into playing games. The best way to avoid playing games is to keep in touch with our own inner core of self-love and love for others. Therapist Miriam Greenspan's parents survived the holocaust both physically and spiritually and taught her that "love is more powerful than oppression,"[18] even the terrible oppression of Nazi concentration camps.

Love is more powerful than playing games. Love is more powerful than those who want to control us. Our inner core of love gives us the strength to say no to being subordinate or dominating others, to being put down or putting others down, and to acting inferior or superior. Love is the power within us that makes game-free living possible.

CHAPTER SEVEN

FEMINIST VERSUS PATRIARCHAL, LOVING VERSUS POWER-HUNGRY LEADERSHIP

The basic dilemma is how women can gain enough money and power to literally change the world, without being corrupted, co-opted, and incorporated on the way by the very value systems we must change.

Emily Jane Goodman
Women, Money, and Power

The master's tools will never dismantle the master's house. ... the true focus of revolutionary change is never merely the oppressive situations which we seek to escape, but that piece of the oppressor which is planted deep within each of us, and which knows only the oppressors' tactics, the oppressors' relationships.

Audre Lorde
Sister Outsider

First they killed my brother Moshe.
Then they killed my father.
Then they killed my brother Bunio.
Then they killed my brother Zachery.
Then they killed my last brother, Herzl.
Only my mother and I were left. I vowed that I would never let them kill her, that I would protect my mother from the Nazis and their collaborators for as long as I lived. Love and hate were what motivated my young mind and heart. Love for my dear, gentle mother--and hate for the cruel murderers.

Alicia Appleman-Jurman
Alicia

Introduction

From age eight to fifteen, Alicia Appleman-Jurman experienced the murder of her father and brothers by the Nazis. The Nazis invaded the Jewish ghetto to take the Jews away and create a "Jew-free" Polish city. After being captured by the Nazis four times, she was tortured in their prisons, but she continually escaped.[1]

At age eleven, Alicia escaped the first time when adults threw her from a moving train headed for a Nazi concentration camp. She survived her second capture because she passed out from the pain of being tortured in a Nazi prison and was thrown on a pile of dead bodies. Some Jewish men saw her body was still warm and smuggled her into their ghetto.[2]

As Alicia was captured the third time, she saw the Nazis shoot two babies in the mouth. As the Nazis and Ukrainians herded the Jews along, many people were "cursing us, and some were throwing stones at us." When Jews fell, Nazis shot them. In the forest, many Jews stood in front of a large trench. When the Nazi machine guns started, Alicia stood paralyzed as people fell into the trench, some dead and others alive. As she was herded closer to the pit, a group of resistance fighters began firing at the Nazis. In the confusion, Alicia and some others escaped into the forest.[3]

Later when the Russians liberated her hometown, Alicia and her mother left their hiding place on a farm and returned. When the Nazis recaptured the town, her mother was wounded as they tried to escape. Since they could not run, they were captured. As they were herded along, a Nazi aimed his pistol at Alicia and pulled the trigger. Her mother stepped in front of her and was killed. Still aiming at Alicia, the Nazi pulled the trigger again, but there was only a clicking noise. His last bullet had killed Alicia's mother.[4]

Alicia was imprisoned with 30 others in a prison cell designed for four people. The next morning, she and 200 other Jewish prisoners, many of whom were turned in by their neighbors, were taken to be shot at a mass grave. When the shooting began, Alicia ran zigzag and jumped into the cold river. Hiding until nightfall, she escaped into the countryside and lived alone with her nightmares. From the age of eight to fifteen, Alicia experienced the murder of her whole family and witnessed the Nazis' ultimate, patriarchal behavior.[5]

The pages of our recorded history are filled with dominating, violent patriarchal activities by conquerors, such as Alexander the Great, Julius Caesar, Hannibal, Attila the Hun, Napoleon, Hitler, Stalin, and the Europeans who slaughtered the American Indians. Murderous conquerors are often treated as "great" men and receive the awe and even the admiration of many. Napoleon has a fancy tomb in Paris that Hitler visited after conquering France.

Loving, feminist behavior is the alternative to power-hungry, patriarchal behavior. Ordinary people such as Alicia have exhibited this behavior in the face of the worst possible destructiveness. Besides the innumerable mass killings that Alicia witnessed, she also experienced and participated in many acts of kindness and love as she struggled to survive the Nazis' murderous actions. When the Nazis asked for her mother, Alicia acted as if she were her mother and went to prison.[6]

When decisions were made about who should hide in the limited space in the Jewish bunkers to avoid being captured by the Nazis, those who were more able were left outside to hide elsewhere. Staying outside herself, Alicia made sure her mother and younger brother were hidden in the bunker.[7]

People helped each other on Nazi marches, because to fall down was to be shot. When a stranger found Alicia still alive on a pile of dead bodies, he brought her home and nursed her back to health. If the Nazis had found out, they would have killed him and all his family.[8]

Although he risked his own life, an old Christian farmer called Wujciu saved Alicia and her mother by taking them in when they were hiding one winter from the Nazis. Alicia saved three other people by getting Wujciu to take them in. In total, Wujciu housed eight Jews and thus saved their lives.[9]

After Alicia's mother was wounded and could no longer

escape, she urged Alicia to flee and save herself. Because she refused to leave her mother, Alicia was captured by the Nazis the fourth time. Her mother died because she took the bullet intended for Alicia. Before her death, Alicia's mom urged her to live and bear witness to the murder of her family and people.[10]

Throughout history, empowering leaders have offered an alternative to patriarchal ways by practicing love. Examples include Buddha, Jesus, Lucretia Mott, Susan B. Anthony, Jane Addams, Gandhi, Martin Luther King, Eleanor Roosevelt, and Mother Teresa. The power of love is the solution for the love of power. Love and feminism as the vision and practice of love are the solutions for patriarchal destructiveness.

Feminism's Power of Love Versus Patriarchy's Love of Power

Although there are as many philosophies of feminism as there are feminists, most would agree that we live in a patriarchy or a dominator social system. According to French, patriarchy is a militant ideology. "To revere power above everything else is to be willing to sacrifice everything else to power." Over thousands of years, patriarchy spread worldwide and only a few societies still exist that are not swayed by it. Almost all American institutions practice the patriarchal value of domination. This deeply influences most people.[11]

The patriarchy socializes females to be submissive and males to dominate women and other men. Being dominated breeds feelings of insecurity. A patriarchal antidote to insecurity is to exert power over someone else. Many males dominate other people, especially women and minorities. Many females buy into the patriarchal value system and exercise control over their children and sometimes over their husbands and co-workers. It does not matter whether it is women or men or the patriarchal system that exerts control. Being dominated negatively affects people's lives.

Whether women work in the home or outside, their function is the same, to serve men's needs. Because serving is considered inferior work, elite white men avoid serving anyone else's needs, while women and minorities are expected to take care of their needs. Feminism wants to make love and serving human needs the highest values. Serving human needs is creative work that is the responsibility of all people, not just women and minorities.[12]

As the vision and practice of love, feminism challenges the patriarchy's world view and its highest values of control and domination. It wants to replace them with its own philosophy and highest values of self-love and love for others. Feminism's purpose is to foster the power of love, while patriarchy's aim is to promote the love of power. The goal of patriarchy's elite is to enhance its own power and control. In contrast, the purpose of feminism is to work for the common good and everyone's self-actualization, while it creates communities of love.

Love is the foundation of feminism, while domination is the infrastructure of patriarchy. Feminism broadens the meaning and importance of love, while patriarchy narrows and distorts its meaning to romance and self-sacrifice.

Patriarchy establishes a hierarchical pyramid that ranks individuals as superior or inferior according to their sex, race, wealth, and power. In contrast, believing that all people are created equal, feminism works to unite them into communities of love that honor their individuality, differences, interdependence, and the sacredness of all life. As the most important and inclusive movement for change today, feminism tries to stop patriarchy's sexism, racism, classism, elitism, militarism, environmental destruction, and all of its other kinds of discrimination and violence.

Feminism offers a vision of a transformed world where all people relate to each other and the natural world with respect, responsibility, understanding, appreciation, equality, freedom, justice, and most important, love. Of course, it is difficult to imagine the details of this new world because our current patriarchal culture offers only brief glimpses of genuine communities of love.

External Domination and
Internalizing Patriarchal Ways and Values

Being raised in the American form of patriarchy, we all inhale its values with every breath. We are dominated in every area of our lives by patriarchal institutions. Without realizing it, we participate in patriarchal ways of thinking and acting, because this is the way things are done in America.

While many of us deny we are dominated, most of us realize we are controlled by patriarchal institutions. Some of us also recognize that we internalize the patriarchy's goals and methods. Usually our awareness of the patriarchy's external control over us comes first, and our recognition that we internalized patriarchal ways comes later, if at all.

The awareness that we use patriarchal ways is crucial to rooting them out so we can free ourselves and our world. Revolutionary movements, like the 1917 Russian Revolution, claim they are working for the people. Looking at the actual results, some cynics describe revolutions as exchanging one set of tyrants for another. This description will be accurate of our attempt to change the world unless we stop using patriarchal ways of thinking and acting.

Lorde states this clearly when she says the master's house will never be transformed with the master's tools. The dominator's institutions will never be changed with dominating methods.[13]

It is just as important to eliminate our own internalized, patriarchal, dominating values and methods, as it is to halt external domination. In fact, external domination will never be stopped until we eradicate our own dominating ways of thinking and acting. External domination and internalizing patriarchal ways are interconnected. As long as one exists, the other will grow from it.

Like everyone else, feminists internalize patriarchal ways. Naomi Wolf advocates feminist values when she hopes that once women get political power, "they use it for justice and with compassion." However, her internalized patriarchal values are evident when she says "it is *only* the master's tools that can dismantle the master's house."[14]

Because Wolf does not distinguish clearly between feminist and patriarchal behavior, she does not recognize some patriarchal ways of thinking and acting, such as mudslinging and the idea that the ends justify the means. Wolf incorrectly claims, in the 1992 U.S. Senate primary race, Elizabeth Holtzman's behavior against Geraldine Ferraro may be "denounced as mudslinging or as self-destructive, but it cannot be denounced as anti-feminist." In addition, she inaccurately says "the electoral process, the press, and money are among the master's tools." These are just tools, not the dominator's tools, because they can be used in either feminist or patriarchal ways.[15]

While advocating power feminism, Wolf criticizes victim feminism or insider feminism, although she acknowledges some of its positive aspects.[16] Although some of her criticisms are valid, her creation of these names is not accurate or helpful.

Feminism needs to condemn patriarchy's victimization of women. It also needs to heal the victims and help them become empowered survivors. Most women who are violated initially identify as victims. It is during their recovery process that they begin to see themselves as witnesses and survivors. When a woman who was sexually harassed for years called herself as a victim, I asked, "would it be helpful to think of yourself as a survivor?" She answered strongly, "No, I am still a victim. When I am stronger, I will be a survivor. Then I want to help others recover from sexual harassment."

It is essential that feminism identify with the women who have been violated by patriarchal abuses and not just those who have been successful climbing the patriarchal hierarchy. As a movement that cares about all people, feminism must identify with and help the people at the very bottom of the power structure. Feminism's universal love includes all people, but especially the suffering.

Besides serving the abused's needs, feminism needs to empower all women by nurturing their loving inner core, encouraging them to use their talents, supporting their

achievements, helping them to unite so that they can transform patriarchal institutions and build communities of love. To
do this, loving, feminist ways of leading must be distinguished
from destructive, patriarchal ways.

Feminist Versus Patriarchal Leadership

A continuum with the two extremes of destructive and
loving behavior applies to all the ways of being leaders, such
as parents, teachers, employers, doctors, lawyers, and
politicians. Some use the words feminist and patriarchal for
the two extremes of leadership, while others name them
constructive and destructive, democratic and authoritarian,
liberating and dominating, empowering and controlling.[17]
Leadership is the exercise of power to facilitate a
dialogue on a group's goals, methods, and actions. Leaders
can be located on the continuum between feminist and
patriarchal using the criteria of the leaders' definition of power,
world-view, systems, goals, methods, values, ethics, and
personal traits.
Examples of authoritarian, fascist leaders at one end
of the continuum are Hitler and Stalin who had power-hungry
goals and used controlling, totalitarian methods. It is more
difficult to decide who are truly empowering leaders, because
even some leaders who proclaim humanistic aims use
dominating methods. Jane Addams, Gandhi, Martin Luther
King, and Eleanor Roosevelt can be placed near the continuum's other end. Although they are loving leaders, they are
not at the very end because each may have failed the ideal
in some way. Most people as parents, employers, and
workers fall somewhere between the continuum's two extremes.
One important sign of empowering leaders is consis-
tency between what they feel, think, value, say, and do in
both their private and public lives. Martin Luther King's work
to liberate African Americans from racism was exemplary in
both its humanistic goals and nonviolent methods. However,
questions have been raised about his private life. Did he treat

women with less than the full respect that he asked for African Americans, if he engaged in extramarital affairs?

Patriarchal leaders' words and actions are often inconsistent. After President Ronald Reagan's words made some Americans feel proud again, was he guilty of unlawful acts in the Iran-Contra debacle? Did he let others take the blame and lie to the American people?

Not all patriarchal leaders are men. Women, too, pursue patriarchal goals and methods. Phyllis Schlafly claims to be defending American women, but she lies about political issues. It is not just misinformation, but a lie, because she knows what she is saying is not true. For example, as a lawyer, Schlafly knows that the Equal Rights Amendment (ERA) will not cause unisex toilets as she has claimed on television and in her anti-ERA campaign.

More than many other people, feminists are aware that women are dominated in many different ways. Despite this, they internalize patriarchal beliefs and practices and need to root them out. Fortunately, many feminists work to raise their consciousness about internalized and external domination as they try to be democratic and empowering in their thinking and actions.

However, some feminists are power-hungry and use dominating methods. While pursuing the feminist goal of equality for women, they use patriarchal methods that mistreat people. Some feminists mistreat men. Despite the fact that they object when women are treated as inferior or as sexual objects, they tell jokes that degrade men. In ridiculing Schlafly, they go beyond fair criticism and legitimate disagreement.

Because the patriarchy insidiously penetrates our beliefs, values, and behavior, we all need to analyze the ways we think, feel, value, speak, and act to see whether they are patriarchal or feminist. Then we need to replace our authoritarian, dominating ways with democratic, partnership ways. The urgency of the task is that manipulating, dominating behavior is unethical and can be destructive. In contrast, empowering behavior is ethical and creates more love. If we

want a less destructive and more loving world, we must
change from patriarchal, dominating ways of leading to
feminist, empowering ways.   (A chart that clarifies the
differences between these two types of leadership is included
at the end of this chapter.)

Characteristics of Patriarchal Versus Feminist Leaders

Two Definitions of Power

For authoritarian leaders, power means domination,
control, and power over others. For democratic leaders,
power means empowering themselves and others to accomplish their goals.

Dominating leadership means giving orders and
expecting obedience. It means being out in front and deciding the group's aims and methods. Most importantly, it
means having power over others. In contrast, democratic
leadership means facilitating dialogue on the group's goals
and methods. After discovering people with knowledge and
skills, liberating leaders delegate responsibilities to them.
They bring out the best in all people by treating them with
caring, respect, liberty, equality, justice, and love.

Values and Worldviews
of Patriarchal and Feminist Leaders

Patriarchal leaders' highest values are domination,
control, and power over others. In contrast, liberating leaders'
highest values are love and caring for themselves and others.

For patriarchal leaders, profit for the self and power
over others are more important than meeting human needs.
For feminist leaders, human need is more important than
profit, wealth, power, and control over others.

Stephen Covey teaches business executives to center
their life and leadership on the most important principles
rather than quick fix strategies. Covey defines these principles as natural laws and "deep fundamental truths that have

universal application." These "inviolate principles" are objective, external, self-evident, and self-validating. As part of the human condition, these natural laws "seem to exist in all human beings, regardless of social conditioning."[18]

Some of Covey's principles are integrity and honesty, which establish the foundation for trust, that leads to equity and justice. Other principles are human dignity, service, excellence, growth, encouragement, patience, and nurturance. Covey does not state that love is the most important principle, although he teaches about "the primary laws of love" and the need to love unconditionally. When we love unconditionally, we encourage others to love. When we attach conditions and strings to our love, we encourage others to violate love. Covey assigned his students to keep diaries with the assumption that they had only four months to live. Their diaries showed love was "the dominant, central theme of their activities, the underlying principle."[19]

Patriarchal leaders believe people are selfish, greedy, power-hungry, and controlling. Because they themselves have these traits, they project them onto everyone else. Considering themselves superior, they believe that elite superior people have the right to dominate the vast majority, including women and minorities, who are considered inferior.

Feminist leaders believe that people are good, caring, and concerned about others. Because they believe that all women and men are created equal, they want to treat others and be treated themselves with respect, understanding, caring, appreciation, equality, liberty, justice, and love.

Dominating leaders believe that the world is a competitive, hostile jungle where selfish, greedy, and power-hungry people win and everyone else loses. The aggressive and ruthless triumph. Assuming power is limited, they conclude that the more power you share, the less you have. Convinced that each person should take care of Number One, they think rugged individualism is the best philosophy.

Democratic leaders believe that the world is a friendly place where all can win and where people cooperate so that all develop their full potential and serve the common good.

Assuming power is limitless, they conclude that the more power you share, the more you empower everyone, the more power there is for all.

Believing that a community thrives when everyone takes care of their own self-interest and promotes the common good, feminist leaders say the best philosophy combines individualism and communitarianism.[20] Stressing both personal liberty and social justice, they work to protect the rights of each individual and encourage everyone to meet their responsibility to the community.

Systems and Structures
of Patriarchal and Feminist Leaders

Patriarchal leaders contend that the best structure is a hierarchy with a rigid chain of command. To exclude unwanted inferiors, they operate closed systems. Manipulation, coercion, the threat of force, and violence are used to ensure obedience.

Liberating leaders believe that the best structure is a cooperative partnership that dialogues about problems and solutions. Wanting to include everyone, they operate open systems of small teams. Dialogue and democratic methods are used to obtain the consent and agreement of the members and group before final decisions are made.

Goals of Patriarchal and Feminist Leaders

Empowering leaders are committed to progressive, humanistic goals. Their stated goals are their real goals. These goals are to empower themselves and others by working for what is good for all people, the common good.

Consciously or unconsciously, dominating leaders' stated goals are mainly used to recruit people and are secondary to their real goal of having power over others. Their unstated goals are their most important goals: their own self-interest, power, wealth, status, prestige, and worldly possessions. Even when they are committed to the humanistic goals, they use dominating methods, which contradict their stated aims.

Budgets, both personal and national, show people's real priorities and goals. The U.S. budget under President Reagan revealed that his highest priority was military weapons. Under his predecessor, President Jimmy Carter, the military budget was about $150 billion. While slashing social programs, Reagan raised the military budget in peacetime to $300 billion. Reagan wanted to raise it to $450 billion, but the Democratic Congress stopped him.

Reagan claimed his goal was to protect the national security. However, this was an excuse to justify excessive military expenditures that benefited wealthy corporations. In contrast, peace activists contend that money and technological genius are wasted on unneeded weapons, when the same money would help national security more if it were used to combat social problems and the national debt.

Authoritarian leaders believe the public good and their self-interest as antagonistic. Their willingness to sacrifice both the group's aims and the common good for their own self-interest shows the depth of their selfishness. In contrast, empowering leaders see the common good and their own self-interest as consistent with each other. Their willingness to sacrifice their own needs for the group's goals and the common good shows the depth of their altruism.

Ethics and Methods of Patriarchal and Feminist Leaders

Patriarchal leaders' top priority is power for themselves and their clique. Only after spending their energy, time, and money gaining power and promoting themselves do they work on the group's goals. Since they are often hard working, they expend tremendous effort to get power. Without regard for what their group wants, they set its agenda to suit themselves.

Partnership leaders' top priority is to empower people

and to help the group decide its own agenda and work for its goals. After spending most of their time, energy, and money promoting the group's aims, they have little left to deal with internal group politics.

Destructive leaders believe the end justifies the means. Consequently, they manipulate, control, and exploit others for their own purposes. Since their main interest is the outcome, the bottom line, they have little concern for the process and use unfair, "dirty," dishonest, dominating, unethical methods. Believing in hard ball politics, they play patriarchal power games.[21] Since they do not object to being dishonest and unethical, they lie to gain and keep power, they lie to destroy those who oppose them, and they lie to manipulate the group to carry out their aims.

Empowering leaders believe the ends do **not** justify the means. They are concerned about both the outcome and the process. Therefore, they use only fair, honest, democratic, empowering, ethical, humanistic methods to reach their goals. Their means are as important as their aims. Their goals and methods are so intertwined that they cannot be separated. To reach peace, the peace movement needs to be peaceful. To achieve equality, justice, and love, the feminist movement needs to treat all people in equal, just, and loving ways.

In political campaigns, the public needs to distinguish between honest, ethical criticism and that which unethically falsifies the other candidate's character and views. Honest criticism of the other candidate's philosophy, actions, voting record, and stated positions on concrete issues is fair and ethical. Lying about and misrepresenting the other candidates' character, philosophy, actions, votes, and positions is unfair and unethical.

Because liberating leaders practice the power of love and care about both the results and the process, they use ethical methods, while striving for humanistic goals. Since dominating leaders are only concerned with the results and not with the means, they step on other people and trammel on democratic procedures. Their unfair, unethical methods contradict any humanistic goals they claim to pursue.

To gain control, patriarchal leaders use different varieties of prejudice and discrimination. They mistreat people by lying, manipulating, exploiting, and abusing them. Some dominating leaders even promote violence to maintain their power. Treating people in a supportive, nurturing way, feminist leaders oppose all forms of prejudice, hatred, discrimination, domination, abuse, destructiveness, and violence, bar none. They consider domination destructive of the dominator as well as the dominated.

Decisions are made by the controlling leaders and their inner circle at small, unannounced meetings. To consolidate the power of their clique, they exclude people who have a legitimate right to be part of the decision making, even elected officials who have important information that would affect the process and outcome. Their inner circle draws up plans to manipulate the group so that it will ratify the leaders' already made decisions. Sharing only the information that leads to the decisions they want, they tell lies to maneuver the process toward their desired aim.

Being inclusive, empowering leaders share decision making and power with all the people. Encouraging participation in the planning, decisions, and actions, they use their personal skills to make members feel that they belong and their contributions are appreciated.

Feminist leaders' planning meetings prepare information and methods for truly democratic decision making. They share all the information available on all sides of the issue. After they tell the truth, both the good and bad news, the group has the data to make reality-based decisions.

Liberating leaders are friendly, enthusiastic, and supportive rather than negative and critical. Respecting all people, they treat them with respect and not with power plays and put downs. Because these leaders use empowering strategies, offer training, delegate responsibilities, and thank workers for their contributions, group members learn new skills and feel a sense of achievement for a job well done. By helping members grow, they turn followers into leaders.

Although dominating leaders are sometimes charming,

their treatment of others is selective. The criterion for how they handle others is whether people agree with, obey, vote with, and act loyal to their wishes. If people obey them, they are manipulated and controlled to accomplish the leaders' purposes. Sometimes these obedient followers are treated in a friendly manner. Other times they are put down, although the leaders claim they are only kidding and being humorous.

If charm and manipulation do not bring obedience, patriarchal leaders use dominating tactics, such as shouting, intimidation, and put downs. They keep escalating their tactics until they get their way. When all else fails, some will even use abuse and violence.

When people resist being dominated and refuse to give up their own way of thinking, personal choices, and independent actions, patriarchal leaders consider them suspect, disloyal, and even dangerous. Those who can be controlled are used to benefit the leaders. Those who cannot are criticized, lied about, ostracized, and excluded. As one patriarchal leader said, "Margo is in my pocket, but we have to watch out for Rose." In other words, we can control and use Margo, but not Rose. Whenever I am tempted to think that patriarchal leaders are not aware of their controlling behavior, I remember this.

Patriarchal leaders' main goal in relating to others is to control them and make them followers. If they cannot turn independent individuals into followers, they will eliminate them from the group so they can't oppose them.

Empowering leaders encourage others to think for themselves, to make their own decisions, and to be independent in their thinking and actions. Rather than asking them to be obedient, they urge them to be loyal to the cause and follow their own conscience. Their respect for all people includes those who oppose them. Their guidelines for discussions are to agree to disagree, while respecting each other. While they do not respect and even hate unethical, exploitative, and abusive actions, they respect the people who use these patriarchal methods. Despite the fact they hate the sin, they respect the sinner.

Dominating leaders defend members of their inner circle even if they have done something egregiously wrong, but they have little tolerance for the minor mistakes of those outside their own clique. Believing the actions of those within their clique reflect on them, they defend their inner circle whether they are right or wrong. In contrast, empowering leaders judge all actions by the same standards. When their friends make mistakes, they ask them to correct them and make amends. Strangers and friends are judged and treated in the same way.

Patriarchal leaders create an us-versus-them atmosphere in order to divide, conquer, and control. By being divisive, they cause conflicts and ask people to choose sides. Telling lies about individuals they view as the enemy, they create tension and hostility within the group. To consolidate their power, they criticize, lie about, ostracize, and exclude those they see as opposing them until they force their critics out of the group. Blaming their own difficulties on others, they turn those who disagree into the devil to be hated. To gain supporters, they speak of a threatening future and promise disaster.

In contrast, democratic leaders create a friendly atmosphere, make peace, solve problems, work for consensus, and build unity. Facing their difficulties honestly, they admit their faults and mistakes. From the depths of their being, they speak of and work for a hopeful future in which the public good is achieved.

When everyone agrees, patriarchal leaders work well with others. When there is agreement, everyone wins. However, when disagreement arises, they use lying, manipulating, and controlling methods to get their way and to retain their power. When there is disagreement, patriarchs want to win, while everyone else loses.

When democratic leaders agree with others, all are winners. All are enhanced and work for humanistic goals. Mutual benefit and synergy result. What is good for the group is also good for the leaders and followers. What is good for the leaders is also good for the group.

When conflict arises and two sides develop, democratic leaders agree to disagree and continue to respect, listen to, and work with both sides. Being unity builders, peace makers, and problem solvers, they urge all parties to focus on the group's goals and work peacefully for a solution that uses everyone's ideas.

Believing in negotiations, empowering leaders work for a compromise that allows all sides to win. If that is not possible, then all sacrificed something, while the work of the group is moved forward. All sides need to agree to a compromise as long as it meets certain conditions: it benefits the group's progress toward its goals, all sides act according to their ethical principles, and any sacrifice is fair, equal, and mutually agreeable.

I often wonder why the world did not learn the immorality and futility of dominating methods with the defeat of Hitler, but power-hungry leaders continue to use them today. For example, Arab fundamentalists who ran in the 1993 election for Jordan's Parliament under the name the Islamic Action Front were against any peace agreement between Israel, Jordan, and the Palestine Liberation Organization. They believe that "the only way to deal with Israel is to destroy it and build an Islamic state on its ashes. Any Arab who thinks otherwise is a traitor to his people."[22]

Personal Traits of Patriarchal and Feminist Leaders

The root causes of the patriarchal leaders' need to dominate are their deep feelings of powerlessness and their lack of self-love. Having low self-esteem and a poor self-identity, they have little or no self-love. The less their self-love, the more insecure they are, the greater their feeling of powerlessness, and the greater their need to dominate others or identify with the powerful by submitting to them.

Patriarchal leaders mistrust themselves and others, because they believe people are selfish, lazy, dishonest, and power-hungry. They think that I'm not OK and you're not OK. Consequently, they use negative, put-down, hostile humor.

FEMINIST LEADERSHIP   145

In contrast, the root cause of democratic leaders' need to love is that they are in touch with their inner core of love. Having a great deal of self-love, they have high self-esteem and a good self-identity. The greater their self-love, the more secure they are, the greater their feeling of empowerment. The more they love themselves, the more they love others, the greater their need to help others and create a better world.

Believing that they and others are basically good, democratic leaders trust themselves and others, until the evidence proves otherwise. They think that I'm OK and You're OK. Because they do not want to harm others even when they are kidding, they do not use negative, put-down, hostile humor.

Possible Ways To Change the Patriarchy and Its Leaders

Since patriarchy and its highest value of domination permeate our worldwide culture, all of us and all institutions are affected by it and have absorbed some patriarchal values and methods. Often we recognize the patriarchy as the cause of dominating leaders before we realize that we carry the effects of the patriarchy within ourselves. How can we rid ourselves, our institutions, and culture of controlling attitudes? How can we change patriarchal leaders who gain power over our groups, even groups with progressive, humanistic purposes?

In Albert Camus' novel, the plague symbolizes more than a physical illness that brings death. It could be a metaphor for patriarchal values. Doctor Rieux and his friend Tarrou work day and night when the plague hits. Tarrou says "each of us has the plague within him; no one on earth is free from it." Although we all have the plague, "there are some people who don't know it, or feel at ease in that condition; others know, and want to get out of it. Personally, I've always wanted to get out of it."[23]

Kay Hagen, a feminist author, uses the "orchids in the arctic" as an image for women in the patriarchy. Female power is like an orchid, the fragile, tropical flower that needs a warm climate. "Male supremacy, woman-hating patriarchy" is like the arctic, a harsh, frigid climate that is hostile to women.[24]

Hagen's image accurately describes the fragility of women's power because of the patriarchy's hostility. However, her image needs to include all people in the worldwide patriarchy. Although women, the poor, and people of color suffer most in our sexist, racist, classist culture, I believe the patriarchy teaches all people, including white males, to feel inferior and to hate themselves.

According to Hagen, for a woman to survive in a misogynist environment, she needs to recognize and avoid male violence. Then her self-love blossoms and "her female power begins to thrive--creativity, vitality, and confidence emerge, along with a refusal to subordinate herself to male power."[25]

Because French does not discuss the fact that all people internalize patriarchal ways, she states there are only two choices in dealing with domination. "If a worshiper of power decides to extend his power over your society, your choices are between surrendering and mounting an equal and opposite power." Either way, the power hungry win because they have converted your society to believe that power is the highest value.[26] If you surrender to domination, the power wielders win, because you live in a patriarchal society. If you fight the dominators with their methods, they win because you adopt their patriarchal ways.

French's statement of the two choices, to surrender to domination or to adopt patriarchal methods, is too pessimistic and limited. Instead, I propose six ways to respond to the fact that we are dominated by our patriarchal culture and we internalize its ways. After experiencing domination, we have six choices: to obey, to flee, to become apathetic, to manipulate the patriarchal system, to rebel, to resist and fight with constructive anger.

Starhawk, a feminist philosopher, describes five responses to dominating behavior: comply, withdraw,

manipulate the system, rebel, and resist.   Her five ways of
dealing with domination have similarities with all but one of
my six responses. Starhawk says her first four responses are
similar to the roles children play in alcoholic families. "The
Hero, the good child, complies.   The Scapegoat, the bad
child, the delinquent, rebels. The Lost Child, the quiet one
who disappears into the woodwork, withdraws. The Mascot,
the child who clowns, entertains, manipulates." The purpose
of these responses is to survive in a hostile environment.[27]

Resistance is the best response. When we realize that
resistance is a possibility, we learn that we can make another
choice in order to survive. As Starhawk says, "none of these
responses are necessarily bad or wrong. At times, any one
of them may be the best possible choice. We play the roles
open to us."[28]

Starhawk speaks wisely when she says, "we cannot
resist all the time, in every area of life. We must choose our
battles." We can withdraw now to conserve our energy so
that we can confront the power hungry on a higher priority
issue. We can obey now because this is not the issue on
which we choose to take a stand. "We can be conscious
when we put on a mask that we are not wearing our true
faces--and so retain the ability to take the mask off." At
another time, we can resist by acting true to ourselves,
speaking with our authentic voice, confronting the unjust
dominators, and creating alternative ways of behaving.[29]

When we experience patriarchal domination, we may
not see all our options. We need to avoid blaming ourselves
for making less than ideal choices, because our first responsibility is to survive as intact as possible. Because resisting is
hard and often brings punishment, we may choose an
alternative to resisting.

1. Conforming, Obeying, and Submitting to Domination

Of the six possible ways to deal with domination, the
patriarchy teaches conformity, obedience, and submission to
authorities. When we experience domination, we conform,

obey, and submit in order to survive. Although we try not to admit it, we live in fear of being controlled. We serve the dominators and become dependent on them in the hope that they will exert power over others, and not over us.

We deal with being controlled by serving the patriarchs so that they will not continue to mistreat us. By accepting our helplessness, suppressing our hurt, denying our anger, and placing ourselves in a subordinate role, we try to win the affection of the power-wielders. In exchange for their protection from harmful treatment, we provide indispensable services for them.

We conform to the aggressors' demands not only in our behavior but also in our self-definition. Women act out the patriarchy's definition of femininity by being emotional, passive, selfless servants of their husbands and children, while men express masculinity by becoming overly-rational, active dominators.

Starhawk says compliance begins with our acceptance of the patriarchal belief system. The patriarchy crushes our belief in our inner core of love by teaching us we are inferior and need to obey those superior to us. We are taught that the experts know more than we do and will tell us what is right for us. Patriarchal institutions construct reality for us by restricting our sources of information and giving us only the data it wants us to have. The authorities' punishments for disobedience range from harsh words to physical abuse, and even death.[30]

Conforming and obeying damage our belief in our own worth and goodness. When we conform to the patriarchy's images of femininity and masculinity, we are not true to ourselves and deep down inside we may hate ourselves for it. A life of conformity is a life of denial. Not being true to our inner core of love, we deny our own definition of ourselves. As Starhawk says, "Obedience has its cost: the destruction of the self." To be obedient is to be unfree. When we conform, we help the patriarchy damage us.[31]

Conformity, obedience, and submission to the power-wielders allow us to feel safe. Because we play the subordinate role, we are exploited for their benefit. The possibility exists that they will order us to harm others. Even if we do not become dominators, we support and strengthen the patriarchal system by serving it. When we obey, the power of the patriarchs grows.

As feminist Flo Kennedy says, "there can be no really pervasive system of oppression, such as that in the United States, without the consent of the oppressed. People who have not withdrawn consent usually deny that they are oppressed." One reason for some men's anger at feminism is their fear that women will withdraw their consent to being dominated. "Where a system of oppression has become institutionalized, it is unnecessary for individuals to be oppressive." Most brainwashed men and women act out their assigned roles without pressure from anyone.[32]

2. Withdrawing and Fleeing from Domination

Of the many ways to withdraw and flee from domination, one is flight to self-destruction. After the dominators preach that we are worthless and no good, we totally isolate ourselves, but we continue to believe that we are not OK. We internalize the abuser's words and carry them with us like records playing in our heads.

When we experience domination, we try to run so far away that no one will ever control us again. We give up on others and become detached, lonely people who keep others at a safe distance. Unfortunately, the original abuse that we never dealt with comes with us in our isolation.

Sometimes our isolation, depression, and self-hatred result in self-destructive behavior, such as alcoholism, drug abuse, and even suicide. Other times our loneliness and unhappiness drive us to become criminals, women batterers, child abusers, rapists, child molesters, or murderers. When we injure others, we also hurt ourselves, because we damage our inner core of love, and thus we become destructive of both ourselves and others.

Sometimes we ignore the rest of the patriarchal world

and try to create our own private world of love for our closest family and friends. Believing in ourselves and those closest to us, but giving up on most other people, we show our concern only for ourselves, our closest family, and friends. One problem we experience in isolating ourselves from the suffering of others is that the sorrow caused by destructive aggression continues to seep into our closed circle disturbing the peace and harmony that we have created.

A different variation of withdrawal is fleeing to liberation by creating a utopian model for future social change. According to Marilyn Frye, some feminists and utopians use "separation as part of the conscious strategy of liberation." Rather than being cowardly escapists, utopians are courageous not only because they attempt to create a new model for a better world but also because they usually experience insults, hostility, economic sanctions, abuse, and violence. As Frye says, "if you are doing something that is so strictly forbidden by the patriarchs, you must be doing something right."[33]

Starhawk describes withdrawal as "another way to respond to an intolerable situation." One form is to withdraw ourselves physically, emotionally, mentally, socially, and spiritually. We deaden our emotions, we think about other things, withdraw physically to another place, and we worship our own Divinity. Another form of withdrawal is denial. We deny what we feel unable to cope with. "Withdrawal cushions us from feeling the full impact of our situation. But it is ultimately dangerous" because we cut off information vital to our survival. By not feeling, thinking, or acting, our minds deteriorate, our emotions die, and our spirits wither. "When we withdraw, our gifts, our perceptions, our energies are lost."[34]

3. Becoming Apathetic Spectators

Another way to deal with domination is to be apathetic and do nothing. When the patriarchy controls us, we give up and resign ourselves, because we believe that nothing can be done by anyone to change the situation. We become apathetic spectators who choose to exert no energy because we feel that any effort is wasted in such hopeless circumstances.

Often apathetic spectators speak cynically and act as though nothing can hurt them, even though being dominated penetrates deep into their souls. Their behavior indicates that they are above it all as they scornfully make fun of both the controllers and the controlled. In reality, apathetic spectators suppress their pain and deny their anger so that they are not conscious of what they are actually feeling. Because they do not help others, they contribute little to the world.

4. Manipulating the Patriarchal System

Another response to domination is to manipulate the patriarchal system for our own benefit. Some of us claim we use power tactics because that is the only way to accomplish anything. After we accept the dominator system as it is and figure out how it works, we use it to serve our own purposes and to gain its rewards for ourselves. As Starhawk says, "when we manipulate the system, we have the illusion of being in control. We can keep the rewards of the system while believing that we are not really complying."[35]

However, when we deceive the system in order to manipulate it, we hide who we really are and thus mistreat ourselves because our ability to act is severely limited. As Starhawk says, "in order to manipulate, we cannot be ourselves, express our true feelings, or share our real perceptions. We literally mask ourselves." When we accept the patriarchy so that we can manipulate it, we buy into its belief that elite white men are superior and have the right to dominate. "We may know everything about how the jail functions and how to get the most out of it for ourselves, but that doesn't change the fact that we are still in jail."[36]

Some of us who attempt to manipulate the patriarchal system for our own benefit try very hard not to harm other people. Others of us are so hurt and angry that we respond with destructive anger and aggression. Bitterness and destructive anger develop when we do not deal with our feelings of hurt, sadness, and powerlessness that result from being mistreated.

Destructive anger is anger that wants to retaliate and get revenge for the injuries we have suffered. Not believing that we can improve our situation or get help from others, we identify with and imitate the dominators by attacking with destructive aggression. Fighting violence with further violence, we assault the oppressors or anyone else available both to protect ourselves from further maltreatment and to get even with those who hurt us.

As Flo Kennedy says, three ways to express hostility are vertically downward, vertically upward, and horizontally. When they are oppressed, some express horizontal hostility by attacking those on their level of the patriarchal hierarchy rather than the dominators above them. Examples of horizontal hostility are sibling rivalry, office competition, and dominating power games in social and political groups.[37]

People who attack those below them on the patriarchal hierarchy express hostility vertically downward. Some examples are supervisors who mistreat employees beneath them, parents who abuse their children, and poor whites who mistreat minorities. As Kennedy says, "oppressed people are frequently very oppressive.... They know best two positions. Somebody's foot on their neck or their foot on somebody's neck."[38]

5. Rebelling against Domination

Rebelling offers an alternative to putting our foot on the dominator's neck. As Sarah Grimke said when she requested equality for women in 1837, "all I ask of our brethren is that they take their feet off our necks and permit us to stand upright."[39]

Rebels express their hostility vertically upward toward the dominators. This is more progressive, but less safe, than vertically downward or horizontal hostility. Vertically upward hostility is aimed at the actual culprit and not surrogate targets.

Flo Kennedy recommends that women practice vertically upward hostility toward the institutions that program us, such as the media and church. She wants us to avoid vertically downward hostility toward our children and horizontal hostility toward our female and male counterparts. "Kicking ass should be only where an ass is protecting the system. Ass-kicking should be undertaken regardless of the sex, the ethnicity, or the charm of the oppressor's agent. As the struggles intensify, the oppressor tends to select more attractive agents, frequently from among the oppressed."[40]

Starhawk makes a distinction between rebellion and resistance. In both rebellion and resistance, we refuse to accept domination, but rebels stand alone, while resisters join with others. "We rebel to save our lives. Rebellion is the desperate assertion of our value in the face of all that attacks it, the cry of refusal in the face of control."[41]

Rebellion does not challenge the patriarchy's system of domination and lead to freedom in the way that resistance does. As Starhawk says, "the choices the system presents us with inevitably increase the system's control." One role the patriarchy offers us that perpetuates its domination is the rebel who disobeys and thus deserves to be punished. "In order to retain control, the system needs to punish, and it needs to single out some individuals for more intensive punishment to serve as an example and warning to the rest."[42]

Starhawk accurately contends that the rebels' disobedience gives the patriarchal system an excuse to punish them and make them outcasts. Punishing rebels intimidates others into compliance. "When the system defines our choices, it channels rebellion into modes that it is prepared to control, into acts that harm the rebel, not the system." Thus, the rebels' acts slowly destroy them without challenging the power of the patriarchy. "To defy reality, alone and isolated, is not the same as to change it." Although "rebellion is our very life asserting itself, willing to settle for nothing less than freedom," it cannot break the bonds of slavery without transforming itself into resistance.[43]

6. Resisting and Fighting with Constructive Anger

The most creative way to respond to domination is to resist and fight with constructive anger. Both rebellion and resistance express our self-love, while resistance offers an alternative to the patriarchy's belief in our inferiority. When we resist, we value ourselves and reject domination. We refuse to numb our pain, because "that prevents us from making any serious trouble for the system."[44]

Resistance starts with awareness of domination and the difference between patriarchal and liberating ways. As Starhawk says, "awareness is the beginning of all resistance." Resisters become aware of the patriarchal beliefs that the superior elite has a right to dominate the inferior masses and that individuals' worth is determined by their role and place on the patriarchal hierarchy. After becoming aware, resisters challenge the basic beliefs of the patriarchy and its hierarchies by affirming their own worth and other people's worth, even their opponents.[45]

Besides awareness, resistance always involves uniting with others to change unjust structures and practices. When we resist, we need to refuse isolation, become connected with others, and transform the patriarchy. Rebels defy alone, while resisters join with others not just to challenge authorities but to reform them. Calling resistance "empowered action," Starhawk says "we do more than defy reality we present its alternatives, communicating our beliefs and values."[46]

When we resist, we try to stop the patriarchy from dominating by turning our constructive anger into creative action that promotes individual and social change. To develop constructive anger rather than destructive anger, we must acknowledge that we are hurt, who causes our hurt, and why. In addition, we need to accept and deal with our feelings of sadness, hurt, powerlessness, and anger that result from being dominated and abused.

Constructive anger is the anger that wants to stop the

activities that cause people, including ourselves, to suffer. This anger fights to bring changes so that harmful practices cannot continue unimpeded. Believing in our capacity to make a difference and in the dominators' ability to change, we work with others for reform or revolution and thus try to make the world a better place for all people.

As Starhawk says, "resistance is only real when it is expressed through action. In turn, the action we take nourishes and strengthens us, for acts of resistance against systems that destroy us are ultimately acts of survival, creation, and nurture." Resistance involves two kinds of actions: first to struggle against all forms of domination and second "to create structures of support that can nurture us and renew our strength." On one hand, we reject the status quo and refuse to be controlled, while on the other hand we create communities of love.[47]

In groups where leaders are dominating, resistance involves challenging these leaders as well as teaching and practicing an alternative way. To become free from power-hungry leaders, we need to recognize them for what they are, people who use controlling, dishonest, and manipulative ways of leading. Next we must identify the differences between the two extremes on the leadership continuum: dominating and empowering, destructive and loving, patriarchal and feminist leaders. After that, we need to teach other group members to tell the differences between the two kinds of leadership.

Before we confront patriarchal leaders, we must scrutinize our own leadership for dominating practices. Since we live in the patriarchy, we internalize its ways, usually unrecognized and unexamined. We must root controlling ways out of ourselves as much as possible before we begin to confront others. The more loving and empowering we are, the more we are aware of our potential to be dominating, because we are socialized to be controlling.

Only after we become aware that some of our own ways are patriarchal are we ready to criticize and confront dominating leaders. We need to demand that they share their power with the group; include all members in deciding the group's goals; discontinue any dishonest, manipulative methods; and begin to use humanistic, democratic procedures.

In addition, we must not allow ourselves to be controlled, to be forced into inferior positions, to be put down, or to be excluded from the decision making. By refusing to play patriarchal power games and by practicing empowering ways, we can set an example of a humanistic partnership and thus offer all people an invitation to change their ways.

When we refuse to be controlled and criticize authoritarian leaders, we can expect a strong reaction in the form of lies and manipulation. When we continue to resist, they will escalate their negative reactions into shouting, intimidation, and abuse. When this does not stop us, they will begin to smear our reputation and exclude us from the group. They will attack us vehemently, because once we are gone, they hope the rest of the opposition will dry up.

Sexist men will stop at nothing to keep their power over women and their male entitlement to use women in whatever ways they want. For example, when the Vice President of a Florida junior college sexually harassed a female employee, college officials defended him even though the evidence against him was strong. These officials protected the male entitlement to sexually harass by dragging out the legal procedures and by lying about the victim and her allies. Eventually the victim was so frustrated and worn down, she left her job. However, she won her law suit and was awarded $60,000.

When patriarchal leaders attack us for resisting, we will be hurt. Resisting is always painful. Getting up after they knock us down and put their foot on our necks is difficult. Successful resistance is getting up one more time than they knock us down.

When liberating leaders try to teach others in their group the differences between dominating and empowering leadership, they will encounter obstacles. Because many members want to think only good things about their authoritarian leaders, they will dispute any criticism of their leaders and their controlling methods. Being ostriches with their heads in the sand is more comfortable than facing the fact that their leaders are patriarchal.

However, if empowering leaders keep educating, the ostriches will begin the painful process of taking their heads out of the sand. After group members understand the differences between the two kinds of leadership, they need to confront the patriarchal leaders and work to elect democratic leaders.

The way to stop patriarchal leaders from controlling groups without resorting to authoritarian methods is to teach enough people to support democratic leaders and to oppose dominating leaders as well as their goals and methods. When enough people disagree with patriarchal ways and promote democratic strategies, they will vote in empowering leaders and vote out authoritarian leaders and everything they stand for. Once the democratic resisters have a majority, they can move the group to revitalize itself and begin to change the larger society.

Resistance to domination liberates us as individuals and changes the collective reality. Resistance challenges the patriarchy's highest value of domination and advocates the value of love for self and others. As Starhawk says, "resistance speaks its own truth to power and shifts the ground of struggle to its own terrain."[48]

Sustained resistance is hard whether we are fighting constructively against domination or creating communities of love. As Starhawk says, "we find it relatively easy to commit a single act of resistance." However, to maintain our resistance over weeks and years as well as over many issues and confrontations requires dedication and stamina. Each act of resistance creates "a rip in the fabric of oppression that has the potential to let another power come through."[49] Enough acts of resistance will transform the patriarchy and create communities of love.

CONTINUUM OF
PATRIARCHAL VERSUS FEMINIST LEADERS

Authoritarian Leaders   Democratic Leaders
Dominating Leaders   Empowering Leaders
Destructive Leaders   Constructive Leaders
Controlling Leaders   Liberating Leaders
Patriarchal Leaders   Feminist Leaders

DEFINITIONS

1. Power means domination, control, & power over others.

1. Power means empowering the self & others to achieve their goals.

2. Patriarchal leadership means deciding the group's aims & means.

2. Feminist leadership means facilitating dialogue on the group's goals & methods.

3. Leaders give orders & expect obedience.

3. Leaders find people with skills & delegate responsibility.

VALUES AND WORLDVIEWS

4. Patriarchal leaders' highest values are control, domination, & power, over others.

4. Feminist leaders' highest values are love and caring for the self & others.

5. Profit, wealth, & power are more important than human need.

5. Human need is more important than profit, wealth, & power.

6. Patriarchal leaders believe people are selfish, power-hungry, greedy, & want to dominate, control, & have power over others.

6. Feminist leaders believe people are good & caring & want to treat others & be treated with respect, equality, justice, liberty, & love.

7. They believe that elite rich men are superior, while the majority, including women & minorities, are inferior.

7. They believe that all women and men are created equal & each has human dignity, rights, individual talents. & uniqueness.

8. They believe the world is a hostile competitive jungle where some lose, while others win, & the most ruthless & aggressive triumph.

8. They believe the world is a friendly place where all win when people develop their full potential & serve the common good.

9. They believe that rugged individual-ism is the best philosophy.

9. They believe that the best philosophy combines individual-ism and working for the common good.

10. They believe power is limited. The more power you share, the less you have.

10. They believe power is limitless. The more power you you share, the more there is for all.

SYSTEMS AND STRUCTURES

11. The best structure is a hierarchy with a chain of command.

11. The best structure is a cooperative team & partnership that dialogues.

12. They use closed   12. They use open
    systems that   systems that include
    exclude anyone   all people in
    not in their   decision making &
    inner circle.   activities.

13. Manipulation,   13. Democratic methods &
    coercion, threat   dialogue are used to
    of force, &   obtain the agreement
    violence are used   of the people and
    to ensure   group.
    obedience.

GOALS

14. Leaders' stated   14. Leaders' stated
    goals are mainly   goals are their
    used to recruit   real goals. Their
    people. The   goals are to
    unstated goals   empower themselves
    are their most   & others & to work
    important goals: for the   common
    self-interest,   good.
    wealth, power,...

15. They see the   15. They see the common
    common good and   good and their
    their self-   self-interest as
    interest as   consistent with
    antagonistic   each other.
    to each other.

16. They sacrifice   16. They often
    the common good   sacrifice their own
    for their own   self-interest for
    self-interest.   the common good.

ETHICS AND METHODS

17. Leaders believe   17. Leaders believe
    the ends justify   the ends do **not**
    the means.   justify the means.

18. They use unfair, dirty, dishonest, dominating, unethical methods.

18. They use only fair, honest, democratic, empowering, ethical methods.

19. They manipulate, lie to, mistreat, exploit, abuse, & violate people.

19. They treat people in a respectful, honest, caring, just, loving way.

20. They are mainly concerned with results, not means.

20. They are concerned with both methods & outcomes.

21. They create an inner circle of decision making from which they exclude people, even officers.

21. They share decision making & encourage all people to participate in every appropriate activity.

22. Planning meetings prepare ways to manipulate people to ratify the leaders' already made decisions.

22. Planning meetings prepare information & methods for truly democratic decision making.

23. They share only information that leads to decisions they want.

23. They share all the information available on all sides of the issue.

24. They tell lies to manipulate people to make the decisions the leaders want.

24. They tell the truth, both good & bad news, so people have good data for decision making.

25. They play patriarchal power games, including shouting, abuse, & intimidation.

25. They deal honestly & respectfully & use empowering methods.

26. They treat people
    as inferiors whom
    they step on to
    gain power & to
    achieve their goals.

26. They treat people
    as equals whom
    they respect, care
    about, listen to,
    & understand.

27. They disrespect
    some people,
    especially those
    who disagree &
    oppose them in
    any way.

27. They respect all
    people, including
    those who disagree
    & oppose them.
    They hate the sin
    & love the sinner.

28. They turn leaders
    into obedient
    followers.

28. They empower
    followers to
    become leaders.

29. They want people
    to think exactly
    as they do.

29. They encourage
    independence &
    free thinking.

30. They take
    disagreement as
    disloyalty & lie
    about, ostracize,
    and expel those
    who disagree &
    oppose them.

30. They agree to
    disagree, while
    listening to &
    respecting all
    people. They
    expect those who
    are loyal to be
    honest & disagree.

31. They cause tension
    & divisiveness as
    strategies to gain
    power.

31. They make peace,
    solve problems,
    build consensus, &
    unity.

32. They blame their
    difficulties on
    others & turn
    those who disagree
    into the devil to
    be hated.

32. They face their
    difficulties
    honestly & admit
    their mistakes &
    faults.

33. They speak pessimistically of a threatening future that promises disaster.

33. They speak hopefully of a beneficial future & promise to work for the common good.

PERSONAL TRAITS

34. The root cause of their need to dominate is their insecure powerless feelings, poor self-esteem, & lack of self-love.

34. The root cause of their need to love the self & others is their loving inner core.

35. The poorer the self-image, the less self-love, the less able to love others.

35. The better the self-image, the more self-love, the greater the love for others

36. The more insecure, the greater the powerless feelings, the greater the need to dominate or submit.

36. The more secure, the greater the empowering feeling, the greater the need to love self & others.

37. They believe that people are selfish & power-hungry, I'm not OK & You're not OK. They mistrust all people, including themselves.

37. They believe that people are good, that I'm OK & You're OK. They trust themselves & others.

38. They are highly critical of people & use negative, hostile, put-down humor.

38. They are caring & supportive of people & do **not** use negative, hostile, put-down humor.

PART FOUR

FEMINISM AND LOVE
CREATE SOLUTIONS
FOR
HUMAN DESTRUCTIVENESS

CHAPTER EIGHT

STAGES OF
PERSONAL EMPOWERMENT
AND WOMEN'S LIBERATION

Women's dearest possession is life; and since it is given to her but once, she must so live as to feel no torturing regret for years without purpose; so live as not to be scarred with the shame of a cowardly and trivial past; so live that dying she can say: All my life and all my strength was given to the finest cause in the world, the liberation of womankind.

Alice Paul stated in 1913

To oppose the essential lovelessness of the sexually hierarchical society is the radically loving act. ... the struggle for justice opens the way to a situation in which more genuinely loving relationships are possible.

Mary Daly
Beyond God the Father

Only when all people, each of us, refuse to submit, will oppression disappear. Each of us is the revolution.

Ti-Grace Atkinson
Amazon Odyssey

More and more women are coming to recognize feminism as a powerful awakening force which opens the mind and heart, a moral force whose message is love of life, love of self and others, love of all forms of life and the earth.

Char McGee
"Feminism: A Vision of Love"

Introduction

In the fall of 1991, I was livid when I learned that the U.S. Senate was going to vote on whether to seat Judge Clarence Thomas on the U.S. Supreme Court without even listening to the allegation of sexual harassment that had surfaced against him. A cry of outrage erupted spontaneously from women all over the country when the information leaked out that University of Oklahoma law professor Anita Hill had accused Thomas of sexually harassing her when he was her supervisor at U.S. Equal Employment Opportunity Commission and Department of Education. The banner headline of Florida's *St. Petersburg Times* said a "Nation of Women says Hill is not alone."

When the vote on Thomas' confirmation was delayed, I hoped that Hill's testimony would be heard in a fair procedure in the U.S. Senate Judiciary Committee. My hopes for a just process were dashed. As I watched the hearings, I became angry and then furious. What unfolded was incredibly unfair.[1]

After hearing Hill's testimony, many women believed her and were outraged at the Republican attacks on her.[2] Some women did not know whom to believe, while other women, many of whom had been sexually harassed themselves, believed Thomas and did not believe Hill. What caused women's passionate reactions?

Men's responses also took many vehement forms. Some of the 98% male Senate were highly critical of Hill, while others were supportive during the Judiciary Committee hearings and in their speeches on the Senate floor before casting the 52-48 vote to confirm Thomas. What caused men's intense responses?

Millions of Americans watched the hearings for hours and days. Like other controversial hearings, such as the 1970's Watergate hearings and the 1980's Iran-Contra hearings, these created tremendous interest and impassioned reactions.

Naomi Wolf claims that Hill's testimony about sexual harassment caused a dramatic shift in the balance of power. "From the fall of 1991 to the present, a new era--the era of the 'genderquake'--has begun. The term genderquake refers to the abrupt shift in the balance of power between U.S. women and men." American women are becoming "the political ruling class--probably the only ruling class ever to be unaware of its status." Women have two options. Since America is in "the final throes of a civil war for gender fairness," women can attain equality that is within our own grasp or we can cling to "an outdated image of ourselves as powerless, inch along for another several hundred years.... The decision is up to us."[3]

While I agree with Wolf that many women's responses to the hearings showed female power, the hearings also demonstrated the strong resistance to taking women serious-ly. In addition, I agree that there are many lessons we need to learn from what happened so that we can move forward assertively toward full equality for women. One lesson is that the Republican attacks on Hill's character, accusing her of being a rejected suitor and having paranoid delusions, were patriarchal methods, blatant lies, and manipulative tactics to ensure conservative domination of the U.S. Supreme Court.[4]

Because of my own deeply held belief in Hill's truthful-ness, I had difficulty understanding why anyone, especially women, would discredit her testimony. After I reflected on my theory of the six stages of personal empowerment and women's liberation, I began to understand the mixed nature of others' reactions. These six stages are a process. Different people are at various places in that process. These stages explain not only the diverse reactions to Hill, but also our own responses to things that happen in our lives.

SIX STAGES OF PERSONAL EMPOWERMENT AND WOMEN'S LIBERATION

What is women's liberation? To understand its true meaning, the patriarchal distortion that surrounds it must be removed. Around the world, women's liberation is a vast movement for respect, liberty, equality, justice, and love for all women and men. Its history in America goes back to Indian women and continues in the present.

Women's liberation is a complex movement that includes every type of woman and an assortment of groups that range from six women in a book club to a quarter of a million members in the National Organization for Women (NOW). The political and spiritual philosophies of these individuals and groups are as varied as their names: liberal feminists, radical feminists, socialist feminists, African American feminists, Chicana feminists, Asian American feminists, global feminists, and Goddess worshipers.[5] Despite their differing ideologies, all women's liberation groups more or less espouse feminism.

Some characterize feminism's goal as criticizing and opposing patriarchy. Shulamith Firestone declares feminism's aim as the "overthrow of the oldest, most rigid class/caste system in existence, the class system based on sex--a system consolidated over thousands of years, lending the archetypal male and female roles an undeserved legitimacy and seeming permanence." Kate Millett speaks of the sexual revolution as ending patriarchy by abolishing the ideology of male supremacy and the traditional socialization that promotes women's status and roles. Bell Hooks says feminism is "a commitment to eradicating the ideology of domination that permeates Western culture on various levels--sex, race, and class, to name a few."[6]

There is much truth about feminism in the above descriptions because feminism's goal is to destroy all forms of domination. Ending patriarchy's belief that one group is superior to another and thus has the right to dominate will help stop men's power over women, the rich over the poor, whites over people of color.

However, this combative aim does not capture feminism's essence, because its purpose is essentially creative. Feminism is a world-wide movement to transform all cultures and institutions so that they practice equality for all people. Barbara Smith says "feminism is the political theory and practice to free all women." Anything less is not feminism, but self-aggrandizement.[7]

Naomi Wolf's broad definition encompasses many women and men who now reject the name feminist. "A feminism worthy of its name will fit every woman and every man who cares about women." Anyone who stands up in any way for women's rights is a feminist. One core feminist truth is "every single woman counts." Another baseline feminist goal is "laying claim to our humanity, all of it, not just the scenic parts." Feminism which means freedom makes women stronger. Sexual liberation is "freedom through caring" for ourselves and others. Feminism is "the ultimate human-rights movement."[8]

Gloria Steinem gives "the equality and full humanity of women and men" as a creative goal for feminism. Robin Morgan offers both combative and creative goals. Feminism challenges man's patriarchal vision of himself as "being at the center of humanity." Morgan's creative goals for feminism are "women's right to freedom, access, self-determination, and empowerment--as a matter of simple justice." Morgan also offers a larger vision. As "the key to our survival and transformation" and the call for the next step in evolution, feminism is "the helix of hope that we humans have for communication with whatever lies before us in the vast, witty mystery of the universe."[9]

French asserts that "feminism is the only serious, coherent, and universal philosophy that offers an alternative to patriarchal thinking and structures." Some feminist tenets are that females are human beings, the two sexes are equal in human dignity, the qualities traditionally associated with women are equal in value to those traditionally identified with men, and equality between the sexes needs to be publicly recognized. Feminists believe that all our relationships are political, "that what happens in the bedroom has everything to do with what happens in the board room and vice versa," and that men are in control in both places.[10]

Espousing feminist beliefs is not enough. As French says, "acceptance of the equality of women and of 'feminine' values is not enough: it is necessary to work for the public recognition of this equality, in both public and private worlds." Feminism is not a set of beliefs which one espouses, while acting in ways that contradict those beliefs. "It is necessarily activist, and thus necessarily political--it involves public expression of personal ideals. Feminism must be lived."[11]

Most advocates of women's liberation believe that feminism is more than a movement demanding entry into existing male structures and their rewards. To be assimilated into the patriarchy for personal self-aggrandizement is to be coopted away from feminism.[12]

In my view, feminism is the vision and practice of love. Feminism is acts of love that work to eliminate all forms of domination; that express respect, liberty, equality, justice, and love for all women and men; and that transform the world by nurturing loving individuals and creating communities of love. Feminism is love in action. Feminism replaces patriarchy's love for power as the highest value with the power of love.

Many feminists do not identify love as the highest value and goal of feminism. French says "the only true revolution against patriarchy is one which removes the idea of power from its central position, and replaces it with the idea of pleasure." Restoring pleasure and felicity as the highest human good helps distinguish between the two kinds of power: power-to is the energy to act and power-over is domination. "Power-to primarily increases pleasure, and power-over primarily increases pain."[13] It is my deep conviction that love is feminism's highest value and goal, not pleasure and felicity. However, since love often produces pleasure and felicity, they are interconnected.

In my definition, feminism is both theory and practice, beliefs and activism, philosophy and mission, vision and action. Feminism is a revolutionary vision of the personal, social, political, economic, educational, and spiritual liberty and equality for women and men so that justice and love become the guiding principles of all the cultures of the world. Feminism takes action to transform our world by eliminating all forms of patriarchal domination. Then it makes respect, liberty, equality, justice, and love incarnate in women and men so they will create communities of love. Women's liberation is the movement that promotes this feminist philosophy and vocation of love.

The feminist methods of pursuing this goal are the six stages of personal empowerment and women's liberation. All six stages produce personal empowerment with its goals of developing self-love and love for others. The fifth stage radiates sisterly and brotherly love outward with the aim of promoting love for all women and men. The sixth stage builds a new world by transforming the patriarchal world through the power of love into communities of love.

Every relationship in a person's life can be at a different stage at the same time. At work, Rose is extremely independent, while at home she bows to her husband's wishes and neglects her own needs. Sometimes her inner feelings are far ahead of her rational expressions. At other times, her head runs in front, while her heart remains behind. There is a constant backward and forward movement as she struggles to free herself.

Personal liberation is both freedom **from** the abuses of the patriarchy and freedom **to** express ourselves spontaneously and fully. Empowering ourselves means shucking the old confining patriarchal stereotypes and getting in touch with our loving inner core and affirming our identity as lovers.

1. The First Stage--Unawareness and Denial of Sexist Status Quo

The point of departure for every woman is to be

unaware and accept the sexist status quo without questioning it. Peggy Way, a theologian, objects to placing outside the liberation process those women who have not climbed up freedom's ladder. To exclude anyone is to speak negatively of them.

A woman in the first stage likes everything as it is. She claims the present sexist situation is fine for women. Believing herself liberated, she says, "I'm free, my husband lets me do anything I want." The possibility that she is discriminated against or that others are being abused has either not occurred to her or has been dismissed by her.

However, the woman who buys into the sexist status quo is not only discriminated against but also dominated, because the control of her life rests in patriarchal hands, and not her own. Many qualities of the dominated person, such as fear of freedom and identification with the oppressor, are true of the woman who accepts the patriarchy.

The most important characteristic of the unliberated woman is her inadequate self-love. Her insufficient self-love causes her to distrust herself and later this distrust extends to other women. With little self-love, she is insecure and not confident. Trying to hide the negative feelings that she has about herself, she conceals who she really is and what she wants.

Because the unaware woman fears freedom, she builds defense mechanisms that emphasize the goodness of the status quo and evade the concrete realities of her subordination. Her fear of freedom cripples her ability to act and causes her to praise passivity. However, her self-distrust and inactivity make her so anxious she feels the need to believe in someone else.

Every young girl is socialized into a patriarchal world where men control almost all the institutions. She is taught to view herself as inferior and consider men superior and powerful. Very early she recognizes her father as the symbol of authority in the home, while the male government and business leaders act as the model for competence and importance in the outside world. The only way for a female to participate in power is vicariously through being connected to a man as his daughter, wife, mother, employee, or sexual partner.

Since the young woman has no faith in her own judgment, she fails to direct her own destiny and accepts the decisions of her father, her male boss, and her husband. Since she fears independence, she becomes dependent on male protectors. The more she believes in the patriarchal world view, the more she distrusts herself and doubts that there is a place for her in the patriarchal world of power and prestige. Her faith in the power of men and her self-distrust are interrelated in a vicious circle. Her self-distrust produces her belief in the power of men that in turn breeds more self-distrust which promotes more faith in men's power.

When troubles exist in our lives, we are not always aware of them. Sometimes we do not want to be aware of them and we deny their existence. Many of us blindly and unquestioningly conform to the status quo, while we ignore or deny the sexist, racist, elitist, power-hungry, greedy, environmentally damaging, drug abusing, criminal, and violent aspects of our culture that are destroying our communities. Sometimes we even pay homage to our country as the best possible way of life.

Denial is a defense mechanism that we use to avoid seeing truths that are too painful. We fear becoming aware of the facts about our patriarchal culture because the truth can cause us to be unhappy and suffer. This ignoring and denying of problems start in early childhood. Alcoholic, dysfunctional, patriarchal, and abusive families teach children to deny the alcoholism, the dysfunctions, the dominating power relations, the psychological, verbal, mental, physical, and sexual abuse within the family.

The family dysfunction is a family secret that is ignored or denied. One way of describing an alcoholic in the family is the elephant in the living room. Every family member is expected to deny there is an elephant controlling the living room and act like the family is perfectly normal. Dysfunctional families often act like everything is fine as the elephant in the living room destroys their psychological well-being.

Robin Norwood, a therapist, claims "we all need to deny what is too painful or too threatening for us to accept. Denial is a natural means of self-protection, operating automatically and unbidden." When our family denies its dysfunction, we as children deny it too, because such serious problems threaten our feelings of safety. Our denial severely impairs our ability to relate to people and situations. We become unable to recognize people and actions that are not good for us and that we should avoid as unwholesome or dangerous. Later as we grow stronger, we may face these problems and the suffering they cause.[14]

Claudia Black, a therapist, estimates that 40% of children in alcoholic families "grow up and leave home without ever being sure of the truth. They either don't know or deny what they know." Alcoholism, patriarchal domination, child abuse, women battering, incest, and other dysfunctions are denied within the family and in the wider society. "Deception begun at home permeates the neighborhood and the community." People look the other way rather than acknowledge dysfunctional families.[15]

The continuum of unawareness and denial ranges from totally blocking out memories to conscious awareness that is suppressed just below the surface. When the suffering from harmful events is too extreme, children and even adults sometimes bar these painful events entirely from their memory. Many victims of incest totally block out the memory of their fathers' sexual molestation and rape for years and even for their lifetime.

Francis Van Derbur, a millionaire socialite, helped establish a home for physically challenged children. Marilyn, the youngest of his four daughters, was crowned Miss America of 1958 when she was 20 years old. Until Marilyn was 24, she completely repressed her memories that from age five to eighteen, her father "sexually violated" her.[16]

To survive, Marilyn claims she split herself into "a night child, who lay awake in a fetal position, only to be pried apart" by her father, and a day child who believed herself happy, although she felt isolated. Until age 24, "the day child had no conscious knowledge of the night child. ... I had no conscious knowledge of what he was doing to me." While Marilyn totally blocked her memories of sexual abuse, the family secret remained hidden behind "the trappings of a perfect family, ... wealth, social status, a handsome father and lovely mother."[17]

Many victims report that they have entirely blocked out their memories of severe child abuse until they are uncovered in adulthood. Even though these harmful memories are suppressed, they still have multiple effects on the victims' lives.

Until Lucy was an adult, she totally blocked out memories of her grandfather sexually abusing her. Before she remembered, she became an alcoholic and suffered from what she called "manic-depression." At age 35, she recalled her grandfather sexually molesting her from her earliest memory until his death when she was 16. As she dealt with these memories, she suffered severe depression.[18]

Another response on the continuum of denial is dissociation. Victims use dissociation as a way to escape from the suffering caused by abuse. While being sexually abused, they dissociate from their own bodies. Some victims "feel physically and mentally removed from what is happening" during a rape. "As with denial, dissociation is a protective reaction that helps the victim survive the experience by not feeling it completely."[19]

Maggie was fully present when a man she had formerly dated punched her, dragged her through several rooms, and threw her on a bed. Then she dissociated, left her body, and stood beside the bed watching. "So there's a period of time where my memory of the rape is real different than my other memories of the rape ... I wasn't in my body. I dissociated from the helplessness. ...there was just this shell on the bed.[20]

Further along the continuum of unawareness is disbelief and denial. A *Ms* study of more than 3,100 college women on 32 campuses shows over 27% of the women experienced rape or attempted rape in one year. 84% of the women knew the rapist. Many acquaintance rape victims

denied they were raped "even in the face of the most excruciating evidence: violence, forceful isolation, restraint, verbal
abuse, and of course, the man's disregard of any negative
reaction by the woman."   Part of the victims' denial was
rooted in the fact that they didn't want to believe that men
they knew would rape them.   Many women repressed the
date rape for years until another emotionally troubling event
brought it rushing back to them.[21]

One major reason why women deny the fact that they
are being dominated and abused is that it is painful to face
and they want to avoid the suffering that they suspect will
result from dealing with it. Another important reason is their
lack of self-love and sense of personal worth. Flo Kennedy
claims that fear of punishment, desire for rewards, and need
for approval are some reasons why people deny they are
dominated.[22]

The dominated believe the patriarchy's teaching that
elite people are superior and have the right to have power
over those who are inferior. Even those toward the bottom of
the patriarchal hierarchy have someone lower to dominate.
After the patriarchy puts some women are on a pedestal, they
begin to act superior and dominate others, especially children
and other women who do not meet the norm of "femininity,"
the norm of being white, wealthy, young, beautiful, domestic,
and submissive. Many people recognize only two positions,
having someone's foot on their neck or putting their foot on
someone else's neck.[23]

Rebellious women who challenge male domination
frighten the unliberated woman. Unconsciously the unaware
woman hears the justice in their complaints, but consciously
she strikes out at them because she recognizes that they
threaten the position which she has slaved so long and
sacrificed so much to achieve. In addition, they remind her of
the deficiency of her own courage. Her feelings of inadequa-
cy make her intolerant of outspoken women's weaknesses
and jealous of their strengths.

Outwardly the unaware woman defends the patriarchy
that dominates her and attacks feminists who offer her

liberation, because inwardly she feels unable to live freely. Her fear of freedom grows out of her fear of losing her safety. Being dominated is a familiar situation. Freedom leads to the unknown, which always feels risky. The dominated woman craves familiarity and safety more than freedom. Moreover, she is attracted to the men who give her security.

Every woman possesses a dual consciousness that includes her socially assigned identity and her loving inner core identity. A fully functioning woman is aware that her socialized self is interrelated with her identity as a loving person. Alienation occurs when the interconnection within the dual consciousness is broken.

When a woman accepts as her self-identity only the imposed patriarchal image of submissive femininity, she is alienated from her own vibrant spirit and her dynamic inner core of love. The imposed image makes her feel like a sex object, instead of a self-determining person. Often the conforming woman internalizes the patriarchal image, even though it causes her alienation, because she fears being punished if she doesn't. It is easier to incorporate a socially assigned identity than to search within to discover her own loving nature.

The dual consciousness is a vehicle for liberation as well as alienation. While no one can live without a socially assigned identity, everyone also possesses an inner core of love. No matter how much the shackled woman distrusts herself and internalizes the traditional picture of passive femininity, she still retains deep within her a loving inner core identity. When this loving nature becomes active, liberation begins.

Women who are violently abused are often the first women to become aware. A maxim wisely says, scratch any woman and you will find a feminist. Every woman feels hurt and angry when her loving inner core is damaged by abuse or by the false patriarchal image of inferior femininity. This unacknowledged hurt and anger smolder under layers of rationalizations until awareness dawns.

2. Stage Two--The Beginning of Awareness, But Remaining Silent

Before I can be free, I must be conscious of my bondage. Awareness is the starting point for liberation. Consciousness raising is the beginning of freedom. When a woman realizes that her patriarchal identity conflicts with her loving inner core, awareness begins. Two courses of action are then possible. On one hand, the dominated woman can deny her own ideas and acknowledge the validity of society's image of submissive femininity. On the other hand, the woman can take the first step toward empowerment by welcoming her new awareness.

Abuse causes personal damage and suffering. In the first stage of unawareness, we deny the injury and the hurt feelings that result. In the second stage, the beginning of awareness, we develop the courage to stop denying the harm inflicted on us. Our courage also helps us become aware of our unhappy feelings and the problems that cause them. We begin to admit to ourselves privately the horror of the abuse, but we remain silent about our troubles, except for what we tell a few close friends.

In the *Ms* college study, only five percent of the rape victims reported the rapes to the police and only five percent asked for help at rape crisis centers. "42 percent of the rape victims told no one about their assaults."[24]

Unlocking blocked memories and becoming aware of repressed injury is a difficult process and takes great bravery. Becoming conscious of what we purposely suppressed because it was too painful is not easily or quickly accomplished. In fact, some exceptionally harmful memories may remain blocked into adulthood and even throughout our entire lives.

Marilyn Atler did not unblock her painful memories of her father sexually molesting her until her former minister broke down her guard when she was 24 years old. "With words I don't remember, he punctured the wall I had built around the secret, and I began to sob. The only words I was able to say were, 'Don't tell anyone'." Shortly after that, in an uncontrolled bout of sobbing, Marilyn told Larry, a long time male friend whom she later married. Then, she revealed her secret to her eldest sister, who responded, "Oh, no. I thought I was the only one."[25]

The negative effects of the childhood sexual abuse continued even after this first revelation to a few people. From age 18 on, even after Marilyn's first disclosures and after her marriage to Larry, she never fell asleep naturally, but took sleeping pills. When her daughter turned five, "I began to have these uncontrollable fits of sobbing." It took ten years for her to understand that she was seeing herself as a five-year-old in her daughter. About that time, she also started having attacks of paralysis although doctors said nothing was physically wrong.[26]

My own mother explicitly advocated a rule of alcoholic families when she said "don't talk about unpleasant things." Even though I was aware, I never talked to anyone for the first twenty years of my life about my father's alcoholism and how negatively it affected our family.

When family members become aware of an alcoholic or other dysfunction in their family, they are expected to remain silent. Children are taught to maintain the family secret. Honest discussion is prohibited either implicitly by changing the subject or explicitly by the parents' admonition not to talk about such things. To admit publicly the family secret is to be disloyal. The secret pact of silence preserves the family's dysfunction. Hiding becomes a way of life that goes unquestioned and unchallenged as the lives of those who keep the family secret are distorted and twisted.[27]

Factors that affect how seriously children are damaged while growing up in dysfunctional families are the degree of secrecy and the degree that the underlying problems are not dealt with and discussed. Norwood claims "what all unhealthy families have in common is their inability to discuss root problems." By diverting the discussion to other people's problems, often ad nauseam, they cover up the family secret. "It is the degree of secrecy--the inability to talk about the problems--rather than their severity, that defines both how dysfunctional a family becomes and how severely its members are damaged."[28]

There are other factors that affect how severely children are hurt. The nature and severity of the dysfunction influence the amount of physical and psychological damage to the child. The seriousness of the child battering affects the extent of the injury. The identity of the abuser influences the severity of the harm, such as whether the child sexual abuse is done by a stranger or the father. The type of destructive behavior against the child affects the seriousness of the impairment, such as whether the incest by the father is sexual touching or rape. The extent of childhood harm is also influenced by the duration of the abuse, such as whether the incest happened a few times or continued over years.

Once women who have been victimized admit the family secret to themselves, and even to a few close family and friends, they often blame themselves and minimize the problem. Not acknowledging the seriousness of the problem, they make excuses for the abuser. Battered women, rape victims, and abused children often believe that the problem is their fault; they blame themselves for not cleaning the house properly, for being out late at night, or for not being good enough.

Carolyn Sapp, Miss America of 1992, told the public that she was battered and terrorized by her fiance, a football player. The first time he went berserk, struck her, kicked her, and threatened to kill her, she felt it was her fault. "I really thought I was the one provoking it." As Carolyn chastised herself, she made excuses for her abuser. After convincing herself that the beating was an isolated incident, she planned to help her batterer.[29]

The second violent incident occurred when her boyfriend tried to strangle her with her seat belt and push her out of a speeding car. After escaping, the bruises covering her neck helped her decide to break off the engagement. "I realized it wasn't right for him to hit me. ... It didn't matter if I had pushed and provoked him." She still thought it was her fault. Battered and betrayed, Carolyn's self-confidence was damaged. "I felt I was weak. ... I was embarrassed. I didn't want people--who look to me as a strong person--to say 'you're a woman who would let a man do this to you.'"[30]

Battered women often minimize the abuse by saying he only hit me a few times, he didn't beat me bloody, or he didn't break any bones. Some rape victims say it was only attempted rape, he didn't complete it, he only threatened me with his fist, or he didn't use a knife or gun. In the *Ms* college study, "only 27 percent of the women whose sexual assault met the legal definition of rape thought of themselves as rape victims." Many rape victims "never named their assaults as rape until months or years later."[31]

Once some people become aware of their problems, they do not want to think about them because dealing with them takes time and often causes pain. Either consciously or unconsciously, they choose not to think about their troubles. The American public has perfected this strategy. Even though the problems of prejudice, discrimination, sexism, racism, homophobia, poverty, drugs, crime, environmental destruction, governmental economic problems, and violence stare them in the face and devastate their children's future, many Americans ignore them.

One reason people use the strategy of avoidance is that it hurts to think about problems. One woman who was beaten by her alcoholic father when she was a child regretfully says, "I remember everything." She avoids thinking about the beatings, because that causes suffering and unhappiness. When some people talk about their abuse, they feel exposed and not supported. Their way of protecting themselves from further injury is not to talk about it. Helplessness and hopelessness cause members of alcoholic families to believe if I just ignore it, maybe it will not hurt and maybe it will go away.[32]

An individual's awareness can develop only so far without the assistance of other people. The foundation on which women's liberation is built is the consciousness raising group. This vehicle of awareness is a small group of women who meet to discuss their past and present lives, their sorrows and joys, the domination that was imposed on them and the subordination that each woman causes herself. Every woman shares her stories of childhood, schooling, jobs, and relationships. Some feminists call the consciousness raising group free space, a place to think about the qualities necessary to become more free and loving.

Among the many discoveries of consciousness raising is the lesson that "the personal is political." The problem that one woman experiences as her own private difficulty also happens to many other women in one form or another. Thus, it is not her individual trouble, but rather a collective problem of all women because of the way the patriarchy mistreats them.

Consciousness grows as each woman recognizes the patriarchy's physical, psychological, political, economic, and religious domination. The aware woman admits that women are dominated because they do not control their own lives; objectified because they are treated as sex objects; exploited because they are used for the advantage of others; discriminated against because they experience stereotyping, limited opportunities, and different treatment than men.

Slowly each woman names the enemy and the pain it causes. Initially she may blame individual oppressive men and then perhaps all men. Gradually she will recognize as the enemy the patriarchy and its institutions that control women and men.

3. Stage Three--Anger and Saying No to Abuse

Abuse, injury, suffering, sadness, and awareness breed anger. Once our consciousness is raised about how we are dominated, we feel tremendous anger and sometimes rage. Anger is the appropriate response to sexism, racism, elitism, and any other form of prejudice, domination, discrimination, abuse, and violence. As Lorde says, "anger is an appropriate reaction to racist attitudes, as is fury when the actions arising from those attitudes do not change."[33]

We are angry because we were abused as small children. We are angry because we were hurt before we developed coping skills and defense mechanisms. We are angry because we were damaged before our self-identities were formed.

As women, we are angry because an impossible body image is forced upon us through magazine ads, television, and movies. We are angry because of all the energy we waste trying to be what others impose on us when it is contrary to our inner core of love. We are angry because doors are closed in our face or opened in false protectiveness just because we are female. We are angry because people ignore our qualifications for the job and concentrate on our looks. We are angry because the patriarchy controls our lives and devalues, objectifies, and abuses us.

As women, our anger grows out of the maltreatment and resultant pain that we experience because of the sexist society. As we become liberated, we feel hurt not only when we ourselves experience discrimination but also when any sister or brother experiences injustice. Since anger follows injury, our anger will continue as long as suffering continues.

Anger can be either destructive or constructive. Destructive anger is the anger expressed by people who have not dealt with their feelings after being abused and injured. It attempts to retaliate against those who harm them. Constructive anger is the anger expressed by people who deal with their feelings after being damaged. It tries to stop the abuser from violating and injuring anyone.

It is not the nature of anger to harm us and make us bitter and hateful, only destructive anger does that. Constructive anger is a creative, passionate energy that empowers us to say no to abuse. As Lorde says, it is not anger that destroys us, but "our refusals to stand still, to listen to its rhythms, to learn within it, to move beyond the manner of presentation to the substance, to tap that anger as an important source of empowerment."[34]

With my consciousness raised and my anger fueled, I am aware that the home, school, church, and business world teach a picture of submissive femininity that conflicts with my innate loving inner core and I say no to this harmful socialization. No, I am not the only person responsible for cooking, cleaning, and child rearing. No, I am not a sex object. No, I am not inferior, ignorant, or helpless. After saying no to the distrust that I previously felt toward myself, I reject the patriarchy and its power over me. Slowly I denounce the hierarchical institutions that make sexism possible.

The first step in liberating ourselves is awareness of the problems that block our freedom. However, when we are aware but do not say no to the injustices, our bondage continues. After understanding our problems, we need to speak out publicly. Our anger at being devalued gives us the courage to voice our troubles. At first, we may only talk to our trusted family and friends about our problems and the pain that results from them. Later we may want to speak publicly.

Why do we need to speak? We only become fully conscious of something when we express it to someone else. We may have an intuition about it, but it remains vague as long as we do not discuss it. As Lorde says, we are never whole persons if we remain silent. There is always one small piece inside us that wants to be spoken and if we keep ignoring it, it gets angrier and angrier.[35] Anger turned inward becomes depression.

Lorde wants us to transform our silence into speech and action. We need to speak about "the poisonous seepage of hatred" that we eat like daily bread and the tyrannies that we swallow every day, until we sicken and die of them. Why are we scared to speak out about abuses that damaged us? We are afraid because "the transformation of silence into language and action is an act of self-revelation, and that always seems fraught with danger." We fear exposure, judgment, contempt, and even annihilation.[36]

What are the roadblocks that keep adults from dysfunctional families from revealing the family secret? One roadblock is the risk of punishment for disclosing it. By overcoming the risk, breaking the silence, and exposing the family secret, they can say things they never could say before and find out things they never knew about themselves and others.[37]

What are the obstacles that keep women from revealing the abuses done to them in the work place? Pointing out sexual discrimination and harassment brings punishment. Once women speak out, their motives are questioned and they are lied about and accused of wrongdoing. Anita Hill received this punishment. If women are not fired for naming the sexist injustices, they are often transferred to a lesser job. If they are fired, they have trouble finding another job because other companies do not want to hire someone who is outspoken about sexist abuses.

After speaking publicly about the problem and the pain it causes, we need to deal with it. First, we may only be able to deal with it indirectly. The final healing comes when we deal with it directly. After awareness and speaking publicly, our focus shifts from what our parents and the patriarchy did to us to what we can do to lessen their power over our lives, empower ourselves, and change our world.

Strategies, such as self-help groups, therapy, and progressive movements for change are available to help us improve ourselves and our society. We can confront our past, heal our wounds, break the cycle, let go of the past, define ourselves, become fully responsible for our actions, and work with progressive and feminist movements to change the destructive institutions in the world.[38]

Phyllis Chesler, a feminist author, asks "at what point do we say no to abuse?" Another important question is at what point do we say yes to life?

4. The Fourth Stage--Affirming Herself, Finding Her Own Voice, Defining Herself, and Learning Self-love

After becoming aware, getting angry, and saying no to abuse, a woman in the fourth stage of empowerment says yes to her own worth, goodness, love, and life. The more she affirms her own loving nature, the more she finds her voice, the more she defines herself, the more she loves herself.

As African Americans assert black is beautiful, we affirm that womanhood is wonderful and sisterhood is powerful. After saying no to the feminine stereotype, we find our own voice and publicly express our own needs, values, and beliefs. Vocalizing our self-acceptance, we express our own thoughts and feelings.

Renouncing patriarchy's femininity, we declare ourselves to be both emotional and rational, passive and active. Socially we demand roles that we choose for ourselves, including the possibility of working not only in the home but also in the world. Politically we reject the almost exclusive male control of institutional power and affirm our intention of assuming responsibility and leadership.

After rejecting the patriarchs' methods of domination, including lying, manipulating, dividing, and conquering, we affirm the processes of liberation, including honesty, communication, support, and unity. Patriarchs promote divisions, while feminists work for unity. While the patriarchal images of femininity cause alienation, we who define ourselves develop loving identities. The patriarchy manipulates us into being sex objects, while feminist support helps us to become our own person and express our sexuality in whatever way we choose. While patriarchal manipulation forces us to be passive, mutual support helps each of us to become active. As Lorde says, the patriarchal "divide and conquer must become define and empower."[39]

When we define ourselves, we become actors instead of reactors. When we recover, we become survivors instead of victims of abuse. Integrating our previous denial, new awareness, anger, saying no to abuse, and saying yes to ourselves, we create a more loving self. Overcoming our previous fragmentation, we achieve a new wholeness and centeredness.

To define and love ourselves, it is essential to affirm ourselves and say I'm OK. In learning to say I'm OK, it is vital to add You're OK. It is crucial to say abusing me is not OK, but it is not growth-producing to claim the abuser is not OK.

It is important to condemn the sin without demolishing the sinner, to halt the violence without destroying the abuser. Mistreating the abuser does not affirm myself. After removing the patriarch's foot from my neck, I need to stand up and love myself, but I should not knock my abuser into the dirt and put my foot on his neck.

A self-defining woman is a self-actualizing person. Being in touch with her loving inner core, she loves herself and others. Having a clear perception of reality, she resists patriarchal socialization and transcends her culture's feminine stereotype to create her own loving identity. Being independent, she is spontaneous and open to experience. With her deep identification with other people, she accepts herself and others and has a democratic way of behaving. Being creative, she forms deep friendships and is a productive citizen of the world.

When a woman defines herself and learns self-acceptance, she liberates herself and develops self-love. Once she loves herself, her love radiates outward into sisterly love for all people. Besides being the fifth stage of personal empowerment, sisterly love and brotherly love give people the courage to transform the world which is the sixth stage of personal empowerment and women's liberation. All six stages lead to personal empowerment, while the last two contribute to personal and communal liberation.

5. The Fifth Stage--Sisterly and Brotherly Love

The world's patriarchal way of relating is elitism, the hierarchy of domination. Some parents want to have power over their children, husbands over wives, teachers over students, whites over people of color, men over women, heterosexuals over homosexuals, rich over poor, employers over workers, clergy over laity, lawmakers and police over people, judges over defendants, doctors over nurses and patients. The liberated woman casts off these dominating ways of relating and tries sisterly love.

To understand the meaning of sisterly love, we need to

comprehend the relationship between two blood sisters. Although they may differ drastically in interests, values, and life styles, they still feel united by the bond of the blood relationship between them. Ideally, the sisterly bond is so strong that it is unbreakable no matter what comes between them. When a feminist calls someone sister, it means that her sisterly feelings are so solid that she recognizes and accepts the differences between them. Sisterhood means that the sisterly bond is so tenacious that it is unbreakable in spite of any difficulty. Sisterhood is indeed powerful.

Sisterhood is sisterly love. Since all kinds of love drive toward self-actualization and communion, sisterly love does too. Sisterly love is universal love, the dynamic power that tries to unite all human beings. Not only does sisterly love strive toward the unity of all people, but it also seeks the personal fulfillment of every person.

While erotic love is exclusive, sisterly love is inclusive. The basis of universal love is the belief that all people are one. Of course, there are important differences between people, such as sex, class, race, nationality, religion, and sexual preference that need to be acknowledged and respected. However, liberated women who experience sisterly love feel that the unity because of their common humanness is greater than the division because of their individual or group differences. If we live on the surface, we perceive mainly the differences that separate us. When we penetrate the depth, we experience the common inner core of love that unites us. When we practice sisterly love, we promote human solidarity.

It is crucial to recognize our very important differences of race, sex, class, disabilities, nationality, religion, and sexual preference. However, it is not these differences that separate us. As Lorde says, "it is rather our refusal to recognize those differences, and to examine the distortions which result from our misnaming them and their effects upon human behavior and expectation." Unacknowledged differences distort our vision, make it difficult to see our different problems, and rob us of our creative insight and energy. "Community must not mean a shedding of our differences, nor the pathetic pretense that these differences do not exist."[40]

Love is "digging the differences." Love is recognizing and appreciating the differences. Although Lorde does not call it love, she stresses the importance of recognizing the differences in order to build community. "Difference is that raw and powerful connection from which our personal power is forged." We need to see difference as a strength, "as a springboard for creative change within our lives."[41]

Most of us love our family and friends. When we practice sisterly love, we love work colleagues and helpless, poor strangers. Sisterly love is born when we have compassion for powerless foreigners. Universal love begins when we recognize and help the needy. When universal love deepens, we see the needy and all people as our own flesh and blood. As Chardin says, "universal love is not only psychologically possible; it is the only complete and final way in which we are able to love."[42]

The woman practicing sisterhood loves unliberated women and liberated ones, controlling men and egalitarian ones. Amazingly, she loves not only the dominated but also the dominators. Although love is creative, it must sometimes struggle against whatever damages love. Love uses its power to oppose whatever is against love, but never the people who act against love. Love attempts to heal the dominators by curing that which harms love within them.

The criterion for recognizing what is against love is anything that makes it difficult to develop self-actualization and unity among people. If I truly love my sisters, I strive to end their subordination. If I truly love the exploiters of women, I work to stop them from doing their harmful deeds. The abusers of women violate themselves as well as their victims. When they abuse women, they injure their own humanness, because they are acting against love and not for it. A feminist with sisterly love in her heart wants to prevent controllers from dominating women and thus harming the women and themselves.

Sisterhood is not only the way that one woman relates to others, it is also a community with a purpose. For Mary

Daly, sisterhood is an exodus community and a cosmic covenant. As an exodus community that leaves behind false sexist identities and the patriarchal society, women join with others on the journey into the liberated future where they create a community of sisterhood. This new bonding is a covenant, a deep agreement that patriarchy must end and justice must reign. Sisterhood is a cosmic covenant because women are renaming the entire cosmos.[43]

Sisterly love promotes respect, equality, and justice. A woman with sisterly love sees every person as her equal and respects her, because everyone has human dignity despite individual shortcomings. Sisterly love promotes justice. In fact, love's relationship to justice is even closer than its relationship to equality. Love is the ultimate principle of justice, while justice is the form in which love expresses itself. Justice is the intrinsic claim of every female that she must be treated as a person, and not a sex object or a servant. Love always includes justice. There is no love without justice. There is no justice without love.[44]

In addition, sisterly love promotes freedom. Freedom is the capacity to direct our life and decide our destiny. Mary Daly claims "sisterhood, like female friendship, has at its core the affirmation of freedom." I believe this needs to be altered to say sisterhood has as its core love and love affirms and creates freedom. To be free is to be in touch with our loving inner core and become fully loving. The first step toward freedom is awareness of being unfree. The final step toward complete freedom is love. The more we love, the freer we become.

Love is not a restraint on freedom, but rather love is the fullness of freedom. The fullness of love that makes possible the fullness of freedom is universal love toward all people and the whole world. Feminists know that no woman is completely free until all women and men are free. No woman is fully liberated until the world and all its patriarchal institutions are transformed.

To speak of feminism and sisterhood as essential to women's liberation is not to exclude men from the movement.

A male is a feminist when he believes in and practices respect, liberty, equality, justice, and love for all women and men.

Voicing feminist rhetoric is not enough to qualify a person as a feminist. It is not feminist to engage in destructive behavior, such as prejudice, verbal put-downs, discriminatory practices, and dominating actions toward women, in fact toward anyone. Feminist men express brotherly love toward all people, while feminist women practice sisterly love. Sisterhood and brotherhood are the heart of women's liberation. Without them, the movement will fail to reach its goals.

6. The Sixth Stage--Building a New World, Communities of Love

The sixth stage of personal empowerment and women's liberation is building a new world, communities of love. The goal of feminism is to build a world where respect, freedom, equality, justice, and love are the guiding principles. When liberated women join together in sisterhood, they briefly experience the freedom and love that will be a persistent reality in the new world. This small glimpse of a community of love gives them the courage to devote themselves to actualizing it.

Some people do not understand the radical nature of women's liberation because they assume what feminists want is their share of the pie. However, feminists vary in their critiques of whether the pie is either partly or entirely rotten. Thus, most feminists' aims go much deeper than just gaining power and wealth in the present oppressive system.

Rejecting domination, feminists make love their highest value. Their goal is to nurture loving individuals and create loving communities. Believing their means must be consistent with their end, they use democratic loving methods to transform the present world. Instead of ordering others around, they facilitate. Rather than manipulating and controlling as dominators do, they respect and care for individuals and the group. One way to determine whether leaders control or love others is to discover whether they inhibit and dominate them or whether they empower them to become freer and more loving.

Feminists treat every individual as a person, not as an object to be used. To strengthen others' self-love and support their diversity, they encourage them to think profoundly and live creatively their own important values. Not only do they work to affirm, empower, and free each woman from her particular subordination, but they also recognize that individual difficulties are collective problems and they strive for collective solutions. They build individual freedom, democratic process- es, and universal love, as they work to eliminate sexism, racism, classism, homophobia, and all other forms of preju- dice, elitism, discrimination, and violence.

After feminists examine every aspect of the contempo- rary culture to distinguish the loving from the destructive, they strive to eradicate whatever is injurious to people and main- tain what is growth producing. From small items such as the title "Miss" to large institutions such as the Roman Catholic Church, they no longer blindly accept the patriarchal defini- tions of the world. Judging everything by the criterion of whether it promotes love or destructiveness, they speak out about how the world can be less dominating and more loving.

Targets for feminist transformation include everyone and everything. Feminists want to change all people, cul- tures, and institutions. In addition, they want to transform all human relationships, including relationships between male and female, parent and child, female and female, male and male, people and institutions, humans and nature, whites and people of color, rich and poor, heterosexuals and homosexu- als, humans and the divine.

Transforming the relationships between women and men includes eliminating the patriarchal stereotypes of masculine and feminine psychological traits and social roles. Feminists want to destroy the masculine stereotype of being rational, aggressive, and adventurous and the feminine one of being emotional, submissive, and domestic. The new feminist vision advocates that each person acquires all the above qualities in different proportions according to his or her unique personality, and not according to sex. Feminists also want to change the institutions that espouse these stereotypes, including the family, media, education, business, government, and religion.

Feminists want to change the current definition that says males are dominating. Since both females and males are innately loving, their human nature is the same. To be a man or woman is to love generously as a friend, parent, partner, lover, worker, and citizen. As William Becker says in his new definition of maleness, to be a man, and I would add to be a woman, is "to give love, without counting the cost;... to be loyal to the true and the good."[45]

The family, school, media, church, business, and other institutions are guilty of encouraging women to maintain exclusive responsibility for the home by suggesting that a woman is a failure unless she is a sex object for her man, an excellent mother for her children, and a super consumer for her spotlessly clean, elaborately decorated home. Rejecting this, feminists advocate both women and men share equal responsibility for raising the children and creating a loving home and world.

It is the equal responsibility of both parents to care for their children's physical, emotional, social, and spiritual needs. Both parents must teach their youngsters to love themselves and others rather than to be obedient. Housework and cooking need to be the shared duty of all family members, except those who are too young or too old to participate.

The relationship between the partners in the home needs to be based on love rather than control. Where domination and subordination are the habitual way of living, love is stunted. Authentic love cannot grow in an atmosphere where one person has power over another. Both partners need to maintain close relationships with their family and friends so that they have sources of support outside their partnership.

An overemphasis on consumerism and setting unattainable consumption goals are serious problems. Many people describe the American dream in materialistic ways and define success by how much money, status, and power they have. They try to acquire a sense of well being by surrendering to the social pressure of keeping up with the Jones and purchasing luxury goods. Television, advertising, social pressure, and corporations stress that purchasing social status goods is the way to happiness. Women are socialized to buy clothes, possessions, and home improvements. Ironically, acquiring more is often an endless cycle that leads to dissatisfaction and unhappiness. Feminists want to change the definition of success to being fully loving people. They value helping themselves and others more than materialistic consumerism.

In the transformed world, feminists want women to control their own bodies in sex and reproduction. If women cannot control their own bodies, they will never control their lives. There needs to be mutual consent before every sexual act. Rape must be eliminated. Safe, effective, available birth control will greatly decrease unwanted pregnancies and thus eliminate the need for abortion. Every child needs to be a wanted and loved child. Children having children must be stopped. Teenage pregnancies must be discouraged through cooperative programs between parents, schools, social service agencies, and caring helpers.

The stereotypes of women as manipulative, petty, distrustful of each other, and competing for men must be abolished, so women love themselves, trust each other, develop friendships, create sisterly love and alliances to fight all forms of prejudice, discrimination, domination, and abuse. The suppression of men's emotional and nurturing natures needs to stop so that they stop competing with each other, develop friendships, and overcome their fears of homosexuality.

The promotion of stereotypical feminine roles does not rest solely with any one organization. Maintaining a solid front, patriarchal institutions advocate women's place is in the home and keep the doors to decision making closed to all but a few token women. Feminists not only want to include women in all decision making, but they also work to transform the patriarchy so that love, and not power, is the highest value not only in the home, but also in the public world of education, media, business, and government.

The current curricula in elementary, high school, and university are male centered. Students do not learn the contributions of women in history and most areas of study. Feminists not only advocate the expansion of Women's Studies in colleges and universities, but they also urge its integration throughout all schools' curricula. In addition, they encourage the growth of multi-racial and multi-cultural studies.

Feminists want schools to teach students to be good citizens who improve their community as well as train them to be responsible, productive workers. Rejecting the current highest value of obedience, they encourage educators to teach respect, liberty, equality, justice, and love, as well as to model these to help students reach their full potential. The maximum class size needs to be 10 students for elementary grades and 15 for high schools.

Particular care must be taken with students whose parents have failed to care for them in loving ways. Until troubled students are healed, schools need special programs for them. Child abuse, family dysfunctions, early difficulties in school, and poverty are factors that predict teen pregnancy, school problems, drug use, and delinquency.[46] To create solutions for these problems, the educational system and social service agencies need more expertise and funding.

More doctors need to make healing, and not money, their top priority. Because adequate, affordable health care is a basic human right, it must be available to all people. After telling their patients the whole truth about their condition, doctors need to consult and make health care decisions with their patients, not with insurance companies.

In both its program content and advertising, the media needs to stop objectifying women and glorifying violence, and focus instead on programs that enrich the human spirit. The legal system needs to be transformed from an adversarial game to a system based on truth and justice. Criminals need to be rehabilitated rather than warehoused and executed.

Guns need to be severely regulated.

Businesses need to include women in all areas of employment and decision making. However, the changes feminists desire are more fundamental than just stopping sex and race discrimination, having women and minorities participate fully throughout the work place, and ending unfair, unequal pay.

Feminists want corporations to change their main goals from building their share of the market and making as much profit as possible to serving authentic human needs by creating safe, useful products, employing workers in meaningful jobs, and contributing to the common good. A just society would provide the necessities of life for all people and make it possible for companies to answer genuine human needs. Then businesses would develop a vision of making the world better, a vision that would motivate their employees to do their best work.[47]

The enormous gulf between the salaries of executives and other workers needs to be eliminated so that all receive equitable pay. Besides a fair minimum wage, there needs to be a just maximum wage and an ethical pay gap between the highest paid executive and the lowest paid worker.

Businesses need to provide humane working conditions that enhance rather than stunt employees' lives, such as providing flexible, reasonable hours and day care near the work place so that both female and male workers can take care of their personal and family needs. Corporations need to value child raising by promoting policies such as paid parental leave. Currently most Boards of Directors and stockholders rubber stamp their corporate executives' recommendations so that the public good is seldom considered. Employee ownership of businesses is an ideal that may help solve many problems in the marketplace.

One idea is for all employees, including executives, to share the menial jobs that no one wants to do, so that all people have meaningful work they can be proud of. For example, one week a year every employee could clean the building. The new responsibilities for cleaning women and janitors would be to train and supervise these weekly workers and do additional work that uses their talents.

Feminists want businesses to take care of their own self-interest but also improve the communities where they employ workers and sell products. Corporations, like all individuals, have a responsibility to care for their own needs and those of their city, state, nation, and world. These responsibilities include more than charitable contributions to worthwhile causes. They include ensuring quality public school education, cleaning the environment, and eliminating poverty.

Interrelated with the shortage of good opportunities for females outside the home is their lack of power. A few elite white men hold most decision-making positions and control almost all the power in patriarchal institutions. The women's movement does not plan to reverse this situation but to equalize it, so that women share the decision making and power. Feminists want to transform institutions by stopping the abuse of power and replacing it with the power of love.

Feminists are exploring ways to use other structures besides hierarchies and involve all people in governing their own family, work place, town, state, nation, and world. Equal, cooperative ways of relating need to dislodge the dominating, competitive style in both the public and private sphere. The power of love needs to supplant the love of power.

Currently our local, state, and national governments are not genuine democracy. Instead, elite groups of wealthy, powerful, white males make most of the important decisions. A truly democratic government is of the people because it is representative, by the people because it is participatory, and for the people because it serves the common good. Our legislatures need to have a fair proportion of minorities and an equal number of females and males. One possible change that would create equality and overcome the monopoly of male power in the U.S. Senate in six years is to mandate one female and one male U.S. Senator from each state.

To have fair ethical elections, negative campaigning needs to be stopped. All candidates need to be provided with free mailing privileges and the same amount of free newspaper, radio, and television advertising. Campaign financing must be changed. One possible reform is the public financing for all elective offices. Then elected officials will owe their allegiance to the American people, instead of affluent contributors. The influence of money needs to be curbed so that elected officials make decisions for the public good, and not for the benefit of wealthy campaign contributors and corporations.

When citizens believe their votes count, they will tell the government what they want done by voting in people who represent their views. Then the government will truly belong to the people. Being proud citizens, they will view paying taxes as a social responsibility to help the government provide needed services, assist the least fortunate, and stop discrimination, poverty, and injustice. Then the government's safety net will be a real support system that ensures all people give according to their ability and receive according to their needs.

Governments need to regulate businesses to ensure just wages, safe products, and an unpolluted environment, until corporations make the shift to serving the common good. All governments, corporations, and citizens have a responsibility to improve the world and protect the natural environment from ecological destruction. Rene Dubos says "think globally and act locally." Rosemary Ruether wisely revises this. "We need to think both locally and globally and act both locally and globally."[48]

In the 1950s, President Dwight Eisenhower warned that the military industrial complex strongly influences government decisions and expenditures. From 1950 to 1990, the United States increased its military spending from $13 billion to $300 billion.[49] In addition, the U.S. and international arms trade drastically escalated. To create a peaceful, loving world, these vast expenditures need to be transferred from destructive military weapons to answering genuine human needs.

The United Nations needs to be strengthened so that it is truly a world government that stops illegal aggression and disarms all nations. Just as Florida is to the United States, so also, in the future, the United States will be to the United Nations.

Feminists are ecologists who want to stop environmental destruction. Going beyond this, they encourage the deep respect for our natural world.

Almost all religions promote spirituality and teach moral values. However, religious leaders often use religion to control people, especially women. Feminists ask all religions to root out any sexist, dominating teachings and practices within their traditions so that they are true to their spiritual and moral values. In addition, some feminists, who have rejected traditional religions because of their sexism, are creating new spiritual and moral movements.

Being treated with respect for their human dignity helps women, men, and children to live up their fullest potential. Therefore, all forms of sexism, racism, homophobia, anti-Semitism, ageism, ableism, elitism, poverty, militarism, war, and violence must be stopped. Because these are interconnected, no one will be truly free until every form of prejudice, domination, and violence ceases.

The feminist goal is to eliminate women battering, child abuse, incest, rape, and all forms of hatred, domination, abuse, and war. Currently many people take out their anger at being mistreated by dominating those below them on the hierarchy of wealth and power. An alternative is using their anger to transform the patriarchal system so that no one is abused.

Some cynics depict revolutions as exchanging the old tyrants for new dictators. If this has been factual about some past revolutions, this will not be true of the women's revolution if it develops its six stages. The mistakes of other revolutions can be avoided if personal empowerment and sisterly love reach the women in positions of power and emancipate them from superiority complexes, elitism, and controllingness as well as free them to treat every person with respect, liberty, equality, justice, and love.

Women's liberation will not lead to a new form of tyranny if feminists reject the patriarchy's highest value of domination and are true to feminism's highest value of love for self and others. Not only must feminists work to abolish the external domination of the patriarchy, but they also need to get in touch with their loving inner core so that they can recognize their own internalized patriarchal ways of thinking and acting. Striving to transform themselves and their world, they must work to root the patriarchy out of themselves and society's institutions and then live the new vision of feminism promoting love.

American women have many feminist role models from the Native American Indian women until today. For example, Jane Addams and Dorothy Day both fought for women's suffrage. Day was arrested and jailed for protesting in front of the White House for women's right to vote. All their adult lives, both Addams and Day helped the poor and fought against poverty and for justice. Both supported the labor movement. Although Day said her vocation was "to love the destitute," she wanted "to change the social order, not just to minister to the slaves but to do away with slavery."[50]

Both Addams and Day were pacifists. Pledging to be a peacemaker, Day said love is not passive, "but a most active glowing force." In 1907 before Addams founded the Women's International League for Peace and Freedom, she wrote of "the latent fellowship" between people and a "new internationalism" which she called "cosmic patriotism." Peace is not just "an absence of war, but the unfolding of world-wide processes making for the nurture of human life."[51]

How effective has feminism been in transforming the sexist, racist, classist world into a world that nurtures loving individuals and creates communities of love? In promoting transformation, the women's movement has been most successful in producing awareness of the problems. It has been productive in developing methods to promote change and less fruitful in creating visions of the ideal future.

In 1837, Sarah Grimke pointed out that women did not receive equal pay for equal work. About the same time, women who worked in factories began complaining about the working conditions and sexual harassment, although sexual harassment was not given that name until the 1970's. For over 160 years, feminists have continued to promote awareness of these problems that have yet to be solved.[52]

In 1848, feminists began creating awareness of the need for women to have the right to vote. They continued to spread this awareness for 72 years as they developed the women's movement that achieved the passage of the women's suffrage amendment in 1920.

The current women's movement has produced widespread awareness of discrimination against women in all areas of their lives, including families, schools, media, medicine, law, economics, politics, and religion. Feminism has created some visions of the ideal future, such as the one that I attempted above, but not enough.

Feminists have tried a multitude of methods to produce social change in the last two centuries, including legislation, education, books, media, petitions, rallies, and marches. By becoming more empowered, they have transformed themselves, their families, and work places. Feminism has existed wherever women were moving forward.

Since the problems created by patriarchy are collective, females need individual efforts and collective solutions. Imagine the reaction if feminists called for a Day to Celebrate the Importance of Women's Work and Women's Equality. Picture all women refusing to do any work in the home or work place in order to celebrate. To achieve unity, all women's organizations would need to publicize this celebration and develop a fund for poor women who need financial help in order not to work. Visualize what would happen if the women's movement made one demand for women's equality that must be met or they would extend the celebration for one week. Envision all women refusing to work until the demand was met. Unity is the strongest power women have.

Imagine what would happen if women and their families refuse to make any donations of time or money until the Roman Catholic Church ordains women as priests. Foresee what would happen if women refuse to buy any products of one multi-national corporation that exploits women at home and abroad until it pays a fair, living wage and provides safe working conditions.

Do women have the power to have their demands met? Studies show women make or influence 70% to 85% of all purchasing decisions. Tom Peters lectures businesses about the women's market and criticizes them for not devising a strategy to cash in on it.[53] When will women recognize their own economic power?

Women alone cannot change the world. To reach its goals, the women's movement needs to form coalitions with other groups working against all forms of prejudice, discrimination, domination, violence, and war. Feminists must unite with female and male revolutionaries to build new communities of love where women and men share equally all psychological traits, social roles, political power, economic power, and spiritual values. For sustained struggle, Ruether says we must build "strong base communities of celebration and resistance" which are local groups that change our own and others' consciousness and form local, regional, national, and international networks to transform patriarchal power structures.[54]

Ending prejudice, domination, and violence is not just a task for future generations. It is our task in this time. All people, women and men, poor and rich, homosexuals and straights, people of color and whites, must move forward together, "hand in hand, not just a few at a time." Only when females and males are as equal as the wings of a bird will both soar to their greatest heights.[55]

CHAPTER NINE

FEMINISM IS A SPIRITUAL AND MORAL MOVEMENT

> Love is what we were born with. Fear is what we have learned here. The spiritual journey is the relinquishment--or unlearning--of fear and the acceptance of love back into our hearts. Love is ... our ultimate reality and our purpose on earth. To be consciously aware of it, to experience love in ourselves and others, is the meaning of life. ... We came here to co-create with God by extending love.
>
> Marianne Williamson
> *A Return to Love*

> The purpose of spiritual life is to recollect that our seemingly separate soul is not separate at all, but part of a Greater Spirit.... In that realization, that remembrance of its oneness with the Source of Life, the soul is mended--healed from its temporal sorrows as it remembers its true identity as wisdom, consciousness, and love.
>
> Joan Borysenko
> *Guilt Is the Teacher, Love Is the Lesson*

What Is Spirituality?

Most people agree that feminism is a political movement. Is it also a spiritual and moral movement? To answer this question, we need to understand what it means to be spiritual and moral. The meaning of spiritual experiences will be described first, although words are totally inadequate.

Spirituality is mystical awareness, cosmic consciousness, dynamic faith, and inspired philosophy of life. It is not just emotional, cognitive, or aesthetic awareness. Spirituality is holistic aliveness. It is feeling and knowing, appreciating and understanding, valuing and loving, all coming together to create a symphonic harmony of deep mystical awareness.

Cosmic consciousness struck Richard Bucke, a psychiatrist, in "one momentary lightning-flash of the Brahmic Splendor" that ever after brightened his life. This caused him to realize "the cosmos is not dead matter but a living Presence," the human soul is immortal, the universe is ordered so all things work together for the good of all, everyone's happiness is "in the long run absolutely certain," and love is "the foundation principle of the world."[56]

Spiritual experiences make it possible to strip away the visible facade of reality and see the hidden truth. Faith results when we go below the surface and experience an awe-inspiring cosmic consciousness of the divine within all people and nature. Spirituality is a mystical awareness of the divine within the human, the holy within the worldly, the infinite within the finite, and the sacred within all of life.

When we look into the depth of ourselves, other people, and creation, we see the divine shining through. The divine is within all of us as our inner core of love. Our faith beholds the luminous splendor of ineffable goodness and love that radiate out of our heart and the center of the cosmos.[57]

To be spiritual is to realize that love as the inner core of life causes the all-encompassing unity of people and nature. Our cosmic consciousness gives us a mystical awareness that we are not separate and that all people and creation are one with the divine. Our spiritual experiences help us see the ultimate oneness of all existence. The mystical awareness that divine love creates the harmonious interdependence of all people and the universe results in indescribable happiness, peace, and joy.

Radhakrishnan, a Hindu sage, claimed that the normal condition of humanity is a conscious separation of ourselves from the divine. When a sudden flame of supreme awareness results in a vision and intimately felt presence of union with the divine, our whole being is "ablaze with purpose."

Realizing our union with the sacred brings "a rapture beyond joy, a knowledge beyond reason, a sensation more intense than that of life itself, infinite in peace and harmony."[58]

Who Is God?

An explanation of spirituality would not be complete without discussing the meaning of divinity, because many describe spirituality as a relationship with God. The word God is a symbol for the Ultimate Reality. The Ultimate Reality is infinite, while words are finite. No finite ideas or images adequately describe the Infinite God. All images of God are analogies, metaphors, or symbols that are only partially true. Because they are finite descriptions of an Infinite God, they cannot be taken literally.

Over 700 years ago, Rumi, an Islamic mystic, used an elephant as a metaphor for God. In a shed where it was too dark to see, people had to feel the elephant to understand what it was like. Touching the elephant's trunk, one said it was like a water pipe. Feeling its side, another asserted it was like a wall. Grasping its leg, the last stated it was like a pillar. Like the people in the dark shed, our ideas about God depend on how we personally experience the divine and yet each contains truth.

The evolution of images of God throughout religious history is a complex topic. Vastly oversimplified, symbols of God include the female goddess, the male god, and images of the sun, moon, earth, animals, plants, and other objects. About 25,000 years ago, the Great Mother Goddess was worshiped in almost all cultures around the world. Later the Goddess, who was often symbolically represented by animals or nature, began to share her pre-eminence with her son and then her husband. Eventually, some religions taught one God whose images were primarily male.

Most Christian religious education fails to present accurately the period when the Goddess was the most important religious symbol throughout the world. Even today, Christians are taught that worshiping the Goddess is a sinful pagan tradition. In contrast, many feminists are rediscovering the worship of the Goddess as an authentic growth-producing way to express their spirituality.

Carol Christ, a feminist theologian, explains reasons why women need the Goddess. The Goddess affirms female power, the female body, female willpower, women's bonds and heritage. Starhawk says "the image of the Goddess inspires women to see ourselves as divine, our bodies as sacred, the changing phases of our lives as holy, our aggression as healthy, our anger as purifying, and our power to nurture and create, but also to limit and destroy when necessary, as the very force that sustains all life."[59]

Most Christians are taught a male image of God in the Trinity. God is the Father, the Son, and the Holy Spirit. Jesus taught his followers to pray to God as Our Father. A less emphasized Christian image is "God is love."

There are many variations of the image where God is described not as a person but as love or another principle. Besides calling God Father and Mother, Mary Baker Eddy, the founder of Christian Science, said God is "Life, Truth, and Love." As "All-in-all," God is "the divine Principle, Mind, Soul, Spirit."[60]

Gandhi believed that "God is love" but he stressed that "God is Truth above all." To find God as Truth, "the only inevitable means is love, that is, nonviolence." In searching for God, Gandhi worked to benefit all people. "I am endeavoring to see God through service of humanity, for I know that God is neither in heaven, nor down below, but in everyone."[61]

For many people, it is difficult to experience and describe God. A standard assignment for my students is to write their own idea of God. This sounds easy, but they find it a perplexing task. Try it yourself. The vast majority of Americans claim to believe in God. However, they have trouble describing God.

Two possibilities are that God exists or God does not exist. One hand, there is no God, no Ultimate Reality. Then people make their highest value into God. In this case, love is my God because love is my highest value.

If there is no God, then humanly created Gods can be rated as creative or destructive. Creative Gods promote life and love. Destructive Gods damage life and love. Examples of destructive Gods are Romans revering the Emperor as God, Europeans believing in the divine right of kings, Germans obeying Hitler as God, and Americans treating money as God.

Many people doubt that God exists. Often atheists justifiably deny God because the images of God presented to them are outmoded and sometimes even ridiculous. For example, the image of God as an old man with a long white beard sitting on a cloud is difficult for educated people to believe.

Despite the fact that I personally have been plagued at times by serious doubts, I believe that the hidden God actually exists and can be experienced. Let's use the air as a metaphor for God. Although we do not see the air, it still surrounds all of us and is within us giving us our life. God is the Invisible, Infinite Mystery. People are visible, finite mysteries. Finite humans help manifest the infinite mystery of God.

I think the most meaningful image describes God as Infinite Love. God is the depth of all existence and the ground of every person's innermost self. As Infinite Love, God is within every person and the universe as our loving inner core. God is within us and yet infinitely beyond us. More than being just part of every person and the universe, Divine Love is our inner core and deepest essence.

Other meaningful symbols include God as the Divine Spirit, Ultimate Reality, Divine Love, Sacred Oneness, the Creator, and Source of life. Our energy and life force help us survive and thrive. As Cosmic Energy and the Sacred Life Force, God is within us as our deepest energy and life force. God is the ultimate foundation of all creation.

Still other meaningful symbols are images that show God as loving. God is Friend, Lover, and Parent. God as Father is more adequately expressed as God as Mother and Father that Ann Lee, the founder of the Shakers, used in the

1700's and Mary Baker Eddy expressed in the 1800's. For all varieties of liberation theology, God is the compassionate Liberator who fights injustice.[62]

Carter Heyward, a feminist lesbian Episcopal priest, believes her vocation is "to live with God, in God, for God." Seeing the divine within all people, she says God is "battered as a wife, a child, a nigger, a faggot." Heyward is suspicious of anyone who claims to have found God, "if the person is not passionately committed to justice for *all* people--black, yellow, red, white; poor, rich; straight, gay; sophisticated, simple; well-educated, poorly educated; sick, healthy; male and female."[63]

God is as near to me as I am to myself, because God as Infinite Love is my inner core. Our inner core of love is the Divine Spirit, Cosmic Energy, and the Sacred Life Force within us. We are all bearers of Divine Love. When I love, I express God's nature. To become our fullest selves, we must transcend finite human love toward Infinite Divine Love.

God as Infinite Love is within us as our inner core of love. We as lovers are within God who is Infinite Love. We are all part of God. God is like the ocean of love. We as lovers are all the drops of love in that ocean.

As Infinite Love, God not only creates all of existence but also causes the unity of everything in the universe. Infinite Love that is God's inner being is the interconnecting life force and the binding cosmic energy that causes the interdependent web of communion of all people and the cosmos.

God is the dancer and creation is God's dance. Creation is God's exuberance.[64] The dancer and dance cannot be disconnected because they are inseparable. God is within creation, while creation is part of the Divine. The Sacred is within all things, while all things are within the Holy.

In 1854, Chief Seattle described Native American spirituality. "Every part of this earth is sacred to my people." Every shining pine needle, sandy shore, and humming insect is holy. The flowers are our sisters. The horse and deer are our brothers. We all belong to the same family. "The earth does not belong to us; we belong to the earth. All things are connected like the blood which unites one family. ... The earth is precious to God and to harm the earth is to heap contempt on its Creator."

Feminist theologians criticize and reject sexist images of God as dominating, controlling, punishing, jealous, and absolutely transcendent. They consider exclusively male images of God, such as God is Father and King, idolatrous and think these symbols legitimize male domination. After being critical, feminist theologians stress the importance of multiple non-sexist images of God, such as God is Spirit, Creator, Lover, Friend, Parent, and Liberator.[65]

How Does Spirituality Develop?
What Are the Paths to God?

Institutional religions teach various ways to become spiritual. Many of these paths to God contain important truths. However, numerous people develop their spirituality outside established religions.

An analogy for the many ways to become spiritual is a mountain with multiple paths to the top where God resides. Some trails that circle around are long and gradual, but less difficult. Other routes are shorter and steeper, but more demanding. Some people try to make it to the top in one gigantic leap. All paths lead to the top and God. There is no right way. All of us must choose the path that best suits who we are as unique individuals. Only I know the right way for me.

I think that the shortest, most direct path to God is love. Our spirituality develops when we have loving experiences with spirit-filled persons, newborn babies, breathtaking paintings, gorgeous sculptures, glorious music, creative thoughts, and deep mutual intimate conversations. Appreciating the exquisiteness of an orchid, the spectacular colors of the autumn trees, and the splendor of a starlit night puts us in touch with the magnificence of creation and its Creator.

Personally I have had many different kinds of spiritual experiences. Most often, I encounter God when I experience the spirit and beauty of people and nature. When I am in touch with a person's inner beauty and spirit, I discover God. When I appreciate a glistening lake overflowing with wildlife, the magnificence of animals' diverse colors and shapes, a majestic valley from a mountain top, and a brilliant sunset from a gorgeous beach, I feel the oneness of life and I experience God.

For some of us, it is easier to encounter the divine through loving nature than to meet God through loving other people and experiencing oneness with them. A possible reason for this is that people hurt and reject us more than nature, so we are less open and more defensive with others than we are with nature.

A way to become spiritual is to become conscious of love as our own inner core and then to experience the indwelling of God as Infinite Love in our own soul. Once we realize that love is our own inner core, we can recognize that other people have the same loving inner core. To get in touch with love as the inner core of all people is to have a mystical experience of God's presence within them. When we open ourselves to see people's loving nature, we find God. When I meet you, I encounter God within you. People and all of creation are dazzling outbursts of divine love.

Tibetan Buddhism teaches ways to enlightenment. To make a Buddhist meditation more familiar and comfortable, I revised it to include God. You can create your own version. Visualize and feel the radiant light in the sky above you as the presence of God, as "the embodiment of the truth, wisdom, and compassion of all the buddhas, saints, masters, and enlightened beings." Fill your heart and soul with the bright light of God's presence.[66]

Then focus on God's presence and pray that all your negative thoughts and destructive actions may be cleansed, all the harm you have done may be forgiven, and your life may benefit all beings. After praying, imagine the brilliant light of God's presence penetrating your heart and soul and purifying all your negative thoughts and actions. See and feel that you are entirely immersed in the sparkling light of God's presence.[67]

Now that you are healed by the gleaming light of God's presence streaming through you, completely merge with the shining light of God's presence so that you are inseparably part of the blissful presence of God. Remain in this Oneness with God for as long as possible.[68]

To help other people, visualize and feel the radiant light in the sky above their heads as the presence of God. Pray that all their suffering may be healed and they may experience ultimate happiness. Imagine the luminous light of God's presence penetrating their heart and soul and healing all their pain. See and feel them merging with the dazzling light of God's presence.

Love is the most direct way to become spiritual and experience God. Suffering is a more indirect and painful road to God. Like death, suffering is inevitable. Because we are finite, we all suffer and die. Suffering is a natural part of being human.

Tillich says suffering is "the door, the only door, to the depth," which is his name for God. Although he accurately claims suffering can lead to God, he inaccurately states suffering is the only door. Love is also a door. As Evelyn Underhill says, mystics see pain as the complement of love and they call love and suffering the wings on which the human spirit can best take flight towards the Absolute. The many ways of loving and suffering are paths to God.[69]

Underhill describes the mystic way as a single process of growth with five phases. The first phase is awakening our consciousness of the divine; second, purifying and disciplining ourselves; third, illumination and enlightenment; fourth, completely cleansing ourselves and surrendering our will; and fifth, union with God, the final goal of the mystic quest. These phases oscillate between suffering and love for God. The mystic way is a progressive growth in love. The end of love is the union of the lover and God.[70]

Love and suffering are interconnected. When we love, we are connected to our loved ones so that their joy touches us. Since we have no requirement that they be happy, their pain touches us. Our love causes us to feel their pain and suffer with them. Our love also creates suffering when we lose our beloved through death or divorce or alienation. The depth of our suffering can often awaken us to how much we love the beloved.[71]

Suffering is natural and unavoidable when it results from experiencing hurricanes, tornados, and earthquakes as well as from being physically ill and dying. Avoidable suffering is caused by prejudice, discrimination, domination, abuse, and violence. People suffer when they are emotionally damaged, socially rejected, spiritually deprived, and when their human dignity is violated. Women suffer when they are treated as sex objects or servants and when they are dominated, beaten, and raped. This kind of suffering is avoidable, because it is unnatural, unnecessary, and contrary to the ultimate good of either the abuser or the abused.

When prejudice, discrimination, domination, and abuse stop, the victims' external suffering ceases, but their internal suffering often continues. The abusers' internal conflicts may or may not end.

One possible response to suffering, whether avoidable or unavoidable, is destructive behavior. Our reaction to unavoidable suffering, such as hurricanes, and even more to avoidable suffering, such as abuse, can be bitterness that leads to destructive behavior toward ourselves or others. We sometimes reason that since life is so unfair to us, we will make others suffer along with us. The saying "misery loves company" has a corollary: misery creates company.

Many people try to control suffering by denying it, because they do not trust their own ability to deal with pain. In denying their sorrow, they often suppress their feelings of happiness. No one can prevent all suffering. To love is to be vulnerable and vulnerability often causes suffering.

Another possible response to suffering is constructive behavior. Whether our suffering is caused by ourselves or others, we can perceive the suffering as a challenge to show our courage in the face of pain and as an opportunity to grow in the face of our insecurity and helplessness.

Suffering and joy are interrelated. What makes us happy is the flip side of what makes us sad. What creates sorrow is the loss of what makes us joyful. Losing those we love creates deep suffering. When we are touched by beauty, we experience sorrow at its passing. Our joy is our sorrow unmasked. When we are sad, we weep for what brings us happiness and delight.[72]

What makes us sad tells us what is important to our happiness; it teaches us what we value; it puts into perspective what is really meaningful to us; it shows us our priorities; and it leads us to our inner core of love. Suffering from a tragedy, such as the death of a dear friend, helps us understand that love is the most important reality. Wealth, success, and power fade in importance when we face the death of a loved one.

Life is full of instances in which it appears that there is no meaning in suffering, especially unavoidable suffering, such as the death of a young child from cancer. For the dying, there may be no meaning in their suffering. For the survivors, suffering has many meanings. One meaning is to help us keep our priorities straight about what is truly important. Another meaning is to show us our fragileness and powerlessness. Yet another meaning is to challenge us to have courage to deal with our pain, helplessness, loneliness, insecurity, and death.

While it is true for some people, as Tillich claims, that "joy is deeper than suffering," other people's suffering may be excruciating and far greater than their joys. Gibran stresses that joy and suffering are inseparable, because "the deeper that sorrow carves into your being, the more joy you can contain."[73]

Although God granted Teresa of Avila spiritual favors for over 40 years, she did not have one day without pain, sickness, and tribulations. Although she admitted that it may not be true for all people, Teresa believed that we can find God through our small and severe suffering, illnesses, trials, and spiritual afflictions. "There is no remedy in this tempest but to wait for the mercy of God." Unexpectedly God calms the storm and fills life with "sunlight and much more consolation." The ordeals make our soul fly higher. All our sufferings are meant to increase our desire to enjoy God.[74]

Tibetan Buddhism offers a way of dealing with suffering that leads to compassion and enlightenment, which are paths to God. Fill your heart with compassion for the suffering of others. From the depths of your soul, pray to God and ask that your own suffering alleviates the pain of others and benefits their ultimate happiness. "Again and again dedicate your pain to the alleviation of their pain." Take on the fear, pain, and loneliness of others to free them from their afflictions. Imagine their suffering in the form of smoke. Watch it leave them and dissolve into your pain. Then breathe in all their suffering and breathe out total healing. Each time, believe deeply that they are now healed.[75]

Since a single right way to God does not exist, there are many different paths. Prayer, fasting, asceticism, detachment from life, involvement in life, work, play, learning, participating in religious rituals, singing hymns, listening to a preacher's sermon, good deeds, leading a moral life, helping others, fighting injustice, faith, and mysticism can all be ways to have spiritual experiences of God or barriers on the road. depending on whether they are done in a loving or unloving way.

Although the spiritual paths of great women and men in the past serve as examples, they are not models to be copied. Each of us has a different path to God, because we are all unique. Since there has never been anyone exactly like me in the world before, I am entirely new and called upon to fulfill my potential in my own way. I must recognize the way to God that touches my heart and then choose it with all my strength.

My own unique path that only I can follow is revealed only in myself and my world. If I do not behave according to my own rung on the ladder, but seize someone else's rung and abandon my own, I will fulfill neither. Only within myself will I find my way to God. My strongest values, actions, feelings, thoughts, and my loving nature reveal what is most precious to me. These stir my innermost being and tell me who I am, what I value, what I love, and what I am called to do.

My foremost task is to express my unique talents and my loving nature. My mission is not to repeat something that another person accomplished, not even the greatest human achievement. My task is not to turn away from people who attract my heart. My calling is to form nurturing relationships so that together we can express our spirit and love. What leads me to God is devoting my whole being to my creative work, experiencing fully my interconnections with nature, and loving passionately myself, other people, and God.

Spirituality Produces Ethical Actions

Spiritual experiences put us in touch with our inner core of love. This makes us want to express our love for ourselves, other people, and creation. Genuine spirituality creates love in all areas of life, in our passionate longing to learn, in our caring for humankind, and in our search for the meaning of life.

Love flows naturally out of our spiritual experiences. Cosmic consciousness produces acts of love. The immediate expression of mystical experiences is love. As Tillich says, "faith leads to action."[76]

What we consider divine affects our behavior. The deeper our commitment to the sacred, the stronger our course of action. The more fervent our ultimate concern, the more passionate our desire to work for it.[77]

Spirituality without any action flowing from it is unfinished. Authentic spirituality demands a response and is not complete without one. The genuineness of faith is gauged by what it produces in dedication and action. The Jewish scriptures teach people to love God by keeping the commandments. The Christian scriptures say "faith without works is dead" and "by their fruits you shall know them."[78] The separation of spirituality from action leads to the deterioration of spirituality and the degeneration of action.

Daniel Maguire sees action-oriented love as part of the moral core of Judaism and Christianity. "Love is an energy that must be incarnated in action." Good intentions that are not lived out are no substitute for action. "Love begets love ... Love is a unitive force, a fusion of vitalities." By melting barriers, love unites without any loss of individuality. "True love accentuates our differences as it bonds us into a fruitful union and is a boon to both lover and beloved."[79]

For AA members, it is not enough to have a spiritual experience. The twelfth step teaches that a spiritual awakening leads to action. Their action is both to practice the AA principles in all areas of life and to carry the AA message to other alcoholics by helping them become sober.

Authentic spirituality produces as a minimum, moral actions, and as a maximum, a lifelong vocation of love. What do the interchangeable words morality and ethics mean? To refer to morality as a set of principles or a doctrine of laws governing human behavior is to lessen its full meaning. To call ethics a code of right and wrong or a standard of good and bad behavior minimalizes it.

Genuine morality is a way of life that promotes love toward myself, other people, and nature. To be ethical is to create more love, life, and full functioning in my every day life.

Decisions can be made arbitrarily or thoughtfully, using a guiding norm or without one. Choices can be made freely or coercively. Some reasons used to make choices are to avoid punishment, receive rewards, gain power, please loved ones, to express the innermost self, and to be ethical. What is a moral decision? Sometimes an ethical choice is a decision between alternatives that are either good or bad, that either promote or harm life. Other times an ethical choice is a decision between different values that are both morally good but are in conflict.

To decide the morality of actions, careers, business practices, political organizations, leisure activities, books, films, television, and even religions, the ultimate criterion is whether they create or harm love. To be moral and to do good is to be loving toward the self, other people, and nature.

Ethical behavior is loving acts that affirm, preserve, foster, and create more love in the present and future. Moral people are co-creators with God.

Ethical people believe that the means and ends are distinguishable, but definitely interconnected. The ends do not justify the means. The methods must be consistent with the goals. The process is part of the end result. To be moral, a person who supports peace must use peaceful means. A feminist who believes in equality for all must treat everyone equally. An individual who preaches love must be loving.

To be immoral is not to be loving. To be unethical is to harm my self, other people, and nature. Whatever denies, diminishes, distorts, injures, or destroys love and life is immoral.[80] To allow myself to be victimized or to dominate others is unethical because both behaviors damage love and life. Evil acts are more harmful, more injurious, and more unloving than wrong ones. Evil acts are hateful, destructive, and violent.

It is unethical to treat women as sex objects, to use people as means to an end, and to manipulate them to serve my own needs. Things can be used. When we use people as things, we abuse their human dignity. We also harm both of us, because we damage the inner core of love within us.

To be immoral is to act contrary to my human nature, my loving inner core. When I act against the love within my inner core, I violate myself. By injuring my loving inner core, my unethical acts distort, contradict, and damage my loving nature.

At the very least, a negative statement of the criterion for ethical behavior is not to hurt or destroy myself, others, and nature. At the very most, a positive statement of the criterion for moral acts is to love myself. other people, and nature. The most moral actions are the most accepting, responding, understanding, and giving acts. They are the most expressive of our loving nature and the best promoters of life and love.

The source of our moral consciousness is our inner

core of love.   Our loving inner core produces our moral obligation to be loving toward ourselves, others, and nature. Since spirituality is the mystical awareness of our loving inner core, it creates a deeper moral consciousness.

The law of love is universal, because it is our own essential nature expressed as law. The only valid law is the law of love. The moral law, the law of life, the natural law, the universal law, and the divine law are all the same. They are all the law of love. To live out the law of love is to fulfill our human nature.

Love provides the foundation and basis for all moral laws. Particular moral laws are valid only when they promote love. For example, Jesus' two great commandments are valid because they are restatements of the law of love.

Tillich calls love "the absolute moral principle." Even though "love is above law," Jesus expressed love as law when he stressed "love one another." As the ultimate ethical norm, "love is unconditional. There is nothing which could condition it by a higher principle. There is nothing above love." Yet love is concrete and can adapt itself in the changing world. "Love alone can transform itself according to the concrete demands of every individual and social situation without losing its eternity and dignity and unconditional validity."[81]

Albert Schweitzer, a scholar who became a medical missionary in Africa, claims reverence for life is "the beginning and foundation of morality." Reverence for life is "the supreme law" and "the underlying principle of all ethics." Is the universal ethic of reverence for life connected to the moral law of love? "Reverence for life is the ethic of love widened into universality." Love for God, love for humans, and "love for all creatures, reverence for all being, compassion with all life" are all interconnected.[82]

For Schweitzer, revering life means removing alienation and suffering, affirming and promoting life, and restoring empathy and compassion. When we have reverence for life, we injure and destroy life only when it cannot be avoided and never from thoughtlessness. We take responsibility for all life and devote ourselves to helping it.[83]

The moral law of love demands that we express who we are and thus we give our love toward ourselves and others. The moral law of love demands that the loving inner core within all people, including ourselves, be respected. To respect the loving inner core means to treat every individual as a person who is a lover, and not as a thing to be manipulated, controlled, exploited, or destroyed by whim or calculation. To treat ourselves and all people with respect is the first step in being loving. To respect and accept individuals as they are gives concreteness to the moral law of love.

People can never be used as means to an end, because their inborn nature is love. Even if there is no evidence of their loving inner core, humans must be treated as persons who deserve respect. No one has the right to deprive people of their claim to personhood and their inherent ability to be loving. Even those whom we consider opponents must be treated with respect.

A Vocation of Love Is the Maximum Action of Spirituality

While genuine spirituality produces ethical actions as a minimum, it naturally leads people to the maximum so that they make their life a vocation of love that nurtures loving people and creates communities of love. Spiritual individuals' ultimate mission is to help themselves and others, to make the world a more loving place, and to love God.

Spiritual people are called to work for a cause outside themselves. Some choose their mission joyfully, while others see it as a duty they must do. All are concerned with the good of their group and more inclusively with the good of humanity. Through a vocation that is precious to them, they devote themselves to the cause of serving humanity by spreading love in the lives of themselves and others as well as in the world locally, nationally, and internationally. Thinking locally and globally, they act locally and globally.

Authentic spirituality teaches us that love for ourselves, other people, nature, the universe, and God is our goal in life.

Our vocation is to love. We must respect and love other people and the earth as we respect and love ourselves, because we are all part of the divine oneness. Our mission is to care for all forms of life, the land, sea, animals, vegetation, air, water, and human beings as well as to take responsibility to stop injustices and end unnecessary suffering wherever it exists.

Our calling is not to remain ignorant about existing injustices or to stand by and do nothing. Our mission is to bear witness against the atrocities and to take nonviolent action to prevent and eliminate them. As Martin Luther King says, the ultimate measure of people is not where they stand in moments of comfort, but where they stand at times of challenge and controversy. Ethical people risk their position, prestige, and even their life for others. On their spiritual path, they lift their bruised and beaten sisters and brothers to a better life.[84]

The ultimate spiritual vocation is to love God by taking suffering and injustice out of life and spreading love personally, locally, nationally, and internationally. Our spiritual mission is to help individuals become more loving, to create communities of love, and to unite lovingly with God.

Living our vocation of love by working for a just cause larger than ourselves makes us happy. Even when progress is slow and defeats come more often than victories, our creative work makes us feel worthwhile and alive. As Gandhi says, "joy comes in the struggle, not in the victory."[85] Dedicating ourselves to a serious cause gives meaning to our lives. When we work with others on a valuable cause, we see their inner goodness, spirit, and love, we feel close to them, and we build beautiful long lasting friendships.

Spiritual experiences teach us that God as Unconditional Love is within us. We are the bearers of Unconditional Love.[86] Unconditional love for myself means I love myself not because of what I do or because I am good. I love myself because I am. We love the birds whether or not they can fly. That is unconditional love. We love horses whether or not they can run. We love the ocean whether it is calm or wild.

We love our dogs and cats whether they are ill or healthy. We do not love them because they love us or because of what they do. We love all the animals and nature simply because they are.

Most parents love their newborn babies unconditionally because they are. Later, because unconditional love is difficult to sustain, many parents change and love their children conditionally because of what they do and whether they are good.

Elizabeth Kubler-Ross teaches that unconditional love for everyone, everywhere, is "the only thing that matters in life." Sadly, we offer children conditional love. We squeeze them into a mold constructed by us. We will only love them if they clean their rooms. If this, if that. In Kubler-Ross' ideal world, unconditional love exists without demands.[32]

Our spirituality enables us to make unconditional love the vocation of our life and thus to become moral activists who teach and live fully unconditional love for ourselves, all people, and nature. This vocation helps us work to transform our world by expressing respect, liberty, equality, justice, and love for all people. Pat Schroeder, a former Congresswoman, asks those who are prejudiced against women, minorities, homosexuals, and the poor, what part of the word "all" they do not understand.

When our spirituality results in unconditional love, we reach our ultimate goal in life. We express all our unconditional love for ourselves, other people, and nature and we create communities of love. Through our love, we are united with God who is Infinite Love.

Feminism Is a Spiritual and Moral Movement

Does feminism have the qualities that make it a spiritual and moral movement? Yes. People who penetrate into the depth of feminism discover love as its spiritual and moral meaning. Feminism is a spiritual vision of love transforming all people and the world. Feminism is the moral acts of love that work to eliminate all forms of prejudice, discrimination, and abuse. It is acts of love that express respect, liberty, equality, justice, and love for all people. Feminism is acts of love that nurture loving individuals and create communities of love.

Mary Daly says women's liberation is a spiritual struggle "because the conflict is on the level of being versus nonbeing." Affirming women is spiritual because it confronts the patriarchal heritage that denies females' humanity. "The women's liberation movement is a spiritual movement because it aims at the humanization of women and therefore of the species, ... because it means the self-actualization of creative human potential in the struggle against oppression."[88]

Daly says patriarchal religion stunts personal realization and genuine community by reducing people to rigidly defined sex roles. The feminist challenge is "a sign of hope for the emergence of more genuine religious consciousness." The becoming of women may be both "the doorway to deliverance" from God as the omnipotent Father and a doorway to a more genuine search for transcendence and divinity. Daly's sisterhood is both revolutionary and revelatory. "It is at war with the idols of patriarchal religion, but it is in harmony with what is authentic in the ideals of the religious traditions."[89]

Sheila Collins says the work of women's liberation is an experience of the holy. Feminists are giving birth to ourselves and to a new order that will focus on life, not death. "Giving birth is a painful labor, but it is made easier if shared in a community. It can even be an ecstatic experience, an experience of the holy."[90]

Carol Christ contends that women's spiritual quest is the foundation for their social quest for equality. Christ defines females' social quest as "women's struggle to gain respect, equality, and freedom in society--in work, in politics, and in relationships with women, men, and children." Their spiritual quest is "a woman's awakening to the depths of her soul." This spiritual quest includes listening to her own experience as she asks and answers such basic questions as "who am I? why am I here? what is my place in the universe?" Her spiritual quest supports her quest for equality.

"Women's spiritual quest undergirds every moment of women's social quest."[36]

Feminism is the spiritual realization of love as the inner
core of life and the moral actions that flow from that realization. Every creative act of the women's movement strives to
make love the essence of our personal and communal life.
Feminism is spiritual because it is the awareness of love as
the inexhaustible depth of life. It is moral because it strives
to express the world-transforming goals of respect, liberty,
equality, justice, and love for all women and men. Thus,
feminism tries to nurture loving individuals and create communities of love.

Many people recognize the validity and the sacred
dimension of the feminist goals, because feminism is a
spiritual vision of love. There is a great deal of controversy
about the means that women's liberation uses to reach its
ends. However, the six stages that feminism uses to achieve
its vision promote love.

All six stages of personal empowerment help us get in
touch with our loving nature and thus find freedom and love
within ourselves. Sisterly love, the fifth stage, teaches us to
love our sisters and brothers as well as ourselves. After
helping us to develop all the love within ourselves, feminism
through the power of love in its sixth stage works to transform
the present patriarchal society into a loving world. The newly
formed communities of love will have respect, liberty, equality,
justice, and love as their guiding principles.

Just as subordination comes in multiple varieties, so
also liberation grows in many ways. However, as Rosemary
Ruether states, "the domination of women is the most
fundamental form of domination in society, and all other forms
of domination, whether of race, class, or ethnic group, draw
upon the fantasies of sexual domination."[37] That is not to say
that women experience the worst kinds of dehumanization
and oppression.

There is no hierarchy of different kinds of oppression.
Thus, it is not appropriate to say that the fundamental
domination of women throughout history is the worst expres-

sion of physical, psychological, social, and spiritual suffering. Nevertheless, it is the starting point and model for all patterns of human prejudice, domination, exploitation, abuse, and violence, because the training for these forms of oppression begins in the home when the husbands assume power over their wives and parents over their children.

Since the type of domination shapes the kind of liberation, Ruether is accurate when she declares that "the liberation of women is the most profound of all liberation movements, the most far-reaching revolution, because it gets to the roots of the impulse of domination." Many feminists call the women's movement "the most important revolution in history."[93]

Calling feminism "transformational politics," Bell Hooks says "embedded in the commitment to feminist revolution is the challenge to love. Love can be and is an important source of empowerment" as we confront sexism, racism, and classism. Hooks calls love "a powerful force that challenges and resists domination." In agreement with Paulo Freire, she sees revolution not only as creative and liberating but also as "an act of love." We need to "work to be loving, to create a culture that celebrates life, that makes love possible."[94]

Char McGee calls feminism a vision of love and believes that it will unfold women's deepest spiritual potential. Women are reconceptualizing the meaning and power of love. "More and more women are coming to recognize feminism as a powerful awakening force which opens the mind and heart, a moral force whose message is love of life, love of self and others, love of all forms of life and the earth." Feminism is revisioning "love as a powerful force which knows the integrity and the interrelatedness of all life forms, and which seeks to manifest this knowing by creating those conditions which best promote the economic, social, political, and spiritual well-being of all womankind, and the abundant welfare of all creation."[95]

Feminism is the most profound revolution not only because it goes to the core of subjugation but also because it questions, challenges, and demands the re-ordering of the meaning and activity of every person and every institution in existence. The women's movement is the vision and practice of love for all people, nature, the universe, and God. Feminism is a spiritual vision of love and the moral actions that flow from that vision. This transforming movement strives to promote love in all areas of life. It is more than a political movement. Because it is love in action, feminism is a spiritual and moral movement.

Act only out of love,

for that is

what you are.

NOTES

Introduction

1. Carol Christ, *Diving Deep and Surfacing* (Boston: Beacon: 1980), pp. 13-14, 23-26 and Mary Daly, *Beyond God the Father* (Boston: Beacon, 1973), pp. 8-9, 33, 37, 100, 167.

2. Kahlil Gibran, *The Prophet* (New York: Alfred Knopf, 1973), p. 28 and Marianne Williamson, *Illuminata* (New York: Random House, 1994), pp. 187-198.

3. Audre Lorde, *Sister Outsider* (Freedom, CA: Crossing Press, 1984), p. 57.

4. Lorde, *Sister Outsider*, pp. 53, 57. Carter Heyward says "love has been romanticized so poorly, trivialized so thoroughly, and perverted--turned completely around--from what it is, we find ourselves having to begin again to re-experience, re-consider, re-conceptualize" it. Carter Heyward, "Sexuality, Love, and Justice," in *Weaving the Visions*, edited by Judith Plaskow and Carol Christ (San Francisco: Harper and Row, 1989), p. 294. Thomas Moore underscores the breadth and importance of love when he says we need to "bring more soulfulness" into all our relationships. "In every gathering of people, from business to politics," friendship and community are more important and valuable than organization, productivity, and functional purposes. Thomas Moore, *Soul Mates* (New York: Harper Collins, 1994), pp. xii, 45, 74, 79, 91, 135, 157.

5. Camille Paglia, *Sexual Personae* (New York: Vintage, 1991), p. 2.

6. Shulamith Firestone, *The Dialectic of Sex* (New York: William Morrow, 1970), pp. 144-145.

7. Lorde, *Sister Outsider*, p. 111. Firestone says that love is not inherently destructive. Firestone, *Dialectic of Sex*, pp. 144-145. Ti-Grace Atkinson disagrees when she says that for women to be oppressed, they must internalize coercion and, in order to do this, they must exist in love, which she calls "a special psycho-pathological state of fantasy" in themselves and in their relationships with men. For Atkinson, love is "the psychological pivot in the persecu-

tion of women." Many values and institutions are the vehicles of women's oppression, including "marriage, family, sexual intercourse, love, religion, prostitution." Ti-Grace Atkinson, *Amazon Odyssey* (New York: Links Books, 1974), pp. 41-44. French contends that love in the patriarchy has often been forced to function as an oppression. In a feminist world, "love too would regain its innocence, since it would not be coerced into playing a role within a power structure and thus function-ing as an oppression--as it often does in the world." French, *Beyond Power*, p. 445. Rene Denfeld calls herself a feminist, but inaccurately portrays and then attacks many feminists' beliefs. Denfeld incorrectly claims "feminism has lost sight of something precious in many women's lives: love." Inaccurate-ly she writes "according to many feminists, this love is implausible, impossible--a lie. Yet ... it will continue to exist, no matter how much feminists condemn it." Denfeld, *The New Victorians: A Young Woman's Challenge to the Old Feminist Order* (New York: Warner, 1995), p. 57.

8. Carol Gilligan, *In a Different Voice* (Cambridge, MA: Harvard University Press, 1982); Nel Noddings, *Caring: A Feminine Approach to Ethics & Moral Education* (Berkeley, CA: University of CA Press, 1986); Eva Kittay and Diana Meyers, editors, *Women and Moral Theory* (Savage, MD: Rowman & Littlefield, 1987); and Julia Wood, *Who Cares? Women, Care, and Culture* (Carbondale, IL: Southern Illinois University Press, 1994). Ruth Sidel advocates a new vision, a new American Dream, a more caring society. "We must develop a vision that recognizes that caring is as important as doing, that caring is doing, and that caregivers, both paid and unpaid, are the foundation of a humane society and must be treasured and honored." Ruth Sidel, *On Her Own: Growing Up in the Shadow of the American Dream* (New York: Penguin, 1990), pp. 241-242.

9. I have found only a few feminists who refer in any way to feminism as the vision and practice of love. Char McKee connects feminism and love in "Feminism: A Vision of Love" in *The Goddess Awakening*, compiled by Shirley Nicholson (Wheaton, IL: Theosophical Publishing, 1992), pp.

249-267. A number of feminists connect feminism and friendship which I believe is a kind of love. Mary Hunt, a feminist theologian, broadens the meaning of friendship and calls it "the foundational relational experience." Friendship is not just a personal relationship but it is also "a political activity." Mary Hunt, *Fierce Tenderness, A Feminist Theology of Friendship* (New York: Crossroad, 1991), pp. 8-10. Janice Raymond, a feminist philosopher, says "female friendship is much more than the private face of feminist politics. Although politics and friendship cannot always go together, we need to create a feminist politics based on friendship." Janice Raymond, *A Passion for Friends: Toward a Philosophy of Female Affection* (Boston: Beacon, 1986), pp. 8-9, 23, 141-145. Letty Pogrebin does not connect feminism and friendship, except to say that there are "feminist friendships" as well as feminine and female friendships. Letty Pogrebin, *Among Friends* (New York: McGraw-Hill, 1987), pp. 285-310. Since I agree with Pogrebin that friendship is a deep, intense kind of love, I disagree with Hunt and Raymond and stress that feminism is a vision of love and not friendship. One reason is that, as a human being and as a feminist, I can love all people with a universal love, but everyone cannot be my friend, because my friend is my soul mate who understands my deepest self and shares with me in a special, fervent kind of love.

10. Marilyn French, *Beyond Power* (New York: Summit Books, 1985); Riane Eisler, *The Chalice and the Blade* (San Francisco: Harper & Row, 1988); Naomi Wolf, *Fire with Fire* (New York: Random House, 1993); Fritjof Capra, *The Turning Point* (New York: Bantam, 1983); and Marilyn Ferguson, *The Aquarian Conspiracy* (Los Angeles: J.P. Tarcher, 1980) stress cultural transformation. Williamson's *Illuminata* claims "there is a spiritual renaissance sweeping the world" and we work for a "global shift" and wage "a revolution based on love." Gloria Steinem, *Revolution From Within* (Boston: Little, Brown, 1992) writes about the need to change ourselves. The feminist slogan, "the personal is political," makes the connection between our personal lives and the politics and power relationships

between the sexes. It points to the need to transform both ourselves and our culture.

Chapter 1 - Love is Our Inner Core

1. Stephen, Covey, *The Seven Habits of Highly Effective People* (New York: Simon and Schuster, 1989), pp. 96-101.

2. Claudia Black, *It Will Never Happen To Me!* (Denver: MCA, 1982), pp. 31-54.

3. Betty Eadie, *Embraced by the Light* (Placerville, CA: Goldleaf Press, 1992), pp. 40, 60, 146-147. Carol Christ, a feminist theologian, began to understand at the time of her mother's death that "love is everywhere. ... love does not ever abandon us." Her mother "was surrounded by a great matrix of love. ... I too am surrounded by love and always have been." After going through despair, Carol realized that "my life would be filled with amazing grace, love abounding and overflowing." Carol Christ, *Odyssey with the Goddess* (New York: Continuum, 1995), pp. 23, 121, 157-164.

4. Professor Bernard Marthaler used this gambit in his teaching.

5. Leo Buscaglia, *Love* (New York: Fawcett Crest, 1972), pp. 77-78; Abraham Maslow, *Farther Reaches of Human Nature* (New York: Viking Press, 1971), pp. 379-384; and Joan Borysenko, *Guilt Is the Teacher, Love Is the Lesson* (New York: Warner Books, 1990), p. 52.

6. In later chapters, I expand on my belief that love is our inner core. Our two most basic needs and drives are within this inner core of love. One drive within love moves toward safety, self-actualization, self-love, self-identity, independence, and solitude. The other drive within love proceeds toward growth, communion with others, love for others, self-change, interdependence, and intimacy. Although the following authors do *not* acknowledge that every human is a lover and the two needs are within the person's inner core of love, they describe two needs within every individual. Abraham Maslow, *Toward a Psychology of Being* (New York:

D. Van Nostrand, 1968), calls the two needs safety and growth. Thomas Moore in *Soul Mates* refers to them as attachment and flight from attachment. Harriet Lerner, *The Dance of Intimacy* (New York: Harper and Row, 1989), names them intimacy and separateness. Stephanie Dowrick labels them in the title of her book, *Intimacy and Solitude* (New York: W.W. Norton, 1991).

7. Doug Bonar, a psychotherapist, uses the metaphor of roots and wings. Catherine Keller accurately contends "we need not be misled by pairs of false alternatives like 'self' versus 'relation'." Unfortunately, she then advocates choosing what she calls the "soluble self" or the "connective" self instead of the "separative self." Keller fails to see that we need both roots and wings, both to be separate from others and at the same time to be connected to them. Catherine Keller, *From a Broken Web: Separation, Sexism, and Self* (Boston: Beacon, 1988), pp. 1-6, 202-215.

8. Like all of us, Carol Christ, a feminist theologian, felt very much alone before her spiritual awakening. After she reached her spiritual realization that we are all surrounded by love and always have been, she correctly concludes "I know that I am not alone and never have been." Christ, *Odyssey with the Goddess*, pp. 157-158. Williamson's *Illuminata* claims that "to the extent to which we think we are alone, we shall have limited power to materialize light," to align our mind with the will of God and to become "the vessel of the world's illumination." Mary Hunt, another feminist theologian, says "as communally oriented as people may be, each person is radically alone." Mary Hunt, *Fierce Tenderness, A Feminist Theology of Friendship* (New York: Crossroad, 1991), p.131.

9. Paul Tillich, *Systematic Theology*, Vol. I (Chicago: University of Chicago, 1951), pp. 195-201.

10. Letty Pogrebin, *Growing Up Free* (New York: Bantam, 1980), pp. 9, 40.

11. Thomas Harris claims there are "four possible life positions held with respect to oneself and others: (1) I'm Not OK-You're OK, (2) I'm Not OK-You're Not OK, (3) I'm OK-You're Not OK, (4) I'm OK-You're OK." Thomas Harris, *I'm*

OK-You're OK (New York: Avon, 1973), pp. 66-77.

12. Maslow, *Toward a Psychology of Being*, pp. 24-39 and Daniel Maguire, *The Moral Choice* (Garden City, New York: Doubleday, 1978), p. 196.

13. Carl Rogers, *On Becoming a Person* (Boston: Houghton Mifflin, 1961), pp. 89-91, 194; Carl Rogers, *Person to Person* (Lafayette, CA: Real People Press, 1967), p. 47; and Carl Rogers, *A Way of Being* (Boston: Houghton Mifflin, 1980), pp. 89-91, 118-120.

14. Benjamin Spock, *Decent and Indecent* (New York: Fawcett World Library, 1971), p. 98. My sister Jane first introduced me to Marianne Williamson's *Illuminata*. Then I read her *A Return to Love*. Although Williamson does not call love our inner core, she says "what we are is love" and "love is what we are born with." Marianne Williamson, *A Return to Love* (New York: Harper, 1994), pp. xx, 31.

15. Lorde, *Sister Outsider*, pp. 53-56.

16. John Gray, *Men Are From Mars, Women Are From Venus* (New York: Harper Collins, 1992), pp. 16-19.

17. William Ouchi contends Japan is "a successful industrial society in which intimacy occurs in the place of work as well as in other settings." William Ouchi, *Theory Z: How American Business Can Meet the Japanese Challenge* (New York: Avon, 1982), pp. 5-9, 44-55. Jane Condon agrees with Ouch on the high value the Japanese people place on harmony and working together. However, Condon spells out the low status of women in the Japanese home and work place that limits intimacy. Jane Condon, *Half a Step Behind: Japanese Women Today* (Tokyo: Tuttle, 1992), pp. 5-18. Williamson's *Illuminata* claims "our primary work ... is to love and forgive. ... Love is the most powerful fuel in any endeavor. ... my only work is to love." Work is "a vehicle for your love." Julia Woods accurately contends there is a "care crisis" in the U.S. because care has been historically assigned to women and devalued as an activity. As a remedy, she proposes that care be broadly supported throughout public life as a cultural value for all and not relegated to women's role. Care must be redefined as "a centrally important and integral part of our

collective public life." To make care an important priority will require changes in government, business, education, individual, and community actions. Unfortunately, Woods' concern is care and not love, and she neglects to recognize care as one of the qualities of love. In addition, she separates care from work and does not see the importance of making love and caring central to all forms of work. Julia Woods, *Who Cares? Women, Care, and Culture* (Carbondale, IL: Southern Illinois University, 1994), pp. 131-169.

18. Alfred Adler, "Individual Psychology, Its Assumptions and Its Results," *Varieties of Personality Theory*, edited by Hendrik Ruitenbeck (New York: Dutton, 1964), pp. 67-77. Camille Paglia's agreement with views like Adler's has already been explained. Paglia, *Sexual Personae*, p. 2. Naomi Wolf claims "all healthy little girls begin with a will to power that is at least as strong ... as their desire for intimacy." Women of all backgrounds have "fantasies of being rulers, queens, empresses; memories of harboring grudges and wishes for retaliation that had elements of cruelty and domination; scenarios in which the girl was lauded on the front pages, ... put her enemies in torture chambers, ruled her colonies, fought alligators, and was knighted by the queen." Wolf, *Fire with Fire*, pp. 262-264.

19. William Grier and Price Cobbs, *Black Rage* (New York: Bantam, 1968), pp. 162-176. Eleanor Johnson claims black women bear the brunt of sexism and racism. Society teaches them "the oppressive process of internalizing racism and sexism, i.e., self-hatred." Eleanor Johnson in *Home Girls: A Black Feminist Anthology* (New York: Kitchen Table, 1983), pp. 320-322.

20. Grier and Cobbs, *Black Rage*, pp. 162-176.

21. Erich Fromm, *The Love of Life* (New York: Free Press, 1986), p. 17 and Pierre Teilhard de Chardin, *Phenomenon of Man* (New York: Harper and Row, 1961), pp. 164-165.

22. Carter Heyward makes a tentative statement, while I am emphatic that we are innately lovers. "If there is one fundamental category that can be appropriately descriptive,

even definitive, of who we are--of what we are here to do in the world--it is that of lover." Heyward, *Weaving the Visions*, p. 293.

23. Gloria Steinem, *Revolution from Within*, pp. 157-160 and Shirley MacLaine, *Dancing in the Light* (New York: Bantam, 1985), pp. 335-345.

24. Shirley MacLaine, *Dancing in the Light*, pp. 335-345.

25. MacLaine, *Dancing in the Light*, pp. 335-345, 348, 387, 396-397 and Shirley MacLaine, *Out on a Limb* (New York: Bantam, 1983) pp. 202, 204.

26. Arleen Lorrance, *Why Me?* (New York: Rawson, 1977), pp. 4-7, 58-61, 73-81, 90, 103-109, 112, 166-168, 173-176, 187.

Chapter 2 - The Essence of Love

1. 1 Cor. 13:4-5.

2. Marie Marciniak, a student of mine at Rutgers University.

3. Plato, *Dialogues of Plato*, ed. by Justin Kaplan (New York: Washington Square Press, 1950), pp. 190-192.

4. Without acknowledging the existence of the inner core of love within every human or the two drives within love, some authors write about the two needs within every person. Harriet Lerner, *Dance of Intimacy*, pp. 2-5; Thomas Moore, *Soul Mates*, pp. 4-11; and Stephanie Dowrick, *Intimacy and Solitude*, pp. 301-303.

5. Paul Tillich, *Love, Power, and Justice* (New York: Oxford University Press, 1960), p. 25. After claiming no one has presented a satisfactory definition of love, Mary Hunt, a feminist theologian, stresses unity in her working definition. "For women friends love is an orientation toward the world as if my friend and I were more united than separated, more at one among the many than separate and alone. Love is the intention to recognize this drive toward unity and to make it increasingly so over time. Love is the commitment to deepen in unity without losing the uniqueness of the individuals at

hand." Hunt, *Fierce Tenderness*, p. 100. Judith Plaskow and Carol Christ introduce some authors in their anthology who write about the "self in relation." Their concept must be scrutinized to see if they stress relation over independence. "The self is essentially relational, inseparable from the limiting and enriching contexts of body, feeling, relationship, community, history, and the web of life." Criticizing the traditional Western view of self as an isolated ego and as "essentially rational, disembodied, and solitary," they describe the "relational self" as "essentially embodied, passionate, relational, and communal." Beverly Harrison, a moral theologian, stresses the primacy and centrality of relationship. "Relationality is at the heart of all things." Judith Plaskow and Carol Christ, eds., *Weaving the Visions: New Patterns in Feminist Spirituality* (San Francisco: Harper and Row, 1989), pp. 173-174, 221-222.

6. Viktor Frankl, *Man's Search For Meaning* (New York: Washington Square, 1967), pp. 176-177.

7. Martin Buber, *I and Thou* (New York: Charles Scribner's Sons, 1958), p. 11.

8. Pierre Teilhard de Chardin, *The Future of Man* (New York: Harper and Row, 1964), pp. 54-55 and Chardin, *Phenomenon of Man*, pp. 264-265.

9. Harriet Lerner, a therapist, stresses the importance of being our self and being self-focused. "Being a self" means we are who we are in relationships rather than what other people expect, wish, and need us to be. We do not sacrifice our self for the relationship and we do not bolster our self at the expense of the other person. Lerner, *The Dance of Intimacy*, pp. 21-23, 201-224. Janice Raymond says it is important to be a friend to our self. Janice Raymond, *A Passion for Friends*, pp. 5-8, 222.

10. Tillich, *Systematic Theology*, Vol. I, p. 177. Mary Hunt claims that attention is essential to building friendship. Hunt, *Fierce Tenderness*, pp. 151-152. Janice Raymond portrays thoughtfulness, which she describes as "concern for others, attentiveness to others' needs, and considerateness for others," as one of the four conditions of friendship.

Raymond, *A Passion for Friends*, pp. 218-222. Attentiveness and concern are part of the love for others that creates union and promotes growth.

11. Abraham Maslow, "Self-actualizing People: A Study of Psychological Health," *The Self*, ed. Clark Moustakas (New York: Harper and Row, 1956), p. 180.

12. Maslow, Self-actualizing People," *The Self*, p. 179.

13. Maslow, Self-actualizing People," *The Self*, pp. 180-183.

14. Mohandas Gandhi, *All Men Are Brothers*, ed. Krishna Kripalani (Paris: UNESCO, 1972), p. 78-84.

15. Gandhi, *All Men Are Brothers*, pp. 4, 65.

16. Erich Fromm, *The Art of Loving* (New York: Bantam, 1963), p. 65. Toinette Eugene, an African American theologian, says "black love confirms and affirms our affection for God, self, others, especially those who have also been oppressed." June Jordan, an African American theologian, stresses the importance of "self-love, self-respect, and self-determination." However, she also says "I will learn to love myself well enough to love you (whoever you are), well enough so that you will love me well enough so that we will know exactly where is the love: that it is here, between us, and growing stronger and growing stronger." Starhawk says "life demands love, because it is through love of self and of others, erotic love, transforming love, affectionate love, delighted love for the myriad forms of life evolving and changing, ... and raging love against all that would diminish the unspeakable beauty of the world, that we connect with the Goddess within and without." Toinette Eugene, June Jordan, and Starhawk in *Women's Consciousness, Women's Conscience*, edited by Barbara Andolsen, et al. (Minneapolis: Winston, 1985), pp. 124-127, 199-207. Although her hunger for freedom surpasses every other longing in her life, Sonia Johnson, a feminist, also wants affection and intimacy. In her discussion of whether freedom and intimacy are antithetical, she stresses the importance of freedom, "doing exactly what we want to do at this moment without negotiation," being in our power, not sacrificing anything we want, and not betraying

ourselves. Johnson claims in the future, women will reunite intimacy and freedom. "Someday women, reuniting love and freedom, would transfigure the world." Sonia Johnson, *The Ship That Sailed into the Living Room* (Estancia, New Mexico: Wildfire, 1991), pp. 128-129, 160-167, 256, 324.

17. Lv. 19:18; Matt. 22:39; Mark 12:31; Luke 10:27; John 13:34.

18. A.A., *Twelve Steps and Twelve Traditions* (New York: A.A. World Services, 1953), pp. 53, 92-93, 115.

19. A.A., *Twelve Steps and Twelve Traditions*, p. 93, 105.

20. M. Scott Peck, *The Road Less Traveled*, (New York: Simon and Schuster, 1978), pp. 166-167.

21. Peck, *The Road Less Traveled*, pp. 166-167.

22. Lao Tzu, *Tao Te Ching*, as quoted by H. Ringgren and A. Strom, *Religions of Mankind* (Philadelphia: Fortress Press, 1967), p. 397.

23. J. Russell Kirkland, "The Roots of Altruism in Taoist Tradition," *Journal of American Academy of Religion* 54(Spring, 1986), p. 69.

24. Lao Tzu, *The Way of Life* (New York: Capricorn Books, 1944), pp. 26, 55 and Kirkland, "Roots of Altruism," p. 69.

25. Barry Stevens, *Don't Push the River* (Moab, Utah: Real People Press, 1970) and Lao Tzu, *The Way of Life*, pp. 26, 55.

26. Gibran says that "to withhold is to perish." Gibran, *The Prophet*, p. 19.

27. Fromm, *The Art of Loving*, p. 18. Beverly Harrison stresses the importance of both giving and receiving. A deeply mutual love is a love that has the quality of both a gift given and a gift received. Mutual love is not the "patronizing love" of the strong for the weak, but the experience of genuinely being cared for and caring actively for another. Beverly Harrison in *Weaving the Visions*, pp. 222-223. Toinette Eugene says "this death-defying capacity of black women and men to go on giving and receiving love has been incredibly preserved within a hostile and racist American

environment." Toinette Eugene in *Women's Consciousness, Women's Conscience*, p. 125.

28. Christine Gudorf, "Parenting, Mutual Love, and Sacrifice," *Women's Consciousness, Women's Conscience*, ed. Barbara Andolsen (New York: Winston Press, 1985), p. 177.

29. Gudorf, "Parenting, Mutual Love, and Sacrifice," *Women's Consciousness, Women's Conscience*, pp. 178-179, 183.

30. Buber, *I and Thou*, pp. 23-24. Rosemary Ruether, a feminist theologian, claims that the I-Thou relation is "a most basic expression of human community" that has been distorted throughout history into an oppressive relationship where women are victimized by men. Ruether, *Sexism and God-talk*, p. 161. Beverly Harrison claims deeply mutual love is the love we want and need. Beverly Harrison in *Weaving the Visions*, pp. 221-222.

Chapter 3 - Love as Dialogue

1. Leo Buscaglia provided important insights about love even though they are couched in some inaccuracies. Incorrectly he says "a human child, newly born, knows nothing of love" and "love is a learned, emotional reaction." Love is not an emotion, as he claims, because love is the innate inner core, the dynamic power of every person. However, he is accurate when he says that we need to learn to become better lovers. "As the child grows, so does his world and so do his attachments." The potential for love is "never realized without work. This does not mean pain. Love, especially, is learned best in wonder, in joy, in peace, in living." Leo Buscaglia, *Love* (New York: Fawcett Crest, 1972), pp. 58-60, 71, 90-95.

2. Gray, *Men Are From Mars, Women Are From Venus*, pp. 132-134.

3. Erich Fromm's respect does not denote the customary honor, but means to look at, since it comes from the Latin word *respicere*. Fromm, *The Art of Loving*, pp. 23-24. Letty

Pogrebin says acceptance is one of the qualities of friendship. Pogrebin, *Among Friends*, pp 42-43. Naomi Littlebear says "I want you to accept me as I accept you." Naomi Littlebear in *This Bridge Called My Back*, edited by Cherrie Moraga and Gloria Anzaldua (New York: Kitchen Table, 1983), p. 158. Linell Cady claims one of love's tasks is to see the other clearly ... without the distorting prism of one's own needs." Linell Cady in *Embodied Love: Sensuality and Relationship as Feminist Values*, edited by Paula Cooey, et. al, (San Francisco: Harper and Row, 1987), pp. 142-143.

4. Daniel Maguire, *The Moral Revolution* (San Francisco: Harper and Row, 1986), p. 81 and Daniel Maguire, *The Moral Core of Judaism and Christianity* (Minneapolis: Fortress Press, 1993), p. 230.

5. M. Scott Peck, *The Road Less Traveled* (New York: Simon and Schuster, 1978), p. 93. Nena and George O'Neill distinguish between the "unrealistic expectations, unreasonable ideals, and mythological beliefs of a closed marriage" and the "realistic expectations of an open marriage." Nena and George O'Neill, *Open Marriage* (New York: Avon, 1972), pp. 81-85, 262-265.

6. Fromm, *The Art of Loving*, p. 23.

7. Martin Buber says "love is the responsibility of an I for a Thou." Buber, *I and Thou*, p. 15.

8. Lorde, *Sister Outsider*, p, 58.

9. Fromm, *The Art of Loving*, p. 23. Julia Wood believes that "caring for others is central to who I am and what my life should be about" and that our culture should be recreated so that "it esteems care as central to public life and invites us all to engage in it." According to Wood, three qualities are prominent in caring for others: partiality, empathy, and "a willingness to serve or nurture others." Wood, *Who Cares?*, pp. 4, 41-50, 160. Since she rejects the notion of universal love, Nel Noddings advocates an ethic of caring that has "fundamental universality." In addition, she distinguishes between "the one caring" and "the cared-for." Nel Noddings, *Caring: A Feminine Approach to Ethics and Moral Education* (Berkeley: University of California, 1986), pp. 5-29.

10. Mary Ellen Curtin (ed), *Symposium on Love* (New York: Behavioral Publications, 1973), pp. 78-79, 107-108.

11. Sherry Henry, *The Deep Divide: Why American Women Resist Equality* (New York: Macmillan, 1994), pp. 57-64.

12. Matthew 7:3-5.

13. Harris, *I'm OK, You're OK*, pp. 66-77.

14. George Schultz, *Turmoil and Triumph* (New York: Scribner, 1993), pp. 346-350.

15. Maguire, *Moral Revolution*, pp. 3-5.

16. Maguire, *Moral Revolution*, pp. 3-5. Toinette Eugene connects love and the worth of every person. "Historically, it has been the religious aspect of black love which enabled black Christians to believe always in the worth of each human life." Toinette Eugene in *Women's Consciousness, Women's Conscience*, pp. 124-125.

17. Maguire, *Moral Revolution*, pp. 3-5.

18. Fromm, *The Art of Loving*, p. 24.

19. Paul Tillich, "Being and Love," ed. Will Herberg, *Four Existentialist Theologians* (Garden City, New York: Doubleday, 1958), pp. 310-311.

20. Abraham Maslow claims the two kinds of knowing are Deficiency cognition or D-cognition and Being cognition or B-cognition or peak experience. Maslow, *Toward a Psychology of Being*, pp. 89-93. Martin Buber identifies two ways, I-It relation and I-Thou relation. Buber, *I and Thou*, pp. 3-6, 45-50. Paul Tillich distinguishes two ways of knowing, surface and deep knowing as well as empirical and personal knowing. The empirical way is cognition of others as things, while the other way is the knowledge of others as persons. Paul Tillich, *The Shaking of the Foundations* (New York: Charles Scribner's, 1948), pp. 52-55, 109-110 and Paul Tillich, "Philosophy of Social Work," *Pastoral Psychology* 4(December, 1963), p. 29. Mary Belenky, et. al., write about five ways women draw conclusions about "truth, knowledge, and authority." Mary Belenky, et. al., *Women's Ways of Knowing: the Development of Self, Voice, and Mind* (New York: Basic Books, 1986), pp. 3, 23-152.

21. Paul Tillich, *The Shaking of the Foundations*, pp. 109-110.

22. Buber, *I and Thou*, pp. 3-6, 45-50.

23. Maguire, *Moral Choice*, pp. 110, 196. Janice Raymond says passion which she describes as "a thinking heart" and "thoughtful feeling" is one of the conditions of friendship. Raymond, *A Passion for Friends*, pp. 223-229.

24. Lorde, *Sister Outsider*, p. 56.

25. Rogers, *Way of Being*, pp. 154-159. Julia Wood includes empathy as one of the three qualities of caring. Wood, *Who Cares?*, pp.41-47. Nel Noddings also claims caring involves empathy. Noddings, *Caring*, p. 30. Maria Lugones advocates empathy. "Thus I recommend to women of color in the U.S. to learn to love each other by travelling to each other's 'worlds.' ... Loving my mother required that I see with her eyes, that I go into my mother's world." Maria Lugones in *Making Face, Making Soul: Haciendo Caras*, edited by Gloria Anzaldua (San Francisco: Aunt Lute, 1990), pp. 390-402.

26. Ram Dass asks what we have to give and answers "Everything. If within each of us is that essence of Being which is in all things--call it God, Life, Energy, Consciousness ... so we have it to share with one another." Ram Dass and Paul Gorman, *How Can I Help?* (New York: Alfred Knopf, 1988), p. 50.

27. Lorde, *Sister Outsider*, pp. 56-59. Letty Pogrebin claims self-disclosure is one of the qualities of friendship. Pogrebin, *Among Friends*, pp. 40-42.

28. Paul Tournier, *The Meaning of Persons* (New York: Perennial, 1957), p. I7.

29. Hugh Prather, *Notes to Myself* (Moab, Utah: Real People Press, 1970), no pagination.

30. Prather, *Notes to Myself*. Deborah Tannen says communication is a continuing balancing act between the needs for independence and intimacy. Males focus on independence and this produces in their communication hierarchical oneupmanship that provides dominance and status. Women focus on intimacy and this results in interde-

pendence, connection, and closeness. Deborah Tannen, *You
Just Don't Understand* (New York: Ballantine, 1990), pp. 24-
48.

    31. Prather, *Notes to Myself.* Virginia Satir believes
"communication is the greatest single factor affecting a
person's health and relationship with others." After she
describes four destructive patterns of communication, placating, blaming, computing, and distracting, she presents one
constructive one, leveling. Virginia Satir, *Peoplemaking* (Palo
Alto, CA: Science and Behavior Books, 1972), pp. 58-79.

    32. Letty Pogrebin says honesty is one of the qualities
of friendship. Pogrebin, *Among Friends*, pp. 43-44.

    33. C.S. Lewis, *The Four Loves* (New York: Harcourt,
Brace and World, 1960), p. 33. Letty Pogrebin says gener-
osity is one of the qualities of friendship. Pogrebin, *Among
Friends*, pp. 40-42. Mary Hunt claims generativity is one of
the elements of friendship. Hunt, *Fierce Tenderness*, pp. 151-
154.

    34. Fromm, *The Art of Loving*, pp. 17-18, 22.

    35.Nick Bruno, a student of mine at Rutgers University.

    36. Antoine de Saint-Exupery, *The Little Prince*
(Harmondsworth, England: Penguin, 1962), pp. 76-83.

    37. Lewis, *The Four Loves*, p. 169.

    38. Williamson, *Illuminata*, pp. 149-150.

    39. Tillich, *Shaking of the Foundations*, pp. 109.

    40. Erik Erikson, *Identity: Youth and Crisis* (New York:
W.W. Norton, 1968), pp. 96-97. Letty Pogrebin claims trust
is one of the qualities of friendship. Pogrebin, *Among Friends*,
pp. 37-40.

    41. Dowrick, *Intimacy and Solitude*, p. 307.

    42. Buscaglia, *Love*, pp. 27, 96-97, 107-108, 148-151.

Chapter 4 - The Social Causes of Human Destructiveness

    1. Andrea Dworkin, **Letters from a War Zone** (New
York: Dutton, 1989), p. 317.

    2. Dworkin, *Letters from a War Zone*, pp. 317-318.

    3. Sam Keen says "love is not primarily something we

make or do, but something we are." In addition, love is "the energy of linkage" and "love is that impulse, motivation, or energy that links us to the whole web of life. Eros is the bond in the ecological communion within which we live. ... It is the mutuality linking cell to cell, animal to environment, without which we would not be." Sam Keen, *The Passionate Life* (New York: Harper Collins, 1983), pp. 35-42.

   4. Keen, *Passionate Life*, pp. 25-42.

   5. French, *Beyond Power*, pp. 25-39.

   6. French, *Beyond Power*, pp. 25-39.

   7. French, *Beyond Power*, pp. 25-39.

   8. Takayoshi Kano, "Bonobos' Peaceable Kingdom," *Natural History* (Nov 1990), pp. 62-71; Rebecca Ostriker, "The Amorous Ape," *New Age Journal* (Sept/Oct 1997), 14; and Frans de Waal, *Bonobo: the Forgotten Ape* (Berkeley: University of California Press, 1997).

   9. French, *Beyond Power*, pp. 25-39. In studying the evolution of apes into humans, Nancy Tanner contends "it is our social life that marks us off as human," including our capacity for learning and communication. Nancy Tanner, *On Becoming Human* (New York: Cambridge University Press, 1981), p. 9.

   10. Many scientists now accept the evidence derived from molecular protein data rather than from fossils. The fossil-based evolution tree proposes the human line split off from the apes about 15 million years ago, while the protein-based data indicates that the divergence occurred just five million years ago. Linda Gamlin and Gail Vines, *Evolution of Life* (New York: Oxford, 1987), pp. 20-21. Evidence shows that hominids existed about three and a half million years ago. French, *Beyond Power*, pp. 25-38.

   11. French, *Beyond Power*, pp. 25-39.

   12. French, *Beyond Power*, pp. 25-39.

   13. French, *Beyond Power*, pp. 34-39.

   14. French, *Beyond Power*, pp. 34-39.

   15. French, *Beyond Power*, pp. 34-39.

   16. French, *Beyond Power*, pp. 25-39.

   17. Marija Gimbutas, *The Goddess and Gods of Old*

Europe (Berkeley, CA: University of California Press, 1982), pp. 9, 236-238.

18. Maguire, *Moral Revolution*, p. 69.

19. French, *Beyond Power*, pp. 39-41.

20. Frederick Engels, *Origin of the Family, Private Property, and the State* (New York: Pathfinder, 1884, 1972), pp. 55, 60-61, 66-68, 71-75, 91-95 and French, *Beyond Power*, pp. 39-41.

21. Merlin Stone in *Politics of Women's Spirituality*, edited by Charlene Spretnak (Garden City, New York: Anchor, 1982), pp. 7-21.

22. Mircea Eliade, *History of Religious Ideas*, Vol. I (Chicago: University of Chicago Press, 1978), pp. 40-41; Stone, *Politics of Women's Spirituality*, pp. 7-21; Sojourner, *Politics of Women's Spirituality*, pp. 57-63; and French, *Beyond Power*, pp. 39-41.

23. Riane Eisler, *The Chalice and the Blade* (San Francisco: Harper & Row, 1987), pp. 1-58 and French, *Beyond Power*, pp. 43-54.

24. Adrienne Rich, *Of Woman Born* (New York: W.W. Norton, 1976), pp. 72, 93-99.

25. Karen Horney, *Feminine Psychology* (New York: W.W. Norton, 1967), p. 115 and Rich, *Of Woman Born*, p. 99.

26. French, *Beyond Power*, pp. 37-42.

27. French, *Beyond Power*, pp. 48, 56-58.

28. Engels, *Origin of the Family, Private Property, and the State*, pp. 65-67, 81-86.

29. Engels, *Origin of the Family, Private Property, and the State*, pp. 65-75, 81-86, 106-108 and French, *Beyond Power*, p. 48.

30. Engels, *Origin of the Family, Private Property, and the State*, pp. 100-101, 106-109 and French, *Beyond Power*, p. 48, 397-402.

31. Joseph Campbell, *Masks of God Oriental Mythology* (New York: Viking Press, 1973), pp. 85-86; French, *Beyond Power*, p. 49; Mircea Eliade, *History of Religious Ideas*, Vol I, pp 40-41.

32. Judith Ochshorn in her *The Female Experience and*

the Nature of the Divine (Bloomington, IN: Indiana University Press, 1981) deals with this question.

33. Gimbutas, *Politics of Women's Spirituality*, pp. 22-31; Eisler, *Chalice and Blade*, pp. 1-58; and French, *Beyond Power*, pp. 43-54.

34. Eliade, *History of Religious Ideas*, Vol I, pp 125-129; Campbell, *Masks of God Oriental Mythology*, pp. 39-60; Denise Carmody, *Women and World Religions*, 2nd ed (Englewood Cliffs, NJ: Prentice Hall, 1989), pp. 155, 160-172.

35. Jill Turner gave this theory in my University of South Florida class.

36. French, *Beyond Power*, pp. 67-76, 299-300.

37. Eisler, *Chalice and Blade*, pp. xvi-xxi, 1-58, 104-105.

38. Peggy Sanday, *Female Power and Male Dominance* (Cambridge, MA: Cambridge University Press, 1981), pp. 210-211, 232.

39. Sanday, *Female Power and Male Dominance*, pp. 163-170, 250-256. Although Sanday's study is extremely important, it has the same problem as other studies of cultures after 3,000 B.C.E.. Once patriarchy began, it corrupted egalitarian societies even when they continued to exist.

40. French, *Beyond Power*, pp. 64, 76-93.

41. Bruce Kokopeli and George Lakey, "More Power Than We Want," *Race, Class, and Gender*, 2nd edition, edited by Margaret Andersen and Patricia Hill Collins (Belmont, CA: Wadsworth, 1995), pp. 450-453 and Marilyn French, *War against Women* (New York: Summit, 1992), p. 15.

42. French, *Beyond Power*, pp. 76-93.

43. French, *Beyond Power*, pp. 76-93.

44. French, *Beyond Power*, pp. 76-93.

45. Anne Schaef, *Women's Reality* (Minneapolis, MN: Winston Press, 1985), pp. 5-6 and Anne Schaef, *When Society Becomes an Addict* (New York: Harper & Row, 1987), pp. 10-11.

46. Horney, *Feminine Psychology*, p. 116.

47. Marilyn Frye, *The Politics of Reality* (Freedom, CA:

Crossing, 1983), pp. 134-136.

    48. Frye, *The Politics of Reality*, pp. 134-136 and Maguire, *Moral Revolution*, p. 115.

    49. Frye, *The Politics of Reality*, pp. 134-136.

    50. Jill Radford and Diana Russell, *Femicide* (New York: Twayne, 1992), pp. xi, 3-7.

    51. Rosemary Ruether, *New Woman/New Earth* (New York: Seabury Press, 1975), p. 182 and Rich, *Of Woman Born*, p. 56.

    52. Rosemary Ruether, *Sexism and God-Talk*, p. 162 and Ruether, *New Woman/New Earth*, pp. 116, 204.

    53. Jesse Bernard, *Issues in Feminism*, 2nd ed, edited by Shelia Ruth (Mountain View, CA: Mayfield, 1990), p. 29.

    54. Pogrebin, *Growing Up Free*, pp. 40-41.

    55. Carrie Chapman Catt said this in 1902.

    56. Naomi Wolf, *The Beauty Myth* (New York: William Morrow, 1991), p. 17 and Jean Kilbourne in her video *Still Killing Us Softly*.

    57. Maslow, *Religions, Values, and Peak-Experiences*, pp. 103-110.

    58. Kay Hagen, *Fugitive Information* (San Francisco: Harper San Francisco, 1993), pp. 82-88.

    59. Hagen, *Fugitive Information*, pp. 87-89, 125.

    60. Hagen, *Fugitive Information*, pp. 84-87, 128.

    61. Hagen, *Fugitive Information*, pp. 84-87, 128.

    62. Robin Morgan, "Theory and Practice: Pornography and Rape," *Take Back the Night*, edited by Laura Lederer (New York: Bantam, 1980), p. 131.

Chapter 5 - The Potential for Violence within Us

    1. Vincent Bugliosi, *Helter Skelter* (New York: Bantam, 1975), pp. 128-129.

    2. Vincent Bugliosi, *Helter Skelter* (New York: Bantam Books, 1975), pp. 128-129.

    3. Erich Fromm, *Anatomy of Human Destructiveness* (Greenwich, CN: Fawcett Crest, 1973), pp. 210-299.

    4. Fromm, *Anatomy of Human Destructiveness*, p. 212.

5. Fromm, *Anatomy of Human Destructiveness*, p. 221.

6. Fromm, *Anatomy of Human Destructiveness*, p. 26.

7. Fromm, *Anatomy of Human Destructiveness*, p. 98

8. Fromm, *Anatomy of Human Destructiveness*, p. 224.

9. Fromm, *Anatomy of Human Destructiveness*, p. 224.

10. Fromm, *Anatomy of Human Destructiveness*, p. 224.

11. C.H. Kempe, et. al., "The Battered Child Syndrome," *Journal of American Medical Association* 181(July, 1962), 17-24 and Ruth Kempe and C. Henry Kempe, *Child Abuse* (Cambridge, MA: Harvard University Press, 1978), pp. 5-6. Vincent Fontana, *Somewhere a Child Is Crying* (New York: New American Library, 1973), pp. 79, 99. Deborah Daro, *Confronting Child Abuse* (New York: Free Press, 1988), pp. 9-10, 28-39.

12. Fontana, *Somewhere a Child Is Crying*, pp. 99, 105.

13. Kempe, *Child Abuse*, pp. 12, 15, 21-22, 36-38. Daro, *Confronting Child Abuse*, pp. 44-69 and Margaret Jay and Sally Doganis, *Battered: the Abuse of Children* (New York: St. Martin's Press, 1987), pp. 44-60.

14. Kempe, *Child Abuse*, pp. 12, 15, 21-22, 36-38. Daro, *Confronting Child Abuse*, pp. 44-69 and Margaret Jay and Sally Doganis, *Battered: the Abuse of Children* (New York: St. Martin's Press, 1987), pp. 44-60.

15. Erin Pizzey quoted in Del Martin, *Battered Wives* (New York: Pocket Books, 1977), p. 23. Maria Roy (ed), *Battered Women* (New York: Van Nostrand Reinhold, 1977), pp. 30-31. Susan Murphy-Milano, *Defending Our Lives* (New York: Doubleday, 1996), p. 42.

16. Roy, *Battered Women*, p. 33.

17. Martin. *Battered Wives*, p. 23.

18. Martin, *Battered Wives*, pp. 23-24 and Murphy-Milano, *Defending Our Lives*, p. 42.

19. Murray Straus, Richard Gelles, and Suzanne Steinmetz, *Behind Closed Doors* (Garden City, New York: Doubleday, 1980), pp. 112-122.

20. Straus, *Behind Closed Doors*, pp. 112-122.

21. A. Nicholas Groth, *Men Who Rape* (New York: Plenum Press, 1979), p. xxi, 2-13. Timothy Beneke, *Men on Rape* (New York: St. Martin's Press, 1982) and Robin Warshaw, *I Never Called It Rape* (New York: Harper and Row 1988), pp. 83-126.

22. Groth, *Men Who Rape*, pp. 98, 101-102; A. Nicholas Groth workshop, "The Victim of Sexual Assault," June 27, 1983; and A. Nicholas Groth, "Child Molester" in J. Conte and D. Shore (ed), *Social Work and Child Sexual Abuse* (New York: Haworth Press, 1982), p. 138.

23. A. Nicholas Groth workshop, "The Victim of Sexual Assault," June 27, 1983 and A. Nicholas Groth, "Child Molester" in J. Conte and D. Shore (ed), *Social Work and Child Sexual Abuse* (New York: Haworth Press, 1982), p. 138.

24. Groth, *Men Who Rape*, pp. 98, 101-102 and A. Nicholas Groth workshop, "The Victim of Sexual Assault," June 27, 1983.

25. Straus, *Behind Closed Doors*, p. 122.

26. Margaret Mitscherlich, *Peaceable Sex* (New York: Fromm, 1987), pp. 224-227.

27. Mitscherlich, *Peaceable Sex*, pp. 224-227.

28. Fromm, *Anatomy of Human Destructiveness*, pp. 26, 32.

29. Kate Millett, *Flying* (New York: Ballantine, 1974), pp. 627-629.

30. T.V. Interview with Diane Sawyer.

31. Maslow, *Farther Reaches of Human Nature*, pp. 34-35.

Chapter 6 - Loving Versus Destructive Behavior

1. Dworkin, *Letters from the War Zone*, p. 319.

2. Virginia Satir, *Peoplemaking* (Palo Alto, CA: Science and Behavior Books, 1972), p. 214.

3. Ashley Montagu, *On Being Human* (New York: Hawthorn, 1966), pp. 80, 93-100.

4. Alvin Toffler, *Future Shock* (New York: Bantam, 1970).

5. Thomas Harris, *I'm OK-You're OK* (New York: Avon, 1973).

6. Covey, *Seven Habits of Highly Effective People*, pp. 206-218.

7. Covey, *Seven Habits of Highly Effective People*, pp. 206-218.

8. Covey, *Seven Habits of Highly Effective People*, pp. 206-218.

9. Covey, *Seven Habits of Highly Effective People*, pp. 206-218.

10. Covey, *Seven Habits of Highly Effective People*, pp. 206-218.

11. Covey, *Seven Habits of Highly Effective People*, pp. 206-218. Carol Gilligan describes two moral perspectives, the morality of fairness and justice and the morality of care and responsibility. Unfortunately, she associates the care perspective with women and the justice perspective with men, because she does not fully acknowledge patriarchal socialization and thus does not see self-love and caring for others as interconnected parts of human nature.

An overconcern with justice can result in egoism. As Gilligan says, "the potential error in justice reasoning lies in its latent egocentrism," defining others in my own terms and confusing my own perspective with truth. Too much caring for others can lead to selflessness. The potential error in the morality of care lies in the tendency to define myself in the other's terms and become selfless. Carol Gilligan, *In a Different Voice* (Cambridge: Harvard University Press, 1982) and Carol Gilligan, "Moral Orientation and Moral Development," *Women and Moral Theory*, edited by Eva Kittay and Diana Meyers (Savage, MD: Rowman & Littlefield, 1987), pp. 19-21, 31.

When people get overly concerned about themselves, they become selfish. This disrupts the balance between self-love and love for others. Once that balance is upset, they often move from an excessive concern for themselves to a jealous clinging to others. Selfish people's love for others is often possessive.

Adolf Hitler's SS or *Schutzstaffel* provide an example of how their excessive concern for Hitler's power caused destructive acts that resulted in an excessive concern for their own power. The SS's adulation of Hitler was carried to such an extreme that they idolized him and carried out his orders in blind obedience. The SS in Nazi concentration camps totally submitted to Hitler's orders to gas Jews and other alleged enemies of the German Reich. On the other hand, while they were being totally subservient to Hitler, their need for power for themselves grew to such an extreme that they brutally dominated the prisoners in substantial and petty ways before they finally murdered them.

12. R.D. Laing, *Politics of Experience* (New York: Ballantine, 1967), p. 58.

13. Rogers, *Person-to-Person*, p. 182 and Rogers, *On Being a Person*, pp. 131-132. The American Psychiatric Association's *Diagnostic and Statistical Manual of Mental Disorders* in the third edition (DSM III) includes a continuum for human behavior that describes a seven point rating scale of levels of adaptive functioning. The scale is a continuum from (1) "SUPERIOR--Usually effective functioning in social relations, occupational functioning and use of leisure time" through very good, good, fair, poor, very poor, to (7) "GROS-SLY IMPAIRED--Gross impairment in virtually all areas of functioning." American Psychiatric Association (APA), *Diagnostic and Statistical Manual of Mental Disorders*, Third Edition (Washington, DC: APA, 1980), pp. 28-30.

14. Rogers, *Person-to-Person*, p. 182.

15. Rogers, *On Being a Person*, pp. 131-132, 158.

16. Eric Berne, *Games People Play* (New York: Grove Press, 1964), pp. 48, 179-183 and Eric Berne, *Sex in Human Living* (New York: Pocket Books, 1970), pp. 116, 154.

17. Robin Norwood, *Women Who Love Too Much* (New York: Grove Press, 1985), pp. xiii-xv.

18. Miriam Greenspan, *A New Approach to Women and Therapy* (New York: McGraw-Hill, 1983), p. v.

Chapter 7 - Feminist Versus Patriarchal Leadership

1. Alicia Appleman-Jurman, *Alicia*, (New York: Bantam, 1988), pp. 32-33, 115.
2. Appleman-Jurman, *Alicia*, p. 95.
3. Appleman-Jurman, *Alicia*, pp. 115-116.
4. Appleman-Jurman, *Alicia*, pp. 219.
5. Appleman-Jurman, *Alicia*, pp. 219-225.
6. Appleman-Jurman, *Alicia*, p. 112.
7. Appleman-Jurman, *Alicia*, p. 114.
8. Appleman-Jurman, *Alicia*, pp. 98-100, 115-116.
9. Appleman-Jurman, *Alicia*, pp. 162-167.
10. Appleman-Jurman, *Alicia*, pp. 219-221.
11. French, *Beyond Power*, pp. 18-19 and Eisler, *The Chalice and the Blade*, pp. 60-61. Rosemary Ruether, a feminist theologian, defines patriarchy as "not only the subordination of females to males, but the whole structure of Father-ruled society: aristocracy over serfs, masters over slaves, king over subjects, racial overlords over colonized people." Rosemary Ruether, *Sexism and God-talk* (Boston: Beacon, 1983), p. 61. Some, who call themselves feminists like Christine Hoff Sommers and Rene Denfeld, criticize other feminists' theories about the patriarchy. Sommers, *Who Stole Feminism?* (New York: Simon and Schuster, 1994) and Rene Denfeld, *The New Victorians: A Young Woman's Challenge to the Old Feminist Order* (New York: Warner Books, 1995), pp. 154-167.
12. Marilyn Frye, *The Politics of Reality: Essays in Feminist Theory* (Freedom, CA: Crossing, 1983), pp. 9-12, 35.
13. Lorde, *Sister Outsider*, pp. 110-113, 123.
14. Naomi Wolf, *Fire with Fire*, (New York: Random House, 1993), pp. xv, 54-55, 132-142, 203-206, 310.
15. Wolf, *Fire with Fire*, pp. xv, 54-55, 132-142, 203-206, 310.
16. Wolf, *Fire with Fire*, pp. xv, 54-55, 132-142, 203-206, 310.
17. My continuum has two extremes of behavior and leadership. Although I incorporate some aspects of their

theories, my description of the patriarchy's love of power versus feminism's power of love differs from the following authors who write about two kinds of behavior, leadership, and organizations. Riane Eisler and David Loye in *The Partnership Way* (San Francisco: Harper, 1990) make a distinction between the partnership way and the dominator way. Alfonso Montouri and Isabella Conti, *From Partnership To Power* (San Francisco: Harper, 1993), agree with Eisler's two kinds of power. French in *Beyond Power* explains the differences between patriarchy and feminism. Charlene Wheeler and Peggy Chin in *Peace and Power: A Handbook of Feminist Process* 3rd Edition (New York: National League of Nursing, 1991) explain how to stop leading in patriarchal ways and start leading in feminist ways. Anne Schaef in *Women's Reality* (Minneapolis: Winston, 1985) distinguishes between the death-oriented White Male System and the life producing Emerging Female System. Anne Schaef and Diane Fassel, *Addictive Organization* (San Francisco: Harper and Row, 1988), write that the addictive organization needs to have a system shift to become an organization in recovery. Marilyn Ferguson in *The Aquarian Conspiracy* refers to the old paradigm of power and the new. Sherry Cohen, *Tender Power* (New York: Addison-Wesley, 1989), names tender power versus plain old power, traditional male dominated power, old boyism. Betty Harragan in *Games Mother Never Taught You: Corporate Gamesmanship for Women* (New York: Warner, 1978) describes the business world as a patriarchal game and gives ideas on how to deal with it. Margaret Henning and Anne Jardin's *Managerial Woman* (New York: Pocket, 1978) explain women and men's different mind sets in the corporate world. Joseph Boyett and Henry Conn in *Workplace 2000: the Revolution Reshaping American Business* (New York: Plume, 1992) want to replace the traditional leadership that practices hierarchy, domination, control, and centralization with new Workplace 2000 leadership that uses partnership, empowerment, self-control, participation, equality, and self-direction. Bruce Kokopeli and George Lakey in *Leadership for Change: Toward a feminist Model* (Philadel-

phia: New Society) teach feminist leadership as an alternative
to patriarchal leadership. Stephen Covey's *Seven Habits of
Highly Effective People* distinguishes between Character
Ethics and Personality Ethics. Covey's *Principle-Centered
Leadership* describes Principle-centered leadership versus
easy, quick fix leadership. Vaclaw Havel, who resisted the
Communist control of Czechoslovakia, went to jail for protesting, and became his country's first President after liberation,
in *Disturbing the Peace* (New York: Alfred Knopf, 1990)
makes a distinction between "an impersonal, anonymous,
irresponsible, and uncontrollable juggernaut of power (the
power of 'megamachinery') and the elemental and original
interests of man as a concrete individual." Douglas McGre-
gor, *The Human Enterprise* (New York: McGraw-Hill, 1960),
writes about two theories of management, Theory X and
Theory Y. William Ouchi in *Theory Z: How American Business Can Meet the Japanese Challenge* offers his Theory Z
by contrasting Japanese and American organizations. James
MacGregor Burns, *Leadership* (New York: Harper and Row,
1978) distinguishes between transactional and transforming
leaders. Alvin Toffler, *Powershift* (New York: Bantam, 1991),
says "this is the dawn of the Powershift Era. ... This crackup
of old-style authority and power in business and daily life is
accelerating. ... A 'powershift' does not merely transfer power.
It transforms it."   John Naisbitt, *Megatrends* (New York:
Warner, 1984), divides various aspects of contemporary life
into two types. Marilyn Moats Kennedy in *Office Warfare*
(New York: Fawcett Crest, 1986) describes old gentlemanly
politics and the new politics of brinkmanship. Morton Mintz
and Jerry Cohen, *Power, Inc: Public and Private Rulers and
How To Make Them Accountable* (New York: Bantam, 1977),
warn about the dangers of unaccountable power and advocate accountable power. Other authors distinguish between
several kinds of power and leadership. Some aspects of
these are included in my two kinds. Cherie Carter-Scott in
Corporate Negaholic (New York: Fawcett Crest, 1992)
describes many kinds of negaholics. Michael Maccoby, *The
Gamesman* (New York: Simon and Schuster, 1976), outlines

four types of leaders: the craftsman, the jungle fighter, the company man, and the gamesman. Andrew DuBrin, *Winning at Office Politics* (New York: Ballantine, 1978), describes five types of office politicians: Machiavellian, company politician, survivalist, straight arrow, and innocent lamb. Arleen La Bella and Dolores Leach, *Personal Power* (Boulder, CO: New View, 1983), name four dimensions of power: powerless, powerful, empowering, and overpowering. Janet Hagberg, *Real Power*, (San Francisco: Harper, 1984), writes about six stages of personal power. William Hitt, *Ethics and Leadership* (Columbus, Ohio: Battelle Press, 1990) lists four kinds of leadership and connects them to four ethical systems, as he stresses the importance of ethical leadership.

18. Covey, *Seven Habits of Highly Effective People*, pp. 33-35 and Stephen Covey, *Principle-Centered Leadership* (New York: Summit, 1991), pp. 18-21.

19. Covey, *Seven Habits of Highly Effective People*, pp. 33-35, 132, 219 and Covey, *Principle-Centered Leadership*, p. 297.

20. Many authors are now saying that rugged individualism has been carried to an extreme and some are advocating communitarianism. Robert Bellah, Richard Madsen, William Sullivan, Ann Swidler, and Steven Tipton have three books, *Habits of the Heart* (New York: Harper and Row, 1985), *Individualism and Commitment in American Life* (New York: Harper and Row, 1987), and *The Good Society* (New York: Vintage, 1992). Christopher Lasch criticizes rugged individualism and advocates populism rather than communitarianism. Christopher Lasch, *The Revolt of the Elites and the Betrayal of Democracy* (New York: W.W. Norton. 1995). Amitai Etzioni stresses communitarianism because it has been neglected, but wants to balance it with individualism. "Individuals' rights are to be matched with social responsibilities." Amitai Etzioni, *The Spirit of Community* (New York: Simon and Schuster, 1994).

21. Harragan in *Games Mother Never Taught You* describes the corporate world as a game modelled on the military and sports. Henning and Jardin's *Managerial Woman*

and Jane Trahey's *On Women and Power* (New York: Avon, 1978) also call the corporate world a game. Hedrick Smith explains that the U.S. Government and those connected with it in Washington, D.C. deal with power as a game and play hard ball politics. Hedrick Smith, *Power Game: How Washington Works* (New York: Ballantine, 1989).

22. Jack Payton, *St. Petersburg Times*, Nov. 9, 1993.

23. Albert Camus, *The Plague* (London: Penguin, 1965), pp. 201, 207.

24. Kay Hagen, *Fugitive Information* (San Francisco: Pandora, 1993), pp. 59-61.

25. Hagen, *Fugitive Information*, pp. 59-60.

26. French, *Beyond Power*, pp. 18-19.

27. Starhawk, *Truth Or Dare* (San Francisco: Harper and Row, 1987), pp. 87-88.

28. Starhawk, *Truth Or Dare*, pp. 87-89.

29. Starhawk, *Truth Or Dare*, pp. 87-89.

30. Starhawk, *Truth Or Dare*, pp. 79-80.

31. Starhawk, *Truth Or Dare*, pp. 79-82.

32. Flo Kennedy, "Institutionalized Oppression Vs the Female," *Sisterhood Is Powerful*, edited by Robin Morgan (New York: Vintage, 1970), pp. 492-493.

33. Marilyn Frye, *Politics of Reality* (Freedom, CA: Crossing Press, 1983), pp. 98-99, 136-140.

34. Starhawk, *Truth Or Dare*, pp. 85-86.

35. Starhawk, *Truth Or Dare*, pp. 87-89.

36. Starhawk, *Truth Or Dare*, pp. 87-89.

37. Kennedy, "Institutionalized Oppression Vs the Female," *Sisterhood Is Powerful*, pp. 495-499.

38. Kennedy, "Institutionalized Oppression Vs the Female," *Sisterhood Is Powerful*, pp. 499-500.

39. Sarah Grimke, "Letters on the Equality of the Sexes," in *Feminism: The Essential Historical Writings*, edited by Miriam Schneir (New York: Vintage, 1992), p. 38.

40. Kennedy, "Institutionalized Oppression Vs the Female," *Sisterhood Is Powerful*, pp. 495-499.

41. Starhawk, *Truth Or Dare*, pp. 82-84.

42. Starhawk, *Truth Or Dare*, pp. 82-84.

43. Starhawk, *Truth Or Dare*, pp. 82-84.
44. Starhawk, *Truth Or Dare*, pp. 82-89.
45. Starhawk, *Truth Or Dare*, pp. 82-89.
46. Starhawk, *Truth Or Dare*, pp. 82-89.
47. Starhawk, *Truth Or Dare*, pp. 82-89.
48. Starhawk, *Truth Or Dare*, pp. 82-89.
49. Starhawk, *Truth Or Dare*, pp. 82-89.

Chapter 8 - Stages of Personal Empowerment and Women's Liberation

1. Jane Mayer and Jill Abramson, *Strange Justice* (New York: Houghton Mifflin, 1994).
2. Mayer and Abramson, *Strange Justice*.
3. Wolf, *Fire with Fire*, pp. xv-xvi.
4. Mayer and Abramson, *Strange Justice*.
5. Alison Jaggar and Paula Rothenberg, ed., *Feminist Frameworks*, 3rd Edition (New York: McGraw-Hill, 1993).
6. Sheila Ruth, *Issues in Feminism*, 4th edition (Mountain View CA: Mayfield, 1998), p. 5; Cellestine Ware, *Woman Power* (New York: Tower, 1970), p. 3; Firestone, *Dialectic of Sex*, p. 15; Millett, *Sexual Politics*, p. 62; and Anne Koedt, *Radical Feminism* (New York: Quadrangle, 1973), p. vii.
7. Ruth, *Issues in Feminism*, 4th edition, p. 5; Wilma Scott Heide, *Feminism for the Health of It* (Buffalo, New York: Margaret Daughters, 1985).
8. Wolf, *Fire with Fire*, pp. 95, 120, 132, 151, 232, 310.
9. Gloria Steinem, *Outrageous Acts and Everyday Rebellions* (New York: Signet, 1986), p. 3 and Robin Morgan, *The Word of a Woman* (New York: W.W.Norton, 1992), pp. 140-142.
10. French, *Beyond Power*, pp. 442-445.
11.French, *Beyond Power*, pp. 442-445.
12. French, *Beyond Power*, pp. 442-445.
13. French, *Beyond Power*, pp. 442-445.
14. Robin Norwood, *Women Who Love Too Much* (New York: Pocket Books, 1985), pp. 5-9.
15. Black, *It Will Never Happen To Me*, pp. 29-39.

16. *People*, June 10, 1991.

17. *People*, June 10, 1991.

18. A victim's story told in conversation.

19. Robin Warshaw, *I Never Called It Rape* (New York: Harper and Row, 1988), pp. 55-56.

20. Warshaw, *I Never Called It Rape*, pp. 55-56.

21. Warshaw, *I Never Called It Rape*, pp. 2, 13, 48-49, 54-56.

22. Kennedy, "Institutionalized Oppression Vs the Female," *Sisterhood Is Powerful*, pp. 492-496.

23. Kennedy, "Institutionalized Oppression Vs the Female," *Sisterhood Is Powerful*, pp. 492-496.

24. Warshaw, *I Never Called It Rape*, pp. 2, 13, 50.

25. *People*, June 10, 1991.

26. *People*, June 10, 1991.

27. Black, *It Will Never Happen To Me*, pp. 29-59.

28. Norwood, *Women Who Love Too Much*, pp. 5-9.

29. *People*, June 10, 1991.

30. *People*, June 10, 1991.

31. Warshaw, *I Never Called It Rape*, pp. 2, 13, 26.

32. Black, *It Will Never Happen To Me*, pp. 49-59.

33. Lorde, *Sister Outsider*, pp. 124, 129, 131.

34. Lorde, *Sister Outsider*, pp. 130-131.

35. Tournier, *The Meaning of Persons*, p. 17 and Lorde, *Sister Outsider*, pp. 40-44.

36. Lorde, *Sister Outsider*, pp. 40-44, 146, 152.

37. Judith Seixas and Geraldine Youcha, *Children of Alcoholism* (New York: Crown, 1985), pp. 131-159.

38. Seixas, *Children of Alcoholism*, pp. 131-159.

39. Lorde, *Sister Outsider*, p. 112 and Paulo Freire, *Pedagogy of the Oppressed* (New York: Herder and Herder, 1972), pp. 52-69.

40. Lorde, *Sister Outsider*, pp. 112-118.

41. Lorde, *Sister Outsider*, pp. 112-116 and Nick Bruno said this in my Rutgers University class.

42. Chardin, *Phenomenon of Man*, pp. 267-268.

43. Daly, *Beyond God the Father*, pp. 157-159.

44. Tillich, *Love, Power and Justice*, pp. 56-71.

45. William Becker, *Feminist Frameworks*, p. 18.

46. E.J. Dionne, "Cooperation Can Curb Teen Pregnancy," *St. Petersburg Times*, p. 20A.

47. "Catholic Worker Positions" in *The Universe Bends toward Justice: A Reader on Christian Nonviolence in the U.S.*, edited by Angie O'Gorman (Philadelphia: New Society, 1990), p. 123 and Boyett and Conn, *Workplace 2000*, pp. 144-149.

48. Ruether, *Gaia and God*, p. 272.

49. Rosemary Ruether, *Gaia and God: An Ecofeminist Theology of Earth Healing* (San Francisco: Harper San Francisco, 1994), pp. 103-104.

50. Irene Franck and David Brownstone, *Women's World* (New York: Harper Collins, 1995); Colman McCarthy, *Disturbers of the Peace* (Boston: Houghton Mifflin, 1973), p. 53; Dorothy Day, *The Universe Bends toward Justice*, p 118; and *By Little and by Little: The Selected Writings of Dorothy Day*, edited by Robert Ellsberg (New York: Knopf, 1983).

51. Dorothy Day in *The Universe Bends toward Justice*, p 118 and Jane Addams in *Instead of Violence*, edited by Arthur and Lila Weinberg (Boston: Beacon, 1968), p. 307.

52. Sarah Grimke, "Letters on the Equality of the Sexes and the Condition of Women," and Harriet Robinson, "Early Factory Labor," in *Feminism: Essential Historical Writings*, edited by Miriam Schneir (New York: Vintage, 1992), pp. 45-46, 49-57. Carol Hymowitz and Michaele Weissman, *A History of Women in America* (New York: Bantam, 1981), pp. 122-139, 234-265.

53. Advertisers becoming aware of women's identity," *St Petersburg Times*, October 13, 1997, p. 16E

54. Ruether, *Gaia and God*, pp. 268-274.

55. Suzanne Pharr, *Feminist Frameworks*, p. 315. Janice Hunt put the wings' idea on a flyer.

Chapter 9 - Feminism Is a Spiritual and Moral Movement

1. Richard Bucke, *Cosmic Consciousness* (Secaucas,

New Jersey: Citadel, 1973), pp. 1-2, 13-14.

2. Raynor Johnson, *Imprisoned Splendor* (Wheaton, IL: Quest, 1971), pp. 326-327 and Evelyn Underhill, *Essentials of Mysticism* (New York: E.P. Dutton, 1960), pp. 21-22.

3. Radhakrishnan in Johnson, *Imprisoned Splendor*, p 332.

4. Carol Christ, in *Politics of Women's Spirituality*, edited by Charlene Spretnak, (Garden City, New York: Doubleday, 1982), p. 74 and Starhawk, *Politics of Women's Spirituality*, pp. 51-52.

5. Mary Baker Eddy, *Science and Health* (Boston: First Church of Christ, Scientist, 1971), pp. 468-469.

6. Gandhi, *All Men Are Brothers*, pp. 54, 59, 63-64.

7. Eddy, *Science and Health*, pp. 16, 517-519; Anne Carr, *Transforming Grace* (San Francisco: Harper and Row, 1988), pp. 134-157; and Sallie McFague, "The Ethics of God as Mother, Lover and Friend, *Feminist Theology*, edited by Ann Loades (Louisville, KY: Westminster, 1990), pp. 255-274.

8. Carter Heyward, "Enigmatic God," in *Spinning a Sacred Yarn* (New York: Pilgrim Press, 1983), pp. 109-114.

9. Anthony de Mello, *Song of the Bird*, pp. 14, 44.

10. Mary Daly, *Beyond God the Father* (Boston: Beacon, 1973), p. 19; Spretnak, *Politics of Women's Spirituali- ty*; Ruether, *Sexism and God-talk*, pp. 47-71; Judith Plaskow, *Standing Again at Sinai* (San Francisco: HarperSanFrancisco, 1991), pp. 121-169.

11. Sogyal Rinpoche, *Tibetan Book of Living and Dying* (San Francisco: HarperSanFrancisco, 1992), pp. 215-216.

12. Rinpoche, *Tibetan Book of Living and Dying*, pp. 215-216.

13. Rinpoche, *Tibetan Book of Living and Dying*, pp. 215-216.

14. Tillich, *Shaking of the Foundations*, pp. 52-63 and Evelyn Underhill, *Mysticism* (New York: Dutton, 1961), pp. 19-23. Matthew Fox describes four ways of developing a creation-centered spirituality. His first positive way of awe at creation and his second negative way of befriending darkness are similar to my ways of love and suffering. His third way of

creativity and his fourth way of transformation are similar to my belief that spirituality produces ethics and a vocation of love. Matthew Fox, *Original Blessing: A Primer in Creation Spirituality* (Santa Fe, New Mexico: Bear, 1983).

15. Underhill, *Mysticism*, pp. 19-23 and Sally Purvis, *Power of the Cross* (Nashville, TN: Abingdon, 1993), p. 89.

16. Underhill, *Mysticism*, pp. 169-170, 428, 446.

17. Gibran, *The Prophet*, p. 29.

18. Tillich, *Shaking of the Foundations*, pp. 59-63 and Gibran, *The Prophet*, p. 29.

19. Teresa of Avila, *Interior Castle* (Mahwah, NJ: Paulist, 1979), pp. 109-114, 126, 143.

20. Rinpoche, *Tibetan Book of Living and Dying*, pp. 219-220.

21. Paul Tillich, *Dynamics of Faith* (New York: Harper and Row, 1957), pp. 116-117; Underhill, *Essentials of Mysticism*, pp. 23-24, 57-85, 209-210; Johnson, *Imprisoned Splendor*, pp. 325-332; Walter Stace, *Teachings of the Mystics* (New York: Mentor, 1960), pp. 26-28; Bhagavan Das, *Essential Unity of All Religions* (Wheaton, IL: Quest, 1973); John White, ed., *Highest State of Consciousness* (New York: Doubleday, 1972); Anthony Campbell, *Seven State of Consciousness* (New York: Harper & Row, 1974), pp. 154-160; Serinity Young, ed., *An Anthology of Sacred Texts by and about Women* (New York: Crossroad, 1994), pp. 75-76.

22. Tillich, *Dynamics of Faith*, p. 116 and Fox, *Original Blessing*.

23. James Fowler, "Faith Development," *Religious Education*, Exodus 20:6, Matthew 7:16-20, and James 2:12-26.

24. Maguire, *The Moral Core of Judaism and Christianity*, pp. 212, 220, 230.

25. Albert Schweitzer, *Out of My Life and Thought* (New York: New American Library, 1963), pp. 124-128, 180-185; Albert Schweitzer, "Reverence for Life," *World Treasury of Modern Religious Thought*, ed. by Jaroslav Pelikan (Boston: Little and Brown, 1990), pp. 237-243; and Albert Schweitzer, *A Treasury of Albert Schweitzer*, edited by

Thomas Kiernan (New York: Gramercy, 1994), pp. 59-77, 125-130.

26. Paul Tillich, *Morality and Beyond* (New York: Harper, 1963), pp. 20-21, 40-43, 88-89, 145 and Paul Tillich, *My Search for Absolutes* (New York: Simon and Schuster, 1967), p. 108.

27. Schweitzer, *Out of My Life and Thought*, pp. 124-128, 180-185; Schweitzer, "Reverence for Life," *World Treasury of Modern Religious Thought*, pp. 237-243; and Schweitzer, *A Treasury of Albert Schweitzer*, pp. 59-77, 125-130.

28. Schweitzer, *Out of My Life and Thought*, pp. 124-128, 180-185; Schweitzer, "Reverence for Life," *World Treasury of Modern Religious Thought*, pp. 237-243; and Schweitzer, *A Treasury of Albert Schweitzer*, pp. 59-77, 125-130.

29. Martin Luther King, *The Wisdom of Martin Luther King* (New York: Lancer, 1968), pp. 145-147.

30. Gandhi, *All Men Are Brothers*, pp. 45, 63-64.

31. Sonia Johnson, a feminist, claims our essence is unconditional love. "I am love. Love is not an act, not something I do. It's what I most fundamentally am. And not just love, but unconditional love. And not just unconditional love, but power and creativity and joy. These are not characteristics of me, but my essence." Sonia Johnson, *The Ship That Sailed into the Living Room* (Estancia, New Mexico: Wildfire Books, 1991), p. 323.

32. Elizabeth Kubler-Ross, "The Process of Aging," in Evelyn Mandell, *Art of Aging* (New York: Winston Press, 1981), pp. 120-123.

33. Daly, *Beyond God the Father*, p. 139 and Mary Daly, "Spiritual Dimension of Women's Liberation," *Radical Feminism*, pp. 263-264.

34. Daly, "Spiritual Dimension of Women's Liberation," pp. 264-266.

35. Shelia Collins, "Feminist Reading of History," *Radical Religion* 1(Spring 1974), p. 17.

36. Carol Christ, *Diving Deep and Surfacing* (Boston: Beacon, 1980), pp. 7-12.

37. Rosemary Ruether, "Women's Liberation in Historical and Theological Perspective," *Women's Liberaton and the Church*, edited by Sarah Doely (New York. Association Press, 1970), p. 26.

38. Ruether, "Women's Liberation in Historical and Theological Perspective," *Women's Liberation and the Church*, p. 26 and Firestone, *Dialectic of Sex*, p. 15.

39. Bell Hooks, "Feminism: A Transformational Politics," p. 497.

40. Char McGee, "Feminism: A Vision of Love," *Goddess Re-awakening*, pp. 249-257.

INDEX

Speakers' Bureau

Ruth Whitney, Ph.D., the author of this book, **Feminism and Love: Transforming Ourselves and Our World**, is available to speak to interested groups about her book and other related topics. She can be reached by contacting:

Whitney Speakers' Bureau
700 14th Avenue North
St. Petersburg, FL 33701-1018

E-mail: WhitneyRA@aol.com
(727) 821-6890